W9-ASM-015

Modes of Imperialism

Modes of Imperialism

CHARLES REYNOLDS

St. Martin's Press · New York

© Charles Reynolds, 1981

All rights reserved. For information write:
St. Martin's Press, Inc,
175 Fifth Avenue,
New York, N.Y. 10010

First published in the United States in 1981
Printed in Great Britain

Library of Congress Card Catalog Number 81-82752
ISBN 0-312-54313-1

832910

LIBRARY
ALMA COLLEGE
ALMA, MICHIGAN

Contents

TO   SARAH, MARY, ANNA, JULIAN, FABRICE

Preface

Like Schumpeter, although for different reasons, I think that there are imperialisms rather than Imperialism. Each imperialism is dependent on the conceptual framework that gives it its peculiar features. Depending on which model of imperialism we adopt, we have a distinct and autonomous picture of the world. They are like prisms that differentially refract as they are manipulated.

Such a framework constitutes a theoretical overview that allows the selection and organization of facts and presents them as a description of imperialism. They are guides to enquiry, a basis for prescription, a framework for our understanding and a complete and coherent account — or so they claim. Each makes a unique and universal claim to knowledge; if we accept one, we are compelled to reject the others. This book is concerned with the nature of this claim. What constitutes a proper ground for their assessment? Do they really explain human actions and experience? And if so, on what basis can their adequacy be established?

These questions are difficult to answer and involve much more than a critical exegesis. They transcend the parochialisms of debate on the nature of imperialism and involve us in an enquiry into the problem of explanation. And so I have been forced to extend my range in seeking to answer them. I am aware that in this book I have wandered into territory both vast and charted by others who will be quick to challenge my navigational competence. Nonetheless, my concern is to establish some measure of common ground between us, and this I seek in the notion of explanation. If we lack common standards to which our claims can be referred for evaluation, then all debate is in vain. We can neither agree nor disagree. Arguments that are void of such reference can succeed only as ideologies, as systems of belief taken on trust. However intellectually exciting, they remain adventures of the spirit rather than a painful and partial exploration of the dark. Creative imagination is necessary to intellectual enquiry, but without direction and means of relating it to evaluation, it cannot be instrumental in producing knowledge.

I have tried to be constructive as well as critical in examining these imperialisms. I have also tried to balance the tendency to treat people as things, characteristic of much of the argument about imperialism. In particular I have offered a partial solution to the problem of explaining human actions and experience through a reconstruction of reasoning. Whatever its imperfections, I believe that if we are to achieve a level of adequate explanation of human conduct it must be capable of reference to explicit evaluatory criteria. Such criteria provide common ground, permitting genuine agreement and disagreement over competing explanatory claims. They enable an enquiry to produce results. We would know in advance of our questioning what would count as an answer and so proceed with a notion of where we were going. In short, I have tried to shift the debate away from the putative phenomenon of imperialism to a discussion of the grounds and conditions appropriate to an explanation of this and any other aspect of human actions and experience.

A book of this kind is totally dependent on an intellectual context created by hundreds of writers, past and present, dead and alive. I am conscious of my debt to these, whose expression, imbued with the spirit of intellectual enquiry for its own sake, has challenged and encouraged my own efforts. What is good in this book stems from their example; what is bad is my own work. My students too have forced me to refine and defend, and sometimes abandon, positions I would otherwise have too complacently accepted. They have been exacting critics. Above all I have taken to heart Montaigne's words *'Que sais-je?'.*

My thanks are due to a number of people who have helped me in the writing of this book but I owe a special debt to Pauline Rowell without whom it would not have been written at all.

C.R.
University of Durham
1981

1

Introduction

Imperialism is an idea that denotes a relationship of dominion — whether explicit, in the form of a political sovereignty asserted by force over subject peoples independent of their will or consent, or implicit, as a system of constraint and control exercised over peoples and territories, independent of their political organization, and directing their activities to the satisfaction of needs and interests themselves generated by the system. Colonialism is distinct from imperialism in that it denotes the settlement of territory by the peoples of a metropolitan power. A colonial relationship is thus established in which indigenous peoples coexist somewhat uneasily with incomers, with their political rights and status unresolved or equivocal. Such colonies may be incorporated in a formal empire, but imperialism does not entail the colonisation of tributary territories. Imperial relations are essentially those of the imposition of rule by one locus of authority upon alien peoples. A variety of forms of dominion may be the result, ranging from the actual absorption of the alien peoples and territory within the state, the establishment of colonies, nominally self-governed, but with basic state functions such as trade, foreign relations and defence, under the control of the imperial state, to relations with states that are formally sovereign but whose freedom of action is constrained in various ways by the imperial power. Whatever the political expression of an imperial relationship, its essence is the exercise of authority or power by one state over other states, peoples and territory. This concept of imperialism is state-centric.

As we shall see in this study, other notions of imperialism, while accepting the idea of domination as central, find its expression in economic or social relationships. The locus might be the state but it can also be economic institutions and agencies, such as multinational corporations, or social groups. Imperialism can even lack a formal identifiable locus and constitute a drive or a dynamic within a set of economic or social relations expressed as a system. Wars, conquest and exploitation become its manifestation.

1

Imperialism is thus used to depict a variety of states of affairs and a number of empirical descriptions are associated with its usage. It is also an ambiguous term in that it is used both to characterize a specific condition and so acts as a descriptive label (states have empires or are imperial powers) to designate a process or causal sequence that produces a particular state of affairs (states pursue imperialism or have imperialist policies). Such a process may be conscious, that is, constitutes a policy actively pursued by individual statesmen or agents. The associated description in this case is heavily dependent upon an elucidation of the reasoning of the agent. Alternatively, the term imperialism may be used to denote forces at work in human relations of which the agent may be unaware or that he is powerless to control. Such a notion implies causality.

So, on the one hand, we have a variety of descriptions each termed 'imperialism', and, on the other, two types of argument. The first uses the concept as a characterization of human action in an historical context, and the other uses it as a theoretical concept in order to derive a general explanation. As we shall see, it is not immediately clear in the literature which form of explanation is being used. My point at this stage is that it is very important for us to determine this question before we can make any assessment of its explanatory adequacy, or accept the associated description of imperialism. Whether we accept the view of the power theorists or that of the proponents of economic imperialism, for example, depends very much on whether the case they have made is derived from an adequate explanatory mode. What this mode is and what its evaluatory criteria are will be discussed shortly.

The problem then is which, if any, of the varieties of imperialism considered in this book provide us with a true or adequate account of this aspect of human actions and experience. Such a problem cannot be answered by comparison or synthesis, that is by attempting some form of evaluation from within these accounts on the basis of their empirical 'findings'. It is not so much that these accounts of imperialism are incommensurable because they contain incompatible assumptions. The economic imperialist argument, for example, selects its evidence and presents its findings within the framework of basic assumptions about *economic* life. The power-security hypothesis does the same, but in terms of what it deems to be political. It is only a valid criticism if their mutual exclusiveness is condemned on grounds that stand outside the framework of their assumptions. And these, as we shall see, are associated with the notion of explanatory adequacy. It is not enough to condemn the former for its exclusion of the political and the latter for its corresponding exclusion of the economic. What counts as relevant depends upon the appropriate criterion of relevance, and this in turn depends upon the terms of the explanatory mode employed and the satisfaction of its criteria of adequacy.

Internal criticisms that concern what might be called the facticity of the putative 'facts' presented in accounts of imperialism, or that concern the conceptual language employed, while useful, cannot of themselves lead to any conclusion as to the relative merits of the competing arguments. Damaging though it may be, for example, that the 'facts' of investment — foreign and domestic — for capitalist countries do not correspond to the theoretical propositions of the economic imperialists, it does not refute the *theoretical* basis of the argument. Facts may be so interpreted as to conform to the hypothesis presented and indeed, as we shall see, this is the case in the literature. Similarly, the ambiguities and inconsistent usages of the concept 'power' in the power-security hypothesis make the argument equivocal to say the least, but do not constitute a refutation of its theoretical status. The point here is that the overriding question is whether or not these arguments constitute *explanations* and this cannot be determined by an investigation of their empirical and analytic failings alone. It can be answered only by establishing what counts as an explanation in terms of the criteria it must meet to be deemed adequate. Putative 'explanations' that are void of such criteria are non-explanatory, however plausible they may appear in terms of their factual descriptions and interpretation of the 'facts'.

So an examination of forms of imperialism must do more than provide an exposition of the arguments combined with an exegetical commentary and criticism. It must provide some grounds for the evaluation relevant to the arguments under consideration. Since, for the most part, writers on imperialism,[1] although frequently critical of each other's work, do not provide such grounds, they must be found. And on my argument they are established in two ways: firstly in terms of what is common for all explanatory modes, which gives its character to an explanation of human actions and experience; and, secondly, in the actual 'logic' of the putative explanation offered.

In the former case there are clear philosophical implications in establishing what counts as an adequate explanation and indeed in what counts as an explanation at all! There is a considerable epistemological literature on this subject.[2] And such an investigation has implications not just for this study of imperialisms but for the whole of the social sciences and indeed for any proffered claim to knowledge in science and history. I can concern myself only with those aspects most directly related to my subject. However, the nettle must be grasped, for unless we can establish criteria for the evaluation of the status and explanatory adequacy of the arguments about imperialism considered in this book, we can progress no further than exegesis. And even this is open-ended, for how can we establish even exegetical criteria without standards external to the exercise? How can we determine good and bad exegesis? Our understanding and interpretation of an argument is not axiomatic and if we base this on intuitive grounds then we may have as many views of a question as we have intuitions. Acceptance of the conclusions of an argument depends upon the satisfaction of explicit criteria of selection and evaluation as a prerequisite of analysis.

This brings me to the second aspect, that of relating the assumptions, implicit and explicit, of these arguments about imperialism to the notion of explanation. At what level is the proponent of a particular argument working? Does he really mean to generalize or are his general statements to be taken as only nominal and not genuinely universal. Does cause really mean cause? For example, in dealing with Marxist and neo-Marxist theories of imperialism, generalizations concerning modes of production and the status of the associated account of political and economic relations are in question. Is capitalism a stage or a state? Is it the product of a process working ineluctably through distinct and necessary pre-paratory stages, or is it simply a characterization of a given economic state of affairs appropriate to historical and unique conditions? If the former is the case, then the logic of a general causal theory is entailed even if it is not explicitly stated or its conditions, logical and empirical, satisfied. If the latter is the case, then since no principle of causality is entailed, other criteria of adequacy are relevant and we would assess it as an explanation in terms of historical evidence. In this case it would not be a theory, although it might prove to be a colligation or a rationalization, and so non-explanatory.

But the implications or entailments of the logical structure of such arguments, where these can be ascertained, are insufficient to enable us to relate them to an explanatory mode. It is not on grounds of logic alone that we can identify such a mode for we are concerned with the larger question of explanatory adequacy.[3] And this in turn depends on extra-logical criteria. An account that is logically valid and complete may be coherent but not true. Logical validity is not the same as empirical truth. I have been using the expression 'adequate' more or less as a synonym for true. The reason for this is that I do not want to suggest that truth is in any sense absolute or objective, dependent upon a universal criterion somehow independent of all empirical enquiry. The notion of truth encapsulated in the term *adequate* is conventional, in that the standards by which we assess putative explanations and claims to knowledge are simply pre-existent and external to them. In other words, while such criteria are independent of any particular explanatory claim, so that we know in advance to what it must refer if its conclusions are to be deemed satisfactory, the criteria themselves are not in any sense universal. They are part of the practice and accepted as such by practitioners. They act both as a means of test for the conclusions of an enquiry and also as a means by which questions can be formulated that are capable of being answered.

I shall develop this argument later on. The point here is that the various forms of imperialism that we shall be considering do not address themselves to the problem of determining appropriate evaluatory criteria. We are presented with arguments that certainly make claims to truth but that pose as finished answers, leaving the nature of the question open. Without anticipating the conclusions of this study, they appear on the face of it to be closed systems of thought and mutually exclusive. By this I mean that question and answer are somehow encapsulated in an account of the world that can only be judged on the grounds of its coherence. Yet such an account appeals to logic, conceptual analysis and empirical evidence, which extend beyond its argument. It purports to explain and to provide us with knowledge. And so we have a problem of how to evaluate it as an explanation.

I have been talking about explanation as a method of establishing knowledge. It is an ambiguous term, for in our language it is also taken to mean a completed account; the answer to the problem, as well as a means of problem solving. What of 'failed' or incomplete explanations, or of explanations that are putative and, while in principle capable, have not yet been submitted to any form of test? A distinction should be made between conjectures that in principle can be referred to external critical criteria to establish their adequacy as explanations, and conjectures that cannot, or that are disguised as finished explanations. The former, potentially at least, are explanatory and are formulated with a relevant test in mind. The latter are *mere* conjectures incapable of any further step. In a sense they are empty speculations.

This distinction becomes important where arguments that lack explicit criteria of reference are under scrutiny. Many of the accounts of imperialism that will be considered in this book are conjectural in both senses. Some of them are incomplete in a manner that admits remedy; others are, in principle and in practice, untestable. They cannot be referred to any critical criteria independent of their argument. To anticipate, genuine or potentially genuine explanatory forms coexist with non-explanatory arguments in the literature on imperialism. Before we can form any judgement or make valid our claims to understanding we must be able to distinguish between them. But having said this we must be clear as to what a genuine explanation is. What conditions must be satisfied before we can say of one argument that it explains and of another that it does not?

What then is explanation? In a general sense we can regard it as being an answer to a problem or puzzle. We judge it according to whether our problem has been solved to our satisfaction. It makes things intelligible; we understand them. But this leaves open the grounds we hold that make particular 'explanations' convincing and others not so. Why did we find *this* explanation more satisfactory than that one? What makes it an explanation at all? The notion of an explanation as being any statement or set of statements that solves problems, confuses a number of related concepts. For example, if we accept this view, explanations need not be true. Explanations may satisfy but may not produce knowledge. Similarly, explanations may be meaningful but not true. It may make sense to 'explain' the Moon as being made of green cheese, or the Earth as flat, or indeed to make any statement about something that is patently ridiculous, albeit meaningful; but whether it satisfies us or not has nothing necessarily to do with its truth. And arguments derived from such statements, however impeccable their logic, are not true either.

The point here is that what is at stake is not the question of making a state of affairs intelligible or making sense of it, but of establishing it as being the case, of it being true. Mere intelligibility can be obtained by postulating an account that is plausible through either a rationalization or a conjecture that 'fits the facts'. But no further reference is necessary for such arguments. Their acceptance is based upon a belief in their credibility. And clearly beliefs of this kind are both subjective and untestable. There is no contact between the proponent of the argument and its recipient on the score of a common ground for their joint acceptance of its validity. An explanation is concerned not merely with making something intelligible but also with the question of its truth. Unlike our understanding, an explanation is either true or false. Intelligibility is a by-product of an adequate explanation.

In short, if we are simply concerned with making things meaningful or intelligible, that is with understanding, the question of the truth of our understanding is begged if it lacks further reference. Being true is not a necessary condition for being meaningful, for if it were then only true things are meaningful, and this is patently not the case. But an understanding based on a satisfactory explanation is grounded on whether or not explicit conditions have been met by the explanation. Such conditions are independent of the explanation as this in turn is independent of the thing explained. Standards have to be set and met before we can accept or reject a putative explanation. Whether this is the case for the accounts of imperialism we are to consider is an important part of this study.

Truth, then, is simply a matter of reference to critical evaluatory standards that are independent of any particular enquiry but that are specific to the general mode of enquiry of which it is a part. This point is important when we consider arguments that purport to be explanatory but that in fact are not susceptible to any form of external test. On the face of it they make things intelligible, they confer meaning and they describe states of affairs, but there is no way of determining their truth. They are also incommensurable accounts: we cannot either synthesize them or have rational grounds for preferring one over another.

Let us now look at the two modes of explanation I intend to use throughout this study of imperialism. The first is that of theoretical explanation commonly associated with the natural sciences but also claimed to be a mode appropriate to the social sciences. Can we establish its autonomy on the basis of its logic and its criteria of adequacy? In what sense can it provide us with explanations whose adequacy is a matter of external evaluatory criteria? A theoretical explanation constitutes a means of subsuming phenomena, whose character it establishes within the framework of a set of propositions derived from a deductive argument and governed by a covering law.[4] If we ask the question why something happens or exists, then we are essentially asking for its cause. From this it follows that the explanation of a particular event or state of affairs moves away from a statement of its unique properties or conditions to a law-like statement that holds good for all such events of that class. A *general* explanation is offered: given the law and given a set of initial conditions, necessary and sufficient, the 'effect' (i.e. the event in question) may be deduced.

Hence we answer the particular question 'why?' by positing a general law together with the necessary and sufficient conditions, and from this we can deduce and predict the occurrence. We can also retrodict the initial conditions etc. from the occurrence itself. The conclusions are a *logical* and necessary consequent of the initial statements and the law. In science, speculative hypotheses, or what Popper calls conjectures,[5] are formulated within an established conceptual framework or general theory. Such conjectures are in principle testable, in that it is known in advance not what would be the answer, but what would count as an answer to the problem. It is the process of test through observation and experiment that establishes the conjecture firstly, as a potential explanation and, secondly, as adequate. The theory proper, the body of concepts and higher level theoretical propositions, is not itself directly testable. The conceptual framework that constitutes the theory provides a logical ground that renders coherent its derived propositions as they are tested. But, for it to act as a basis for explanation, the hypotheses derived from it must be empirically testable. *Their* test constitutes a test of the theory.

Such a test, either through a confrontation of the derived hypotheses with experience in the form of observations or through experiments, or both, while helping to establish what counts as an answer, does not provide us with certainty. As Popper and others have argued, no matter how many times testing may confirm a hypothesis there is no empirical or logical means of proving a genuine universality.[6] The correspondence between the hypothesis and the observation or experiment that tests it is temporal and finite. Conjectures can only be falsified and not verified. And neither is the parent conceptual framework indubitable, for it too is susceptible to change, either as anomalies or theoretical 'gaps' are explained through the formulation and testing of conjectures that require a new coherent framework, or as it is modified to subsume advances on the empirical level.

In scientific practice there are a number of subordinate grounds used to choose between competing or incommensurable hypotheses. They include the criterion of excess empirical content, where a hypothesis establishes new facts as well as subsuming those explained by a more limited explanation. Simplicity, or the principle of Occam's razor, is another one. A complex theoretical argument is rejected in favour of one that covers the same empirical ground but with fewer supporting hypotheses or riders.[7]

My point here is that theoretical argument, if it is to be deemed to be explanatory, must satisfy two sets of conditions — one appertaining to its causal logic, and the other to the tests of its adequacy in empirical terms. A conceptual framework that only satisfies the first set of conditions is non-explanatory, however plausible it might appear to be in 'fitting the facts'. It is fundamentally the method of test that qualifies argument as explanatory. And in the case of theoretical explanation it is based upon a mode of testing that pre-exists any claim to knowledge. Conjectures are formulated in the light of commonly accepted grounds of adequacy. It is this method of test that permits scientific knowledge to exist and also to change.

To sum up; speculative hypotheses are formulated positing general propositions about things that are then referred to 'facts' through experiment and observation. Anomalies, in the form of facts or events that do not conform to the theoretical conclusions, refute the attempted explanation. It is inadequate. But an unrefuted explanation does not constitute truth because there is no means of establishing the assumption of the uniformity of nature necessary to the assertion of the continual or infinite validity of its conclusions. We can never know that the next repetition of the test will not falsify it. Nor can truth be based on an inductive principle since this leads to infinite regress. Thus all such theoretical generalizations that are explanatory are only probabilities. But it does not follow from this that they are either purely analytic statements or statistical in nature. Untestable hypotheses, symbolic or conceptual schemes, etc., do not constitute empirical explanations. They may indeed be closely related to such explanations in that they provide the hypotheses or higher level propositions, or the variables, concepts and definitions from which those propositions capable of an empirical test are derived. They may be the theoretical structure that provides coherence to the empirical level, or they may be part of the method by which potentially fruitful conjectures are formulated, but without the level of empirical testing they cannot provide us with an explanation.

Turning back to accounts of imperialism, we can see that where we have a general conceptual scheme presented as a theoretical basis for imperialism then, potentially at least, we have an explanatory form akin to the one discussed above. If this is the case, it is the relation between the conceptual scheme and derived hypotheses, and between these and references to empirical testing through observation and experiment, that must be determined before we can make any explanatory claim. If all we have is an irrefutable conceptual framework, void either of testable hypotheses or means of test, then we have no explanation. The conditions that require satisfaction in terms of explanatory adequacy should be stated as part of the argument. Where generalizations and general conceptual categories are encountered in the literature on imperialism, we should be able to refer them to some form of test relevant to the theoretical mode of explanation. If it claimed that such accounts fall outside this rubric, then alternative grounds for establishing adequacy must be stated. If there are no such grounds, then we are entitled to dismiss them as explanations of imperialism.

I turn now to the other mode of explanation — the historical — that I posed as an alternative means of explaining imperialism. This is not specific to history but provides an explanation of human action in terms of reasoning. Essentially it takes the form of reason-giving explanation and it is important to distinguish between this and rationalization. A normative notion of rationality can either be imposed upon a class of actions in terms of appropriateness, according to notions commonly accepted by men in that situation as being rational, or it can be referrable to the conceptions of the individual agent. The importance of making such a distinction lies in the truth conditions of the reference. If we 'explain' an action by asserting a normative principle that permits a statement of what is appropriate action in a given situation, then the reference of such an account is to the principle itself. But on what grounds is this justified? Why should an agent accept it as a basis for his actions? Did he in fact accept it as such? This latter question is of course begged. But it is this question that is important in explanation; if we wish to refer an account of an action to something that validates it, it is insufficient to cite a normative principle of rationality in the absence of evidence that it was to that the agent himself appealed. As in the case of causal argument, which may be accepted by the agent as a theoretical basis for his actions, the point is not the substance of such arguments but whether they are actually cited as reasons. We are not constrained in explaining his actions to validate the grounds on which they are based. In short, if he has reasons then these, and these alone, can constitute an adequate reference for an explanatory account of his action. The question whether the observer thinks them reasonable is irrelevant, as is the question of their nature and status as reasons. And the question whether the agent considers them as reasonable is nonsensical, for they *are* his reasons. He may, of course, seek to justify them, but this is a different argument.

Thus the imposition of an observer's criterion of rationality on an agent's action is non-explanatory, given the absence either of a theory containing such a principle as a covering law and susceptible to an empirical test or of an alternative means of validation. In effect what is being done here is not explanation but judgement. The judgement consists of stating a criterion for an appropriate relation between reasons and actions, either in terms of means—ends, or in terms of the belief system of the agent. Here again the distinction between a reference to the observer's reasons and those of the agent becomes blurred. In the case of the former, the judgement takes the form of asserting on various grounds appropriate conditions and actions for the fulfilment of a stated purpose. Selecting these, and acting on them, not only will in effect succeed in achieving the end for which they are a means, but is the only rational way of proceeding. The degree to which the agent conforms to the model is a measure of his rationality. But we may ask again what justifies this argument? In the absence of an adequate explanatory basis that would permit prediction, and a testable statement of necessary and sufficient conditions, we have to take it on trust. The point here is that the argument as it stands points to a non-explanatory model of rational choice. And judgements of rationality or prescriptive statement are not explanations of acts.

If, however, we examine the agent's own reasoning and discover that he in fact adopts this procedure, that is, he too refers to such a model, while we are not in a position to establish whether his reasoning was sound in terms of reference to a validated explanation, we can distinguish between forms of reasoning or establish whether it was reasoning. Where we have evidence of reasoning that somehow connects means to ends on the basis of the agent's own conceptions, then we are in a position to refer an account to such evidence in a way we are not when we make a reference to external notions of rationality that are alleged to govern action. Either these last are normative or imply a general theory; if the former, no explanation is forthcoming, and if the latter, specific truth conditions are entailed that need to be fulfilled if we are to make good any claim to explanation.

No judgement as to the reasonableness of an agent's reasons is necessary in formulating a reason-giving explanation. We can know what his reasons were on the basis of evidence, but we cannot presume the knowledge that allows us to say that they will produce specified consequences. The question of what constitutes a good reason is decided by the agent. The observer, if he wishes to explain rather than to judge, is constrained by that decision. To understand an action or to make it intelligible is to understand the intention or purpose that coexisted with it. The meaning of the action lies in this; and it is the meaning it had for the agent. But to *explain* the action all we need to do is to relate the evidence of intentions to it. It is at this point that the observer begins to construct an account. This is to argue that explanation lies in making such a reference and that meaning and understanding are its products. There are a number of difficulties in doing this, most notably providing evidence of reasons, but the point here is that no judgement as to the rationality of the belief system of the agent, his conception of the relation of means to ends or of the ends, or the appropriateness of his proffered reasons, is entailed by this notion of explanation. While all these might be questioned in practical discourse, they are not relevant to the historian. Nor are we constrained to formulate any general law or causal hypothesis in adopting it.

The substitution of the rationalizations of the observer for those of the agent is innately anachronistic. What is deemed reasonable or rational, as I have argued, can be referred to causal explanation or to normative judgement. In the former case the theory is atemporal and treats a particular action as an instance of a class; and in the latter case the principle either is inseparable from the society that considers it relevant or appropriate, or is metaphysical and outside time. But even if the rationalization consists of no more than making an inference from the evidence of action of what would be reasonable as an intention or purpose, and citing this as a reason that makes the action intelligible, it is still anachronistic. The observer who does this is treating himself as a homologue for rational man and is referring past actions, for which he has no direct evidence of intentions, to what he conceives of as reasonable under the circumstances. And this will vary from observer to observer.

To explain in terms of the agent's intentions, rather than in terms of the 'consequences' of his actions perceived by the observer, is to show what was actually known to the agent at that time. It not only presupposes cognition but confines the explanation to the unique in terms of the individual, the place and the time. And it also follows that the appropriate focus is *action* and not events, that is with acts related to intention, purpose, motive, etc. generally subsumed under the rubric of 'reasoning'. Hence consequences and results are those perceived by the actors on the basis of their intentions and expectations. The observer can, of course, draw attention to successes and failures (but not 'mistakes') and to the unintended consequences of human acts, but only through reference to the reasoning of the historical agents.

What is being explained, it should be stressed, is the nature of the action. When we have an adequate account, we know 'what actually happened'. The adequacy of such an account depends on its relationship to evidence of the associated reasoning. This constitutes a truth test. The degree to which inferences enter into the account, or the use of indirect evidence, is an indication of its relative strength or weakness as an explanation. The more direct the evidence, the more adequate it becomes. And from this we are able to make comparisons and evaluations of different accounts (or histories) of the same actions.

Considerable difficulties exist in formulating such an account. It is difficult to determine what constitutes 'reasoning' as apart from *ex post facto* rationalization or special pleading. The reasons given by an agent may not, of course, be his 'real' reasons, so there is room for interpretation in any given case. The materials we have to work on are survivals from the past and incomplete in a way that cannot be known. But it must also be said that we can have no explanation in the absence of such evidence, however sophisticated or subtle an attempt at rationalization may be.

I want to stress that the mode of explanation described here is particularist and not general. It tells us about the actions of the agent and not why he holds his reasons for them. All we have explained is the act itself and we have done that by making it clear what it was in terms of the agent's view of it. To step outside this relation is to engage in some other exercise, including perhaps the theoretical mode of explanation. If this is done, then on my argument such an account still requires the satisfaction of criteria of adequacy specific to that mode.

From this it is clear that the criterion of an external test is met by this mode of explanation. It has a very different logic from that of the theoretical mode. Like it, it must satisfy two sets of conditions for an account within the mode to be deemed adequate or satisfactory as an explanation. The first is a specification of action in terms of the intentions, purposes, reasoning, etc., of the agent in a context of time, place and personality. Actions that are not referrable in this way — because they either are treated as involuntary, or are part of the external reasoning of the commentator or belong to a theory of action or a conceptual framework not shared by the agent — are outside this mode. Secondly, the test of adequacy employed constitutes rules governing the selection and status of evidence of reasoning. As with the convention of empirical testing in the theoretical mode, this criterion does not provide us with objective truth or certain knowledge. There can be no means of establishing in any absolute form a connection between the reasons an agent actually gives for his action and evidence for them. But, as in the case of legal evidence, in practice rules exist that stand outside the level of action itself and to which the latter may be referred in order to establish reasoning. By this I do not mean rules that assess the rationality of action but rules that assess the validity or worth of the evidence of reasoning attributed to the action that is the subject of explanation. Such an explanation stands or falls on the assessment of this evidence. Where the evidence is scant or suspect then the explanation is a bad one. Where there is no evidence then we have no explanation.

This necessarily abbreviated discussion on explanatory forms indicates the basis of the method I have adopted in this analysis of the imperialisms considered in this book. Throughout there is a conscious application of two kinds of reference for the arguments under review. Is the appropriate reference to the kind of general theory with its specific evaluatory criteria posed as one explanatory mode, or is it to the other reason-giving mode? Given that the proponents of these arguments do not themselves specify what conditions need to be satisfied for their enquiries or conclusions to be deemed adequate as explanations, it is up to us to make the appropriate reference. As I have argued, this is both difficult and debatable. It may be that the two postulated modes of explanation I have outlined and treated as possible sources of reference are not acceptable on various grounds. But while they might be open to criticism, some such reference is necessary if we are to treat the proffered arguments as explanatory and a means of achieving knowledge.

Turning now to the four main chapters in this book, I have treated each of these as constituting a model of imperialism, distinctive in content although not necessarily in terms of their explanatory nature. What each claims about the world and the place imperialism has in it constitutes a selection and ordering of 'facts' subsumed under a general theoretical argument. But, accepting their incommensurability as arguments that 'explain' imperialism and positing a family resemblance between the various arguments that constitute the model, they possess, as we shall see, similarities as well.

The idea of power in inter-state relations, for example, is distinctive in one sense, but competition for power itself can be explained in terms of fear. The hypothesis of a competition for material resources between states is explained on the one hand as the consequence of the organization of peoples into sovereign autonomous nation-states each concerned to protect its own security and knowing no higher form of morality or rule of law, and on the other by their capacities for aggression linked to the consequent fear aroused by such capacity. In the one case the idea of a power struggle is central to the argument, but in the other it is subsumed within a larger argument about human nature. For each model claims to be objective and universal. The power-security hypothesis asserts the primacy of politics, the economic imperialist thesis that of the dominant capitalist mode of production, the ideological view the supremacy of belief and its practical consequences, and the sociobiological argument that of the human psyche and its genetic conditioning. In terms of knowledge of imperialism each asserts a unique and superior claim.

These four models have been chosen not as definitive or encompassing the whole range of arguments about imperialism, or even as complete in themselves, but as a selection of the major viewpoints in the literature. They are not models in any rigorous sense, for their ambiguities, the lack of explicit criteria of reference for their evaluation, the way in which their basic concepts dissolve and translate into one another under critical analysis, exclude any treatment of them as tightly organized conceptual schemes. They are embryonic in this sense. I take a model in the social sciences[8] to be either a method of investigation or an elaborate analogy designed for some heuristic purpose. In the former case certain factors or variables alleged to be present in a given situation — of economic choice for example, or of political decision — are extrapolated, and projected relations and consequences are postulated. The point in doing this is that some relationships between variable factors that would not otherwise be accessible through observation might be elicited. There is an explicit analogy with the use of mathematical models in the natural sciences.

There are a number of unresolved problems in this type of modelling in the context of human actions and experience, not the least being that of the relation between the model and theory. Instead of isolating key variables in human behaviour, the model constitutes a form of theorizing that assumes an explanatory level either untested or untestable. The technique of modelling in the natural sciences is designed to suggest possible testable hypotheses within the framework of a pre-existing theory whose adequacy has been established. In the social sciences the model is often a substitute for theory. In any case, in the absence of a tested theory the use of models is simply a voyage in the dark. The framework of assumptions about human actions and decisions is carried into the model, which naturally reifies them. The exercise is circular.

Similarly, the use of models as a homology with some aspect of human behaviour is merely another way of stating an understanding of the latter. The formality of such a model, with its attempt at precise definition and measurement of categories and its conceptual elaborations, only masks its descriptive nature. It cannot provide us with an *explanation* for it is derived from what we already know, merely turning this into re-description. The categories are not made more precise through being closely defined or put in some quantitative form, for they cannot be extended into any testable empirical hypothesis. And as with the use of models as a method of enquiry there is no means of testing their assumptions, whether these are implicit or explicit.

The notion of model used in this study is that of a characteristic and developed argument taken from the literature on imperialism. Such an argument takes its main features from a number of writers, whose theses have a family resemblance differing only in degree and detail. Differences between them certainly exist, and in some cases, notably that of economic imperialism, these are deemed sufficiently important to stimulate a continuing debate and an increasing elaboration of the central argument. Nevertheless, even here there is a cohesion and an agreement on the central features of the imperialism they purport to explain. Their contentions are only an extension of the common thesis. Where there are ambiguities and lacunae in the development of the argument I have tried to clarify and fill them. In so doing I have tried to follow the spirit of the thesis and to trace its implications as far as they can be taken within its logic.

In particular, I have not postulated any countering thesis or adopted a position that is implicitly opposed. Thus, in tracing the power-security theory of imperialism, I have not subjected it to criticism, explicit or implicit, derived from an alternative hypothesis such as that of economic imperialism. The point is not that the power theorists reject economics, or that the economic argument conceives of politics as mere epiphenomena, or that both reject the relevance of ideological views and the beliefs of individual agents; it is their status as *explanations* that matters. A criticism based on the postulates of an alternative hypothesis itself requires justification in terms of its explanatory power. If one of these models of imperialism were right then it would indeed refute the others or reduce them to incoherence. But it is the manner in which such arguments can be judged right — or wrong — that is important. Their claims to an exclusive truth require examination.

And this brings me back to the problem of explanation. The four models of imperialism considered in this book are not compared or contrasted with one another. No empirical grounds for such an exercise exist. The data and the empirical material to which they refer, and that they subsume, are made relevant by the conceptual framework that they deploy. On the empirical level it is not a valid criticism, for example, that the economic theory of imperialism neglects the data employed by the sociobiological theorists. Their categories of empirical reference are exclusive because of the central hypothesis employed. In this example, economic data are important because it is the mode of production that determines everything else. The ethologists, however, are concerned with the fundamental biological basis of human behaviour, and so reduce their area of reference to biological generalities. Other aspects of human action and experience are either 'explained' by their thesis or are irrelevant. At this level not only can there be no synthesis between the arguments on imperialism but there is no common ground either. The imperialism each depicts is a closed system. They are incommensurable arguments.

The common ground I seek lies not in what they say about the world of human action but in their nature and status as explanatory arguments. And here they share a number of characteristics. I have tried to relate these to the two modes of explanation discussed earlier on this introduction. All of these models of imperialism seek to make general statements about human behaviour. They are mutually exclusive. But in doing so there is an explicit claim to a level of generalization that purports to be explanatory. They seek to formulate a ground for explaining a broad category of human activity. And so it becomes important to ask what validates this ground. The logic of a general explanation of human behaviour is thus a common point of reference for all these arguments. In this respect they are all trying to do the same thing. So, such aspects as, for example, the relationship of an elaborated conceptual scheme to empirical materials, the way in which the latter is organized and presented as a narrative illustrating the concepts employed, the selection of pertinent data and the element of rationalizing about human action, are all common to these various notions of imperialism. The question therefore arises as to what grounds require satisfaction before we can consider any of them an adequate explanatory account of imperialism.

Equally, we have to consider the alternative: that they are really forms of historical explanation specific to time, place and the individual. Quite different grounds exist, as we have seen, for this type of explanation. Again we have to stiuplate what they are before we can evaluate the 'historical' part of these arguments. The level of generalisation in this case is not logically central to their explanatory force but constitutes a kind of colligation or organizing principle. Their adequacy is determined not by the relation of empirical generalization to some form of atemporal test, but by the relation of evidence to the rationale of the narrative.

The actual empirical examples to which these models are referred in the book — security competition between the major powers in the pre-nuclear and nuclear periods; the relationship between the capitalist and non-capitalist states and multinational companies; Hitler's foreign policy; and Japanese imperialism in the 1930s — are in one sense arbitrary. All these models in principle explain a form of imperialism that makes its appearance when the conditions stipulated by the theory come into existence. The nation-state itself, once it acquires the material capacity to engage in major violence, is caught in the power-security trap and consequently engages in imperialist policies. Capitalist states are imperialist once they enter into that mode of production and are forced to compete for economic territory. A commitment to ideological beliefs such as nationalist-socialist ideology forces the believer to embark on a course of action that includes imperialism. And the latent aggressive drives in man impel him into forms of violent competition that at their highest level become imperialism. All manifestations of imperialism — the phenomena of violence, conquest, domination, expansion and war in the world at large — are in principle explained by each of these models. Their specificity in historical terms is merely contingent and while they are applied to cases of imperialism in the immediate past (only the sociobiological thesis seems to be truly universal) they present themselves as general explanations, capable of extension beyond any particular historical reference. The form of imperialism that they postulate supersedes all others. It is *that* which constitutes imperialism.

So the selection of these empirical examples is not intended to reduce the scope of these models, or to suggest that they are confined to these specific cases. Although in its theoretical postulates each model singles out particular phenomena as directly relevant — security fears and arms races in the power-security hypothesis;

capitalist modes of production in economic imperialism; racist and autarkic ideas in ideological imperialism; and aggressive drives and atavistic instincts in the sociobiological argument — the historical or empirical references merely *illustrate* each model. I do not say *prove,* for reasons that will be made clear in my discussion of each case. They could in principle be referred to any nominal case of imperialism in the past. But they are atemporal arguments that apply equally to the past, present and future. My intention in using these particular examples is to try to establish their explanatory adequacy in the two senses of explanation I have discussed earlier. They are thus test-cases for each of the models of imperialism I have considered. In principle they should be interchangeable. If this were done we would then have a different explanation and an associated description according to which model we used. Our view of war, for example, would be fundamentally different according to whether we used the power-security hypothesis, the economic theory, the ideological view or the sociobiological argument. When applied to specific historical wars their empirical character would be determined by the argument selected. The focus shifts according to the prism selected.

NOTES AND REFERENCES

1 For example, see the debate in Roger Owen and Bob Sutcliffe (eds) *Studies in the Theory of Imperialism* (London, Longmans, 1972) and also D. K. Fieldhouse *The Theory of Capitalist Imperialism* (London, Longmans, 1967).

2 See, for example, Daniel Taylor *Explanation and Meaning* (Cambridge, Cambridge University Press, 1970); G. H. Von Wright *Explanation and Understanding* (London, Routledge and Kegan Paul, 1971); Alan Ryan *The Philosophy of the Social Sciences* (London, Macmillan, 1970); E. Nagel *The Structure of Science* (London, Routledge and Kegan Paul, 1961).

3 See the debate in Imre Lakatos and Alan Musgrave (eds) *Criticism and the Growth of Knowledge* (Cambridge, Cambridge University Press, 1970).

4 See the account of explanation given by C. G. Hempel and Paul Oppenheim 'Studies in the logic of explanation' in *Philosophy of Science* Vol. 15 (1948) pp. 135-78 and C. G. Hempel *Aspects of Scientific Explanation* (Glencoe, Free Press, 1965).

5 See Karl R. Popper *Conjectures and Refutations* (New York, Basic Books, 1963) and *Objective Knowledge* (London, Oxford University Press, 1972).

6 Popper *Objective Knowledge, op. cit.*

7 See Paul Feyerabend 'Consolations for the specialist' in Lakatos and Musgrave, *op. cit.,* pp. 197-214 and 'How to be a good empiricist' in P.H. Nidditch (ed.) *The Philosophy of Science* (London, Oxford University Press, 1965) pp. 12-39.

8 See May Brodbeck 'Models, meaning and theories' in May Brodbeck (ed.) *Readings in the Philosophy of the Social Sciences* (London, Macmillan, 1968) pp. 579-598.

2

Imperialism as Power

Power has a long tradition of usage in political literature. Terms such as 'power politics', 'balance of power', 'power vacuum', 'the pursuit of power', 'the struggle for power', etc., abound in accounts of international politics.[1] Not all writers use these expressions either consistently or systematically, but they seem to share a common conception, firstly, that power is some form of capacity or quality and, secondly, that international politics is anarchic and violent in nature, and that the political activities of states constitute a struggle for survival.

The only major constraint on states and their freedom to pursue their own interests is the countervailing force of rival capacities for exercising violence. All other constraints — such as the existence of economic exchange relationships of mutual benefit, relative dependence on external sources of raw materials, on markets or on investment income, contractual obligations incurred under treaties or formal alliances, the existence of international organizations designed to resolve disputes peacefully, competing priorities in internal resource allocation, and domestic political conditions — only mitigate this fundamental anarchy. International law is vestigial in its jurisdiction and in its effects. Given this general condition of international anarchy, the state that enjoys most power not only can act as a predator on other states but can also protect itself. There is a major advantage in seeking and gaining power in the world, for by doing this a state can create its own security. Underlying all inter-state relations is the problem of national security, and all other interests, however momentarily dominant in the political life of a nation, are subordinate to it.

What is this problem and why does a national concern for security lead to imperialism? What is the connexion between power and imperialism? I intend to try to answer these questions firstly by examining what I have termed the power-security hypothesis[2] in the context of the post-war nuclear arms race and then, secondly, by

19

assessing this essentially *political* characterization of imperialism in terms of its explanatory adequacy. As will be seen in the treatment of other modes of imperialism in this study, what is at stake is whether a general thesis that characterizes imperialism in terms of specific categories of factors — political, economic, ideological, and sociobiological — has any capacity to *explain* inter-state relations. Clearly they are incommensurable as theories or world views. In choosing one as a valid characterization of world politics and apportioning it explanatory power, we are compelled to reject the others. Any attempt at synthesis breaks down inevitably into a form of argument that is neither general enough to constitute a theoretical explanation nor specific enough to constitute a historical explanation, for reasons that I hope to make clear.

The power-security thesis conceives of the world as made up of sovereign states each responsible for its own well-being and security. A minimal definition of security is the preservation of the state as a political entity and the maintenance of its territorial integrity. The two are not synonymous, for a state may by fortunes of war or of diplomacy lose some of its territory and still remain a state. France, for example, lost Alsace-Lorraine after the war of 1870, and Czechoslovakia lost the Sudetenland in 1938. It is rare for a state to be extinguished altogether, Poland in the eighteenth and nineteenth centuries being perhaps the most notable example. The division of Germany after the last major conflict is something of an anomaly.

However, no government is willing to lose territory and this is deemed as constituting part of the identity of the state that its primary function is to protect. Consequently, governments create a military capacity for what they somewhat euphemistically call defence. All statesmen, regardless of the polity they serve, or of its resources, prepare for the eventuality of international violence inimical to the existence of their states. Regardless of other objectives that might be served by the use or the development of a capacity for violence, the minimal requirement of national defence is to provide national security. As we shall see, the nature of the potential threat and the range of options open to states in countering it are variables. The security problems of Switzerland are different from those of China or France. And such problems are not immutable. Although factors such as spatial relations, topography, political geography and even climate are relatively constant, rapid changes in other factors, such as weapons technology, political relations, types of government and their will or ability to deploy national resources, popular sentiment, ideological commitments, etc., all combine to produce a highly unstable and unpredictable network of mutual actions and reactions largely uncontrolled by any one state or groups of states. It is this inherent instability in the international and domestic environments that is at the core of the power-security hypothesis and its related imperialism.

The history of the nation-state has also been the history of war and of the technology of war. Considerable progress, if this is the appropriate word, has been made in the development of engines of destruction. The background to this development and to the kaleidoscopic pattern of inter-state affiliation and animosity has been the constant threat of war. War appears as normal; as a basic fact of international politics. And so any study, either of the domestic politics of a state or of relations between states in times of peace, that ignores this salient feature of world politics is inevitably distorted.

The need to prepare for imminent violence, whatever its postulated form, permeates all aspects of political life even where it is least apparent. There is never a genuine choice between guns and butter, for both have to be provided for in reality. Defence has a high priority in the allocation of resources within the state. Of course variations between states in terms of this allocation exist in practice, depending on whether the immediate security problem has been deemed to be resolved, if only temporarily, by a government. As we shall see, even when the immediate threat appears to have been allayed, as in the case of Britain and France after the last major war with the defeat of Japan and Germany, the security problem simply reappears in another guise. Even neutrals such as Sweden and Switzerland, and those smaller states such as Finland, Belgium and the Netherlands, whose role in recent world history has been that of victims of aggression, have defence policies.

But this apparently sensible policy, that of providing for the defence of the state, creates the condition that it most seeks to avoid. The paradox stems from the notion of security central to this argument. A condition of security only exists when the state possesses the capacity to fight successful wars against any potential aggressor, and defence policy is concerned in the main with relative war *capacities* and not with the *intentions* of other governments. The point is that the allocation of resources for defence is based on the current and projected military capabilities of other countries. In crude terms unalleviated by political relationships or economic conditions, this means that a national defence capacity must be equal to or superior than that of any other state or combination of states. Obviously this calculation does not take into account alliances or diplomacy as countering ploys. But, given the relative instability of the political world, contracts between governments are prone to revision or abrogation and those between allies are no exception. Governments may be overthrown or go out of office and radically new policies may be adopted by their successors, and so on.

Although the foreign policy of a state is designed to promote national interests, security being but one of them, it is clearly linked to short-term considerations. The very instability of international politics exacerbates this element of expediency. But weapons development and procurement take a long time to come to fruition in the form of a viable force. Consequently, decisions involving defence and the allocation of resources tend to overlap and to produce effects independently of policies and decisions made in the political sphere. Defence contingencies are not the same as political contingencies and the two tend to be out of phase. In short, there is a tendency amongst defence planners, including the military, to ignore the short-term political world and to concentrate on questions of relative capacities for violence as concrete factors on which to base their decisions. Intentions might change with governments, but their capacities for violence remain as constant factors. Politicians thus find themselves inhibited, or perhaps tempted, by a capacity for violence created in the past that has unforeseen consequences for a crisis or a political relationship in the time of their office.[3]

The consequence of this duality in the conduct of politics in the world arena — the pursuit of national interests through diplomacy and the pursuit of national security through the creation of a capacity for war related to other national capacities — is an exacerbation of the security dilemma. The central problem is that one state's security is always another state's insecurity. Whatever a state does for its own defence has inevitable repercussions on other states and their capacity for violence. This is especially the case when a radical innovation in weapons technology takes place. There is a built-in incentive for those states with the requisite resources to adopt a policy of research and development in new weapons in order to forestall innovations made by other states. This is true even of those weapons formally or informally banned by international convention or by tacit agreement — research is undertaken on chemical and biological weapons by most major states.

The result, so the power-security hypothesis has it, is a competition between states. This takes the form of arms races, combinations of states for mutual defence or collective 'security' and the social and economic organization of the state for war. Such a competition is ultimately decided by war itself. In attempting to achieve security through preparations for defence, the nation-states succeed instead in creating anarchy and violence in the world. Yet war can decide the question of national security, or, to be more precise, *which* nation is secure, only if that nation succeeds once and for all in monopolizing violence in the world in the same way as its government has monopolized violence within the state. In theory, security can be achieved through the establishment of a world hegemony or empire, or by the creation of a world state. In historical times neither of these possibilities has ever been realized, although hegemonial dominion has been established, as in the case of the Roman Empire, over large areas and over a variety of peoples. Such empires were established through war and disappeared in the same way. No state has ever won a war, for victory and defeat have never been total. The end of every war has seen the beginning of another one.

Such preparations, and the need to counter possible developments in war capacities made by other states, appear on the face of it to be rational. Theodore Roosevelt's remark 'Speak softly but carry a big stick' is but one reflection made by many statesmen of the maxim 'he who wants peace must prepare for war'. And indeed, quite apart from the fundamental question of national security, other national interests are served by the use or threat of violence. As Carl von Clausewitz has it, war is policy by other means.[4] But, as he also pointed out, war is a rational course of action only when the ends are unchanged by the means employed. War is indeed rational if political objectives are realizable through the use of violence. But how is this to be guaranteed?

The main determinant of the kind of war actually fought, according to the power-security hypothesis, is not any political limitation set in advance by the contestants, or even the nature of the actual issue in dispute, but the material capacity of states to inflict damage on each other, created for the purpose of providing for national security. This capacity, although designed for the *defence* of the state and so unrelated to any specific political crisis or dispute, nevertheless acts as the ultimate parameter for the scale of violence in inter-state conflicts. It impinges upon the rational use of violence by changing what is nominally at stake into the larger question of national survival. The comparatively minor issues in inter-state disputes become occasions rather than causes of war — the war that is actually fought. It is not the tone of the statesman's voice that matters but the size of his stick. The scale of the conflict is thus a function of the scale of armaments created in the interests of national security.[5]

Hence a threat of violence in pursuit of lesser objectives than national security becomes irrational if the war that is actually fought becomes one of national survival. It would become rational only if the victor power in its triumph succeeded once and for all in achieving world hegemony and so finally resolving its problem of security by eliminating all its competitors. Victories that fall short of this never succeed in resolving the security problem. In short, violent contests between states, whatever the nominal issue, have this security dimension, which makes such contests inherently irrational. This is not to say that limited wars have not been fought successfully in the past and their limits maintained by the contestants so that the means have been commensurate with the ends. But these wars — Crimea, Korea and Vietnam come to mind — were attended by special circumstances and were at best stalemates and inconclusive. The point is that there is always a possibility of general war even where such limits are consciously adhered to, given the existence of a capacity for this type of war created on grounds of national security. The temptation to increase the scale of war in the event of imminent defeat is always present.[6] Moreover, the constant pressure of weapons development means that this capacity not only is constantly changing but is indeterminate. The consequences of its use are not evident in peace-time, nor the consequences of any counter-measures taken by an opponent. This introduces a 'mechanical' effect into warfare that might take the conflict beyond its prescribed limits. The effect of submarine warfare in the First World War and of air warfare in the Second World War are examples of this. The development and effect of such weapons can, as we shall see, change the prevalent conception of national security.

What then is the consequence of this characterization of the world as an anarchy, its perpetual violence tempered by relatively brief interludes of peace? The emphasis so far in the argument has been on the security dilemma posed by the existence of a number of sovereign states each providing for its own defence and in so doing creating a general and permanent condition of insecurity for all. It is the existence of this dangerous and anarchic environment for the state that impels those that possess the requisite resources into attempts to control it. The power-security hypothesis postulates the pursuit of power as the primary objective of the state in its relations with other states. And this is supported by the creation of a war capacity, which in turn generates the reciprocity between states, making the need to provide security ever more acute. Hence the attempt to provide security for the state in a world made anarchic and dangerous by this open-ended competition compels the state to try to control its own environment. In practice this means the extension of its influence over other states. Such control directly challenges the security of these states and so the competition becomes a conflict over rival spheres of influence dominated by the technological capacities of the competing systems of 'influence'. Imperialism is thus a direct consequence of the security dilemma. The world becomes a world of 'mice ruled over by lions'.[7] The lions continually quarrel.

Now, expressed in these terms the power-security argument appears both abstract and over-simple. I have termed it a hypothesis and this implies at least a conjectural explanation of a general nature. In essence what is suggested is that the primary reason for a state firstly to develop and then to use a war capacity is fear for its security. This, translated into a world composed of sovereign states, similarly preoccupied, means that the only secure guarantee of territorial integrity lies in the exercise of authority beyond the nation-state through diplomacy backed by force. It is this that provides the impetus to imperialism. And so we have a general explanation, through security fears, of a whole range of phenomena, from the allocation of resources to defence, a defence policy and its domestic political and economic implications, to arms races, technological innovations in weapons, alliances and 'war' diplomacy, and war itself. Imperialism takes the form of the extension of authority through the subjugation of other states by force or by diplomacy, the physical seizure of territory, the establishment of security-dependent relations with weaker states as a pre-emptive denial of resources or strategic positions to the putative 'enemy', and so on. The kind of politics characteristic of these activities is designated *power politics.*

Fundamentally, this argument depends on the primacy of security fears emanating from the nation-state and producing an interactive system of mutually insecure states. This insecurity is self-reinforcing, given the inability of any one state to create a lasting hegemony over the others, and the necessity of responding to changes in political stance, government, weapons technology, etc., likely to affect the overall security 'balance'. The condition of international anarchy is both produced and perpetuated by the actions of states designed to achieve a measure of security.

Now, for this conjecture to be genuinely explanatory, a distinction has to be made between the explanation and the phenomena it seeks to explain. In other words, the argument must not be circular in that the phenomena of arms races and wars are taken to mean anarchy, and this in turn taken to represent national fears for security. Otherwise we are confronted with a conceptual framework — a set of abstract definitions of related concepts, such as state, security, power, etc., — void of empirical application. Or, alternatively, we have a description of a particular past situation couched in this type of language and so normative in nature. To impose the power-security argument on political acts and decisions without reference to the actual reasoning of those engaged in action is to indulge in rationalization. To engage in refining the logic of a model is to remove the argument from the realm of explanation and to theorize without empirical application. Whether these two possibilities actually apply to the power-security hypothesis and its version of imperialism will be considered later on.

Before examining the power-security hypothesis in terms of the contemporary relations of states and their 'imperialism', some preliminary discussion of the two concepts — power and security — would appear to be useful. The theoretical and explanatory implications of this argument will be considered at the end of the chapter but, given the problems of defining power and the indeterminacy of the notion of security, some clarification at this stage is necessary.

The notion of power blends two quite distinct notions, that of power as a capacity and that of power as an exercise. The former lies in the notion of a relation between pre-conditions for, and the successful accomplishment of, an action. The latter is less precise and consists of action itself, a state rather than a condition. In our context the former refers to the creation of a capacity to fight successful wars or to create a condition of security for the nation-state; the latter consists of actual involvement in world politics in which the purpose of the involvement is to advance the 'power' of the state. This may be done through the use of violence, threats or diplomacy, but in all cases these actions are related to specific objectives, whether it be the general end of winning a war or some more limited objective such as the successful conclusion of a negotiation. We tend loosely to associate the former notion with defence policy and the latter with foreign policy, in all its guises — political, economic, cultural, and so on. We conceive of a road to power, that is power as a means, and the successful enjoyment of a state of power. In our context, the creation of a war capacity as a pre-condition for security constitutes one form of power; the attempt to control other states, and its concomitant political and economic activities, constitutes the other form of power.

This is to say that, although the two are related in that the former is a pre-condition for the latter, they correspond nevertheless to two quite different notions of power. Power as a capacity constitutes a set of attributes or dispositions to perform an action or category of actions. In a general sense any projected course of action entails an assessment of capacity. We make estimates of probable success in terms of our possession of as many of the attributes — the means — we deem necessary to attain our end. National security is the goal of defence planning and the creation of a capacity for national defence is based upon estimates of resources, their deployment, the dispositions of other states, friendly, neutral or inimical, and their likely reactions in times of crisis. It is the basis of the power-security hypothesis that this capacity has a destabilizing effect impelling the state not merely to develop this capacity further as other states compete but to seek to control its environment, that is to exercise power.

These two notions of power as a capacity and as an exercise are combined in a form of imperialism pursued by the most 'powerful' states. Their 'power' is not only derived from their success in dominating other states, that is on the basis of their performance in controlling their environment, but is also based on an estimate of their capacity to do so. The notions of power as a capacity or potential for action and power as an exercise or fulfilment are united in political estimates of the relative strengths of states and the formulation of strategies designed to achieve the goal of national security.

However, the blurring of this distinction is a mistake if we wish to base an explanatory hypothesis on the concept of power. We must distinguish between power and its exercise if we wish to explain in terms of a set of pre-conditions, necessary and sufficient, for a given level of activity to take place. In what sense does power as capacity explain imperialism as an effect of the exercise of this capacity, as the power-security hypothesis has it?

Power as a capacity is essentially a theoretical concept both in its practical and in its explanatory aspects. It comes of course from mechanics. A generalization is entailed that relates a set of pre-conditions for an action to the successful completion of that action. In this case the creation of a defence capacity and the creation of a position of 'power' in the outside world are means to the end of national security. In a theoretical sense such means need to be related to a precise and definable end in terms of its fulfilment. If such a relation cannot be stipulated and its terms are left imprecise, then the 'theory' only amounts to a practical estimate of possibility and probability such as that made by politicians on the basis of Stalin's famous comment 'How many divisions has the Pope?' A genuine theory that treated power as capacity would have to state, firstly, the necessary and sufficient conditions for a postulated action and, secondly, produce an explanatory hypothesis in terms of a general covering law. Such a construct would clearly show that the level of action explained is entailed by these conditions being satisfied within the law. The explanation would consist of showing how the fulfilment of these conditions and the consequent result are together explained by the associated law. Wherever and whenever this association exists, the resultant state of affairs occurs. The necessary and sufficient conditions and the covering law are logically independent of the phenomenon that is the subject of the explanation.

Power would thus have a precise meaning in terms of the

predictable achievement of a desired state of affairs. While it would be synonymous with capacity it would not be as open-ended and as ambiguous as it is in the absence of such rigorous treatment. As we shall see, there are considerable difficulties in using the concept power in empirical explanations of political action.

Power as an exercise, what might be called the actualization of power, is somewhat different from the idea of power as a set of pre-conditions or capacity for action. This notion on the face of it does not seem to be theoretical. In the context of international politics it becomes confused with the condition for which an explanation is sought. The quest for power in terms of the power-security hypothesis leads to imperialist policies. But imperialism is a state of affairs as well as a type of practice. An empire places the metropolitan state in a position of power *vis-à-vis* its subject territories. But seeking to achieve such a position of hegemony is also imperialism. In this sense both pre-war Germany and Britain were imperialist powers, the former seeking to gain an empire and the latter to preserve one.

The characterization of international politics as power politics thus blurs the distinction between the achievement of power as a pre-condition for security and the exercise of power as an extension of the rule or authority of the state over other states. The power-security hypothesis does not make this distinction clear, but it is apparent that the former is deemed to be the means for achieving the latter. Both are necessitated by security fears and this is the core of the argument, and indeed of the asserted paradox that these fears induce power politics, which in turn exacerbates the general condition of insecurity and so promotes power politics. Power is the ultimate goal and this is equated with empire, which alone provides a guarantee of national security. Short of this, the pursuit of power politics as a means of solving the immediate problem of security, while apparently rational, is inherently irrational, since it creates further insecurity.

Rationality in this sense depends not on normative judgement but upon the assertion of a dynamic at work in inter-state relations. Insecurity is an *unintended* consequence. Indeed intentions are irrelevant. The dynamic operates independently of the reasoning of the politicians, for presumably if they were aware of the problem, or could control the factors contributing to it, it could then be resolved. The essence of the power-security hypothesis, if it is to be considered as a *theoretical* explanation of imperialism in inter-state relations, is that the relation between the capacities created, whatever the immediate reasoning, for national defence produces the unintended effects of security competition and its political consequences. Such a relation is independent of the will of rational agents whose actions, while apparently corresponding to the rationality of providing for the nation's defence in a hostile environment, actually create that hostility. So in assessing the power-security form of imperialism we must distinguish between causes and effects. The creation of a capacity for the exercise of power in national defence policies directly leads to the pursuit of power in order to offset the condition of insecurity that it creates. Is such an effect, firstly, separable from a set of pre-conditions that constitutes its cause, and secondly, can the notions of power and security be used as explanatory concepts in this way, or are they in turn open to explanation? Given the ambiguities of the expression *power* this last seems a distinct possibility.

If power can be treated as an attribute independent of the reasoning of the agents who are engaged in political action, what of security? This was rather loosely defined earlier as the preservation of the territorial integrity of the state from aggression or a threat of aggression. In an absolute form this would constitute a condition of complete independence and freedom from constraints imposed through coexistence with other states in a world of states. Almost any form of relationship can be construed as a potential threat to national security. Trading and economic exchange relations, for example, can be viewed as constraints on a state's freedom to act. Paradoxically the more beneficial the terms of trade, the more dangerous they are to the state, given the possibility that they are open to curtailment by forces that are not controlled by the beneficiary. The more enmeshed a state is in a condition of economic interdependence with other states, then the less freedom it has to act in its own interests. As we shall see in later chapters this condition of interdependent economic relations has been conceived of as constituting a form of imperialism. Marxist commentators argue that capitalism of necessity constructs a network of dependent relations between capitalist states and a subordinate 'economic territory'. Conversely, national—socialist and fascist writers argue that a state is only genuinely sovereign when it enjoys a complete autarky and is free of any form of dependence, however immediately beneficial, on external sources of supply and markets. This sentiment in less extreme forms has been echoed by liberal democratic politicians in their attack on intergovernmental economic agreements such as the EEC.

The notion of security thus has implications beyond that of the relative ability of a state to defend itself against a potential aggressor in terms of material capacities for violence. The identification of the state and its territorial integrity with that of its political regimen is a complicating factor. Insurrection, subversion, terrorism and radical forms of politics have all been interpreted in practice as constituting a threat to national security, where in fact no challenge to the territorial integrity of the state is involved. Politicians are fond of identifying a variety of national interests under the rubric of security. A good deal of this can be regarded as a form of political rhetoric in which the legitimacy of forms of government, or their policies, rather than the survival of the state is at stake. The point here is that security, unlike the concept power, is essentially a normative concept. It is not a theoretical concept that can be used independently of the reasoning of agents in order to explain their actions. The idea of security is innately subjective. Hence its use in any form of explanation must be related to the actual reasoning of the agents and to actual historical situations rather than to any generalized or analytic approach. It has an emotive aspect in much the same way as insecurity corresponds to fear.

Moreover, it is a relational term; that is, it does not designate any absolute or general condition or quality but is defined in practice by reference to a concrete state of affairs that is a compound of national capacities, intentions, relations and other variable factors most of which are contingent. The indeterminacy of the concept security in general terms makes it essential to relate it to a specific historical context and to the reasoning of politicians responsible for defence and foreign policy. It is *their* aspirations and fears that provide the empirical content of the notion of security. And it is *their* policies and actions that translate them into practice.

An example might clarify this point. With the appearance of the long-range heavy bomber[8] it was generally feared by European politicians, with their relatively densely populated states and heavily concentrated industries, that there was no defence against this new weapon. Their fears were strengthened by the experience of Guernica in the Spanish Civil War where studies of the destructive effects of the bombing indicated that large cities could be devastated without any effective defence. The bomber consequently took on a significance that had its effect on contemporary notions of security. Chamberlain in his negotiations with Hitler believed himself to be at a disadvantage given the superiority at that time of the Luftwaffe.[9] Paradoxically, while this weakened the British negotiating position, it also exacerbated Britain's security fears. A large navy and the Channel were no defence in modern warfare. The only solution to the new security problem was the development of an equivalent force and the elimination of the German threat. Apart from disarmament, and this had failed as a collective measure in the inter-war period, there was no *political* solution to this problem. It was a matter of relative capacities. Whatever the diplomatic and political disputes of the late 1930s, it was the existence of a superior German capacity to use this new weapon that constituted a threat to security.

In the event it turned out that the significance of the bomber was exaggerated. A defence was possible and it did not have the decisive effect on warfare as had been feared. The point here is that it was the expectation that it would and the consequence it had for security that mattered. This played no small part in pushing Britain to the point of fighting a total war rather than continuing a policy of 'appeasement'. Diplomatic 'solutions' could not get over the fact of this new destructive capacity. This ascription of the notion of security to agents places any explanation that uses it in an historical, rather than a theoretical form.

If the power-security hypothesis has any general theoretical force, it lies in showing that a specific security problem and its 'solution' in historical terms is the product of conditions and forces that exist independently of the reasoning of agents. In other words, while security fears are subjective, their manifestation and the particular form they take are the product of external forces beyond the control of the agents. Whether this can be done will be examined later on.

But what of the possibility that with this form of imperialism we are dealing with an argument that is really historical in nature? If the explanation of power politics and its resultant imperialism lies in the security fears of political agents and their conceptions of the environment in which they practise, then it may be that further explanation is unnecessary. We may find in an examination of motivation that the pursuit of national security did indeed impel statesmen into imperialist policies. It might also be the case that security is wrapped up with ideological, economic or political considerations, so that the direct relationship between national military potential and international conflict is either more complex, or more peripheral, than the power-security hypothesis has it. But whatever the case, this form of explanation is rooted in evidence of the reasoning of those politicians engaged in international politics and is historical in nature. No *theory* is entailed by an explanation of imperialist policies adopted by those who consciously pursued them. The characterization of imperialism in terms of security motivation depends entirely on the nature of the evidence. It may be that in specific historical cases politicians sought to extend their authority over what they considered to be a violent and dangerous environment on the grounds of national security. If this is the case and such justifications are not rationalizations or cover for other motives, or political rhetoric designed to win support or acceptance of unpalatable measures, then we have made out a case for this form of imperialism. But such a case only fits that particular set of circumstances and its associated reasoning. It is an exercise in history and by no means easy to do.

No statesman, on this argument, is *compelled* to pursue imperialist policies by reason of his fears for the security of his country. And should such a relation exist in past historical situations, it does not provide a confirmation of the power-security hypothesis. The relation between reasoning and action in such cases is contingent and not a case of logical or empirical necessity. Only where we can show imperialism to be a necessary consequence of the relation between security fears and a quest for power in international politics would this argument be a genuine hypothesis. Such a hypothesis would then be theoretical in nature and permit a valid level of generalization about imperialist phenomena. Evidence of reasoning does not fall into the rubric of test or reference relevant to this form of explanation. The motives of politicians and their alleged disposition to act in this particular way are themselves a product of external forces. Such forces are causal in nature and so a quite different type of explanation is involved subject to terms of reference and evaluatory criteria distinct from those appropriate to a historical explanation. Whether this is in fact the case for the power-security hypothesis will be left open at this stage. The point here is that these two quite distinct modes of explanation uneasily coexist in the logic of the power-security hypothesis.

Let us now look at an example of international politics in order to see what kind of application this argument has and whether there is a distinct form of imperialism stemming from the problem of security. If the power-security hypothesis and its variant of imperialism has any explanatory force, whether historical or theoretical, then we should see a direct connection between security fears and expansionist policies pursued by the major powers. Leaving in abeyance the question of the nature of this connection for the moment, I want to examine the nuclear arms race and its associated policies as an empirical test of the thesis. In what sense were the politics and policies pursued by the major powers following the Second World War products of the security dilemma? Were they imperialist in nature?

But before doing this I want to consider the period immediately preceding the advent of nuclear weapons. If the power-security hypothesis is a *general* explanation of imperialism, then the nature of the weapons making up a national capacity for violence, and the reasoning surrounding their deployment, should be immaterial. It is the capacity itself and the resultant competition that matter. Consequently, there should be no difference between the application of the thesis to the so-called 'conventional' and the nuclear forms of war and their associated international politics. Is this the case?

There are three additional reasons for considering the 'pre-history' of the present nuclear arms race. Firstly, the power-security argument itself emerged after the First World War and was concerned with explaining the two world wars of this century. The phenomenon of the Anglo-German naval arms race preceding the first of these wars drew attention to the possibility of major wars occurring as an unintended consequence of competition in *defence* provision. Subsequently, Hitler's use of military threats to force territorial concessions in his European diplomacy and the consequent war of *matériel* between the major powers emphasized the importance of military capacity and its economic concomitants to national security and to the achievement or maintenance of national policy objectives. If peace was desirable as a condition for maintaining the political status quo in the world at large, then it had to be based on an equivalence of forces shared by all the major powers. Such a consideration was fundamental to any peace-keeping organization such as the United Nations. The impotence of the League of Nations was attributed to its lack of teeth. So preparation for war in terms of relative military capacities was deemed to be an essential condition for peace. Disarmament was chimerical. Such thinking preceded the nuclear arms race.

Secondly, although the power-security argument is a general one, in principle applying to all nation-states whatever their actual capacities for violence, it was primarily concerned with what are now called conventional weapons. Whether the development of *nuclear* weapons makes a qualitative difference to the argument is important in assessing its status as an explanation. So some comparison between the conventional and the nuclear forms of war is clearly relevant. And, thirdly, this examination will serve to illustrate some of the more abstract points made in the preceding discussion in a context void of the 'theorizing' of the nuclear strategist and other exponents of the *science* of war.

What was the security problem in the inter-war period and in what sense did imperialist policies emanate from it? The World Disarmament Conference illustrates the practical aspects of security. All the participants presented a different solution to the problem of inter-state violence. Britain, an imperial power with the largest European navy, favoured the demobilization of land forces. France, with the largest European army, favoured naval disarmament. Germany, ostensibly disarmed under the Versailles and Locarno treaties, argued for a progressive rearmament[10] so that disarmament could then proceed on an equal footing and thus provide her with security relative to the other European states. The smaller powers and the 'neutrals' were in favour of a general and total disarmament. Not surprisingly, the conference broke up without reaching any tangible agreement. The nation-states contented themselves with empty gestures such as the Kellogg—Briand Pact, which 'outlawed' war. In the meantime national defence policies proceeded with the task of providing a national solution to the security problem.

The problem of security, however, became acute with rapid German rearmament beginning in 1935.[11] Britain, although concerned about this development, was ready to reach an agreement with Hitler by which he pledged himself not to challenge the British navy. The Anglo-German Naval Treaty of 1935 conceded British naval superiority and so guaranteed British trading and imperial interests. France, of course, was in a different position, and French security was defined not in naval terms but in terms of a capacity successfully to fight a land war in Europe. This capacity, apparently guaranteed by the disarmament provisions of Versailles and subsequent treaties, was directly challenged by German rearmament and Hitler's unilateral breach of treaty obligations. The countering strategy of creating an alliance system with states bordering Germany, far from adding to French strength, became a liability since the German challenge was directly to these states and not to France. France, once the German challenge to the political status quo in Europe was under way, found herself in the position of providing these small states with security and thus directly challenging Germany. In 1938 the French government accepted the Munich settlement and so broke her treaty obligations to Czechoslovakia. The Czech government was informed that France would not intervene in the event of a German attack. It was only when Britain abandoned a policy of non-involvement in political alliances in Europe that France was able to present a direct challenge to Germany. In terms of the power-security hypothesis, the growth of German military strength presented a threat to France regardless of the actual substance of Germany's political claims on Europe. The French were compelled to rearm and to counter the German challenge on grounds of national security. The apparent political crisis only masked the realities of security competition.

But what of Britain? Was it so axiomatic that German demands on Poland in 1939 — the occasion of war — constituted a threat to British security? On his part Hitler certainly believed that although he had broken previous agreements with his opponents, including the Munich agreement, his demands did not conflict with British interests. So far as Eastern Europe was concerned they were non-existent. But the British guarantee to Poland after the German annexation of Bohemia and Moravia, with its apparently unequivocal character, was a radical change not only in British policy towards Europe but in the situation itself. It made the issue one of power politics and excluded a diplomatic settlement. The consequent manoeuvrings in attempting to persuade the Poles to negotiate on what, on the face of it, were a less exacting set of demands than the unfortunate Czechs had been faced with, and the equivocal position of the USSR, simply highlighted the underlying contest between relative military capacities. Britain had identified the future of the Polish state with her security and had done what the French alone had tried to do but failed. Apart from security, Britain had no clearly identifiable interest in Eastern Europe.

In removing the Soviet Union from the situation by the Molotov—Ribbentrop Pact, Hitler apparently thought the deadlock was broken and the way paved for a *political* solution, albeit realized by force of German arms. Given the isolation of Poland and the consequent inability of the French and the British to intervene in the East, then it was rational for them to accept the inevitable. The inevitable meant a new partition of Poland between Germany and the Soviet Union. Clearly the Poles had no incentive to negotiate. The prospect of following the Czech example was not encouraging. Hitler's 'minimal' demands, as in the case of Czechoslovakia, were only the prelude to conquest and he had already demonstrated his attitude towards the inviolability of international agreements arrived at through diplomacy.

The French too had an interest in preventing another Polish partition, especially one involving the Soviet Union. A *de facto* alliance between Germany and the USSR meant that any future German aspirations towards territorial aggrandizement in Europe could only be achieved at the expense of France. Alsace-Lorraine remained a bone of contention. French security was directly involved and indeed French policy was consistent on this point ever since the refusal of the United States and Britain to honour the joint security pact negotiated as part of the post First World War settlements.[12] French policy over the inter-war period, and now in 1939, can be explained in terms of security fears. Equally clearly the Soviet Union was motivated in the same way. Her neutrality was due to a reluctance to confront Germany in a way that would place the chief burden of protecting Poland on the Soviet Union. There was no guarantee that the Soviet Union's nominal allies in such a conflict would intervene to save *her* in the event of defeat. At the same time, the USSR embarked on massive rearmament and prepared for a major war. German encroachments on Poland presented a clear security threat to the Soviet Union whatever their ostensible intentions.

But in what way was there a security threat to *Britain* in German demands in Eastern Europe? One of the major factors inhibiting the British position at Munich was an awareness of military inferiority relative to the German armed forces. This, combined with the prior acceptance of the piecemeal revision of the Versailles Treaty;

recognition that, however suspicious, German demands for the Sudetenland were based on the very principle of self-determination that was supposed to have guided the post-war settlements; and the lack of any direct British interest in Czechoslovakia, led to what has been called 'appeasement'. Yet, given the lack of any clear reason for the use of force to preserve Czech national integrity, it is difficult to see what was appeasing in British policy where no national interest was sacrificed for peace. Even if Britain had the capacity to intervene, the Sudetenland issue seemed neither to present a challenge to a tangible British interest, as would perhaps have been the case if it had been Romania that was the target, or Greece, nor to threaten British security. Why then did Britain directly challenge Germany one year later? Why did British policy change from one of non-involvement in European politics to one that directly posed a major war on the scale of the last conflict?

Leaving out such considerations as Chamberlain's domestic political difficulties, with the emergence of a war party and pressure groups that opposed Hitler's policies towards minorities it seems that British policy was reversed in 1939. Following the power-security hypothesis, this reversal would appear to be a response not to the actual demands made by Hitler — the nominal content of his proposals as it were — but to the underlying force that supported them. It was not what he apparently wanted that mattered, but his ability to achieve it by force. The realization of the disparity of forces led Chamberlain both to see Germany as a security threat and at the same time to avoid conflict in 1938. In 1939 it was assumed that Germany's apparent capacity to fight successful wars had to be checked. Only large-scale rearmament would do that. Negotiation had to be through strength. And even this would not succeed until political and diplomatic recognition of the mutual constraints of balanced military capacities had been established. As Hitler had so clearly demonstrated in the case of Munich, agreements made in the absence of such a balance would not be respected. But in the case of Poland it was too late and the hope of deterring a German invasion by pooling military resources through a countering alliance that included the only state that could practically assist Poland — the Soviet Union — disappeared with the Molotov—Ribbentrop Pact. The central issue then became not the question of the existence of Poland, but one of security. The war that was threatened by France and Britain, if the threat was to be taken seriously, was a total war. Hitler, on the contrary, reasoned that, given the favourable opportunity presented by the relative military and political weaknesses of his opponents, *his* war would be a limited political war. The changes in Europe he wanted would be accepted by Britain and France, given that he could make them with speed and given that the question of national survival, for Britain if not for France, was not endangered by his eastward thrust. On the first point he was right but not on the second. His *blitzkrieg* against Poland was successful but the allies refused to accept the result and the war became total.

On this argument then, although the actual occasion and timing of the war were contingent on the politics and diplomacy of the states involved, the recognition that force confronting force would determine the issue was implicit in the British and French guarantees to Poland. Capacity rather than intentions was the dominant factor. It was not the specific demands made by Hitler on Poland that were so unacceptable[13] but his capacity to achieve them by force. A challenge to this was to present a countering force, but one that was inherently open-ended. The threat of war implicit in the crisis diplomacy of the later 1930s was a threat to national security in terms of the territorial integrity of the state. Such a threat could not have been posed in the eighteenth century and the contest that was threatened was a very different kind of war to the Cabinet wars of that time. In short, the ostensible *casus belli* — the question of the integrity of Poland — concealed the actual cause — the capacity of Germany to force political and territorial changes in Europe unilaterally. In the eyes of his opponents Hitler was pursuing imperialist policies. His progression from revision of the post-war settlement to radical change in the political status quo implied a quest for power in Europe that was unacceptable.

The major change in policy on the part of Britain in 1939 is thus explained not in terms of a change in the parameters of political reasoning, in the assumptions made by politicians about each other's intentions, but by the operation of an underlying rationale. This rationale is the logic of the power-security hypothesis and its emphasis upon relative military capacities and consequent competition. As these change, so does policy. Created out of security fears, they exercise a pervasive influence upon all levels of policy. All aspects of external relationships between states are thus directly or indirectly related to security. This last becomes dominant in times of crisis where, whatever the apparent substance of the dispute, its real nature is derived from the fundamental competition in capacities for violence possessed by the contenders.

Thus Chamberlain came to recognize that an all-out struggle with Hitler was 'inevitable', although this did not preclude him from trying for an accommodation. In this he was trying to buy time so that rearmament would redress the imbalance of forces. His relative impotence in terms of the use of force, or its threat, to induce Hitler to moderate his demands made for a weak policy, yet paradoxically led him directly to war. Only direct confrontation with Hitler could produce any kind of political influence in Europe. Yet the irony of this posture is that it entailed total war and, given the totality of consequent defeat, clearly *any* kind of influence or demand could be indulged by a victor. The reason for this is that the threat of this scale of violence to achieve a limited political end — in this case the preservation of Poland — meant that means and ends were incommensurable. It was not a limited war that was threatened. With the neutrality of the Soviet Union, the only hope for Poland was Western success in a major war with Germany. Yet this prospect imperilled the security of all the belligerents. On this argument the prevailing concept of security, linked to a material capacity for total war, conflicted directly with the notion of war in the Clausewitzian sense as policy by other means.

Hitler, in believing that the *blitzkrieg* was not only possible but could produce the political gains he wanted, was mistaken. It was not the political objectives he sought, so far as he made these clear, that produced such opposition, but the military capacity he had created to achieve them. This capacity was exaggerated by his opponents and initially he had luck as well as skilful judgement on his side. But what destroyed the prospect of any negotiated peace was a general recognition that any negotiation based on relative weakness would not lead to a successful or lasting settlement. The strength of the fears aroused by his successes and his apparent capacity to achieve them was the determinant factor in deciding the kind of war to be fought. It was to be total both in victory and in defeat. All other issues paled into insignificance once this had been realized. Even had Hitler been successful in his invasion of the Soviet Union, any peace would have been a Peace of Amiens.[14]

It would seem that, if we accept this argument, the problem of security was the dominant factor in determining the power politics of the inter-war period and of the world war that followed it. Whatever the nature of relations between states and their acceptance of contractual obligations in the forms of treaties and alliances, the determinant influence in international politics was the security dilemma caused by the creation of differential national capacities for violence, paradoxically created in the interests of defence. But defence came to mean a superior capacity and security lay in controlling an inimical environment. As we shall see, Hitler himself justified his policies and his wars in terms of providing for the security of Germany. Security for his opponents too consisted in eliminating rival capacities for opposition. This is one view of the power-security hypothesis. What of the imperialist aspect?

The question is not that the major powers pursued imperialist policies *per se,* that is, that they sought to extend their power and influence over their environment, absorbing territory, asserting hegemony over some states and maintaining dependent relations with others. This in itself is a common phenomenon in the history of the nation-state. Rather, the *explanation* of such phenonema lies in relating them to the power-security hypothesis in such a way that motivation is shown to emanate from security fears, or that politicians are compelled to act in this manner by the dynamic of security competition.

Now all the states central to the crisis of the late thirties were imperialist powers. They all possessed empires or aspired to empire. It is curious that the former category — the imperial states — are somehow deemed to be respectable while the latter — the imperialist powers — are not. The opponents of Germany, Italy and Japan were seeking to maintain enormous empires acquired by means no more legitimate than those the aspirant imperialists themselves sought to employ. The redistribution of the German and Turkish empires at the end of the First World War was a division of the spoils rather than an acceptance of Wilsonian liberalism. The Mandates system that the victor powers adopted gave only nominal recognition to the principle of self-determination or to the primacy of the welfare and rights of the indigenous inhabitants. Britain, for example, felt able through the Balfour Declaration to promise a national home to the Jews over the heads of the Palestinian Arabs who at that time were the overwhelming majority in the Mandate of Palestine. By the end of the 1930s Britain was fighting a major colonial war in Iraq. The French were similarly occupied in the Maghreb.

One of the aspirant imperialist powers was the Soviet Union. Sharing with Germany in a new partition of Poland, Stalin did not deviate from his demands for territory in the Baltic and in Eastern and Southern Europe and for foreign bases, whether his negotiating partner was Germany, Britain or the United States. Even when his very existence as a political leader and the survival of the Soviet Union were at stake, Stalin made these demands a central part of his negotiations with Britain.[15] He wanted recognition of his absorption of the Baltic states, of territory from Finland and of his hegemony over that state, of his gains from Poland and of his claims to Bessarabia and N. Bukovina, as much from the Western allies as from Hitler.

In his negotiations with Britain and the United States after the war, Stalin insisted that the Soviet Union had the right not merely to acquire specific territories, bases in the Dardanelles and a colonial trust in North Africa, but also to maintain a sphere of influence in the border states. The issue of Poland and her government was a major bone of contention in these negotiations, and while Stalin conceded the paramountcy of, for example, British influence in Greece and American influence in Italy, he did not deviate an inch over Poland. The USSR had been invaded three times from Poland in this century. For Stalin it seemed self-evident that a major power had the right to stipulate conditions for its security. He conceded the right of Britain to regain her empire from the Japanese. (The United States revealed more ideological prejudices on this issue than did the Marxist Soviet Union.) He accepted the predominancy of the major maritime powers in the Atlantic, the Mediterranean and the Pacific. He even conceded the American 'presence' in China and urged Mao-Tse Tung to compromise with the Kuomintang government. He made no complaint about the dominant position of the United States in Latin America. What he wanted, and his grounds were based on the security needs of the Soviet Union, was a dominant Soviet influence in all the areas directly bordering the USSR. He could compromise on some areas, notably Yugoslavia and Hungary, but not on Poland.[16]

In the Soviet case, security appeared to be paramount and, if taken literally, explains the insistence by Stalin on controlling the border areas. He was consistent in his demands and in urging Soviet security as their justification. This was endangered by the presence of alienated, or hostile, weak border states, themselves bordering on powerful expansionist states such as Germany and Italy. The game of power politics in which these states had coerced and manoeuvred the weaker countries in the past was dangerous to the security of the USSR. The disarmament of Germany after the First World War had proved illusory as a means of solving the problem. General disarmament had equally failed, with each state insisting on the primacy of its own security needs. In the event a relatively weak state like Poland had first allied with France, then with Germany, and finally with Britain and France again, but had never contemplated friendly relations with the Soviet Union. It had proved a gateway for invasion.

So in Stalin's view the uncertainties posed by the independence of these border states, and the distinct possibility that Germany would rise again, meant that his control over the border states was essential to Soviet security. What he could not mention was the fact that the United States with its nuclear monopoly was also a potential danger. If the Soviet Union did not create a border zone of neutralized or allied countries then major Soviet industrial zones were exposed to attack from forward American bases. This could not be mentioned in negotiations for obvious reasons. The presumption of allied unity and cooperation was necessary for any agreement to take place. But in security terms the position was that both a new state and a new weapon had emerged that potentially endangered the Soviet Union.

The Soviet Union itself possessed no means of countering this potential threat, for it had no nuclear weapons, long-range aircraft or forward bases. The proof of American and British sincerity in precluding such a possibility lay in conceding the reality of the Soviet position and allowing Soviet control of the border states. When this was not forthcoming, the Soviet Union acted unilaterally and created her own imperial control over these areas. She also, as we shall see, bent all her efforts to creating weapons that could strike directly at the United States.

So far, then, the actions of the Soviet Union can be seen as consonant with the power-security hypothesis. They were imperialist and directly linked to the problem of security. What of the other aspirant imperialist powers — Germany, Italy and Japan? Both German and Japanese imperialism will be considered in other chapters where very different explanations are provided for their attempts at expansion. Something can be said here, however, of the central aim of their imperialism. Both wanted to secure economic self-sufficiency and a form of autarky that limited foreign intervention and dependence. Both were major industrial countries that were badly hit by the world economic recession of the early 1930s. They had suffered from trade slumps, and in the Japanese case from a cessation of migration possibilities. Overpopulation and its consequent strain on resources was seen in both countries to be a major problem. The solution to these problems was seen to be the acquisition of resources through conquest. On the face of it their attempts at expansion could be seen to be a form of economic imperialism. But there was a security dimension too. A state was only secure if it possessed an independent economy capable of withstanding adverse changes in the world market economy and of supporting armed forces equal or superior to its neighbours'. For Germany, the effects of a naval blockade in the First World War and the blasting of incipient economic recovery in 1929 by the collapse of the world market economy, together with the burden and humiliations of reparations and French intervention, all provided arguments for the creation of an autarkic system. When this appeared either too costly or impossible to put into practice, conquest and the acquisition of the necessary resources were solutions. Similarly, when Japan realized that the conquest of China was illusory as a solution to her economic problems, she faced the consequences of a 'blue water' policy. Expansion into South-East Asia and the Pacific was likely to be opposed by the United States. Such opposition inevitably would take the form of naval warfare. And in this respect Japan was particularly vulnerable, lacking domestic oil resources capable of sustaining a prolonged sea war. This weakness was emphasized when the

American and British response to the Japanese invasion of Indo-China was the imposition of oil sanctions. To accept this threat and to withdraw meant a complete abandonment of the major premise of Japanese imperial policy — the creation of economic self-sufficiency — Pearl Harbor was the answer.

But these two cases, which will be discussed at length elsewhere, do not show the primacy of security in terms of imperialist policies. The pursuit of autarky and an aggressive nationalism were dominant elements. It is true that the idea of security included that of autarky. The security of the state lay not merely in defending itself against any aggression, and so preserving its territorial integrity, but in creating the appropriate conditions under which this could be fulfilled. A viable capacity for defence had to be created through a self-sufficient, independent economic structure. If this did not exist then it had to be provided. But this broadening of the idea of security into ideological and economic dimensions weakens the power-security hypothesis by making it more complex. A circularity is introduced in which economic conditions for security, and security conditions for economic benefits, are inextricably intertwined, with neither element emerging as the determinant of political action in the form of imperialism.

Nevertheless, in the case of Japan, a primary condition for Japanese security was the exclusion of any major maritime power from dominating the Pacific and the exclusion of any major power from the mainland of Asia. In the circumstances of the later 1930s this meant the United States in the former case and the Soviet Union in the latter. The preoccupation of the Soviet Union with European politics, together with the more immediate problems relating to oil supplies and the American presence in the Pacific, resulted in the 'blue water' policy prevailing. Security considerations were thus important although, as we shall see, whether these were fundamental or simply contingent upon the immediate situation and on other policy objectives, are open questions.

So far as Germany was concerned, the immediate problem was to avoid isolation and the prospect of a two front war. But ultimately the security problem, as Hitler saw it, lay in creating a military capacity capable of matching the combined resources of the other European powers. This meant insulating the German economy from outside interference and, through conquest, acquiring the resources necessary to maintain her armed forces as well as to support a large population. An expansionist policy, if successful, would thus provide Germany with a viable economy as well as a guarantee of security, even when faced by a coalition between the continental powers, France and the Soviet Union, and the maritime powers, Britain and the United

States. Again, security was linked with specific conditions — economic, military and political — that, if fulfilled, would provide a permanent solution to the problem. Imperialism provided a 'permanent' solution as diplomacy did not. As in the case of Japan, this admixture of elements makes the power-security hypothesis appear oversimplified. Nevertheless, a case can be made for the primacy of security considerations in German imperialism.

Italy was perhaps the most vulnerable of all the contending states in this period, faced with fundamental problems of geography and resources. She was faced with dangers from land and sea that compelled her, unlike the other aspirant imperialist states, to create both large land and naval forces. In the past, aggression had come from across the Alps as well as from the Mediterranean. The diplomatic solution to this problem — an alliance with Germany — left her at the mercy of German intentions as well as forcing her to challenge the other imperial powers, France and Britain, if her imperial aspirations were to be satisfied. Her paucity of resources both in manpower and in materials, particularly oil, meant a dependency upon Germany. The explanation for Italian imperial aspirations is complex, for they had both an ideological and an idiosyncratic character deriving from Mussolini's leadership and the fascist system. Economic factors were important too in seeking a solution for an impoverished Mezzogiorno after the United States had blocked Italian immigration.

Nevertheless, Italian imperial aspirations were linked directly to the problem of security. The Mediterranean was to be Italy's *mare nostrum,* with Italy the dominant naval power. Given an alliance with Germany as an essential element in Italian policy, thus 'securing' the North, the chief danger to Italian security lay in French and British naval dominance. The support given to Franco during the Spanish Civil War was intended to counterbalance their superiority in this respect. But command over the Mediterranean depended on control of its littoral, especially where major naval bases existed, and Italian policy in North Africa, as well as in the Balkans, was intended to achieve this control.

It would seem from all this that security fears were certainly relevant in explaining the imperial aspirations of these states. Clearly other factors existed and the question whether the policies adopted were means to an end or ends in themselves is an open one. Whether the security aspect was a predominant motive depends on evidence of the reasoning of the principal agents. The case of Germany will be examined in some detail in terms both of the power-security hypothesis and its implications for imperialism, and of its problems as an explanation. However, there is nothing in what has been said so far to indicate that Chamberlain, Daladier, Stalin, Mussolini, Matsuoka or Roosevelt were *compelled* to pursue imperialist policies, either in defence or as aspirants, because of the dynamic of security competition. The rationale for their actions, if this existed, was a conscious one, which may indeed have produced unforeseen and unintended consequences but was not in any sense independent of their reasoning. There is no evidence to support the theoretical argument of the power-security hypothesis so far as this period is concerned. The implications of this will be considered later. For the moment it can be said that the link between imperialism and security postulated by the thesis appears to exist in the reasoning and actions of politicians in this pre-nuclear period. Security was construed in terms of creating conditions that did not exist in the international environment. Such conditions consisted of creating a national capacity for violence with its appropriate economic base, alliance policies and diplomacy (designed to eliminate or deter potential rivals or competitors), control over strategically important bases in terms of the available military technology, intervention in the domestic politics of other states so as to ensure their neutrality or partiality, the acquisition of territory or the maintenance of existing possessions, and so on. In this respect there was little difference between those states seeking to maintain the existing political system and those seeking to change it. The only discernible difference was in their respective justifications of their policies and actions.

The quest for power in the world at large and the imperialism associated with it, although stemming from a variety of motives, seem directly related to the security fears of nation-states and their consequent competition. In the crisis of the later 1930s these fears appeared to be paramount. In the final analysis, diplomacy and the attempt to resolve this competition through peaceful means, as well as through countering threats, were abandoned in favour of the last resort — war itself. The Second World War can thus be seen as a war between imperialist powers whose imperialism stemmed directly from the problem of providing state security in a world of states.

The Second World War did not, however, resolve the security dilemma once and for all. Indeed, the power-security hypothesis appears, superficially at least, to receive further confirmation in the celerity with which the victorious alliance disintegrated and reformed into countering alliances. Former enemies became allies and vice-versa. A new arms race began. The most obvious change was the arrival of a new power that dominated international politics — the United States. And this power possessed a monopoly of the most destructive weapon known to man. Was the United States primarily motivated in her post-war policies and actions by security fears? Did these, if they existed, result in the pursuit of imperialism in the world at large? The power-security hypothesis, if it is genuinely explanatory, should provide us with an explanation that encompasses the nuclear age as well as the previous period of security competition in conventional weapons.

The United States had been concerned with the problem of her security long before she was attacked by Japan. Well before Pearl Harbor, the United States conceived of security in naval terms. Alone or in conjunction with an ally, it was necessary to possess naval superiority in both the major oceans. The denial of land bases to foreign powers on the continent of the Americas and the naval technology of the day made the United States secure. But the vulnerability of capital ships to air attack, and the necessity for forward bases to provide protection for battleships, extended American interests well beyond the Western hemisphere. The eclipse of Japan saw the United States dominant in the Pacific. The major Japanese bases, including Okinawa, were taken by the USA. Under the sketchy pretence of trusteeship, a number of strategically placed Pacific Islands became part of the American domain. Japan herself was occupied, with the United States retaining sole authority to the exclusion of her former allies.

But this extension of authority was based on a conception of security in terms of a capacity to deter or repel any aggression upon the homeland. In other words, it was a traditional view based upon the importance of long-range aircraft. If these could be deployed from foreign bases they could not only destroy an opponent's ships, submarines and air fields, but they could also deliver the atomic bomb. In spite of the revolutionary character of this new weapon, its effectiveness depended upon the same delivery system used for conventional bombs — the long-range heavy bomber. Consequently the same factors of space-relations and the relative capacities of potential opponents were predominant in defining the conditions for American security. Forward bases were essential if the United States was to be secure. The utility of the new weapon depended upon a strategic airforce capable of reaching distant targets. The United States needed global reach for her security. This was relatively easily attained in the Pacific given the possession of island bases and the existence of a superior carrier fleet. The Atlantic posed problems because of the existence of sovereign states each with its own conception of security. Before the United States could extend her military capacity in this area, some accommodation had to be made. In the short run there was no possibility of any major threat being made by a foreign power, given the American monopoly both of the bomb and of an effective long-range bomber. But this state of affairs could not be presumed to last for ever. The Soviet Union, as well as Britain and France, were embarking on nuclear programmes and sooner or later the advantage that the United States possessed would disappear. If the Soviet Union extended her authority in terms of territory, then the United States would herself be faced with an opponent she could not attack, but from which she could receive an attack. Spatial relations and the technology of air warfare were dominant factors in this reasoning.

The solution was seen to be a form of collective security in which the Western European states were protected by the American nuclear capacity to attack the Soviet Union, and that gave the United States herself the necessary forward bases for her own protection. NATO was initially the answer to the security problems of both the United States and the Western European states. But all depended upon maintaining the capacity to attack the Soviet Union without significant retaliation. And this depended upon the United States keeping the lead in the ensuing nuclear arms race.

This policy of maintaining an outward chain of forward bases from which virtually all parts of the world could be attacked with nuclear weapons, while at the same time isolating the United States from similar attacks, was reminiscent of British imperial policy in the nineteenth century. Security was seen in terms of space combined with the limitations of the most advanced military technology. Sea power was the factor behind the British creation of a chain of foreign bases that could both protect British economic and commercial interests and provide security for the homeland. Air power spelled the end of the capital ship, but in turn demanded its own network of bases. So the early containment policy pursued the objectives of forming alliances with European states thus securing bases and of unilaterally creating a similar screen in the Pacific.

But of course there was a competitive aspect to this. The identification of British and French security with that of the United States, masked the provisional nature of the nuclear umbrella. They embarked on nuclear programmes of their own as an additional precaution in spite of the protection accorded them by the United States. The long-term danger to their security lay in the possibility of the Soviet Union developing a force equivalent to that of the United States. They could agree with the United States that the westward expansion of the Soviet Union should be checked and provision made for the defence of the forward bases essential to their joint security. But these conditions for security were not immutable. Nor were the European states concerned with the Far East and the Pacific as a security zone. Their interests in this area were parochial and not directly concerned with security. A divergence of interests existed between the Western allies outside Europe.

On the Soviet side, once it became clear that the United States and Britain were not prepared to accept her demands for a sphere of influence in her border areas, a unilateral policy of extending control over Finland, the Baltic, Poland, the Eastern European states and those in Southern Europe was pursued. Territory, or space, was important to Soviet security, and if this could be secured only through the creation of a number of subordinate or puppet regimes in the border states in the face of Western opposition, then it was justified by the compelling needs of Soviet security. It was the United States that had the advantage in terms of her capacity for violence. Once it became clear that the United States had no intention of accepting Soviet demands and, moreover, was herself establishing foreign bases from which to attack the Soviet Union, then the need to secure as much territory between potential Soviet targets and American bomber bases was paramount.

By 1954 two alliance systems confronted each other over a divided Germany. The Korean War, the first armed conflict involving the major powers in the post-war period, brought into focus the limitations of nuclear weapons. It also indicated to the United States the dangers posed by Soviet exploitation of opportunities presented by the existence of political instability. It was hard to justify the use of nuclear weapons against the Soviet Union or China, or the extension of the ground war, in terms of national security. Yet the alternative — an acceptance of communist success in changing the political affiliation of a state through such an intervention — would constitute a dangerous precedent. The same identification of security interests under the cover of a nuclear umbrella as in Europe could not be made in the Third World. Yet Soviet encroachments in this area could eventually present a direct challenge to American security, by eroding the chain of bases necessary given the technological limitations of existing aircraft.

Consequently the United States found herself having to be prepared for intervention, direct or indirect, on a worldwide basis. A challenge might be made almost anywhere in the non-communist area. The policy of global containment was ultimately concerned with national security in that it was designed to restrict Soviet control over territory and hence protect the American posture of global reach. But it was also innately open-ended in that a major condition for success was the preservation of the political status quo in terms of a network of friendly or allied regimes. Unlike Europe, where compatible interests coexisted with stable governments prepared to maintain their contractual obligations, this element of political stability existed nowhere else.

The attempts made by Dulles to create alliance systems similar to NATO in South-East Asia and elsewhere were only nominally successful and masked the inability of signatory governments to maintain power.[17] Their very instability meant a permanent commitment of the United States to maintaining friendly regimes in power in order to safeguard the American position. This led to an involvement in the domestic politics of other states that came eventually to produce more 'communists' than it contained. For domestic opposition in these states came to identify itself, and to be identified, as anti-American and so by definition pro-communist. The regime in power had an interest in promoting such an identification and so providing a basis for American support. Political dissent not only found no legitimate outlet but invited American intervention; and of course also provided an opportunity for the Soviet Union to do the same.

The consequence, then, of the policy of global containment was an attempt on the part of the United States to prevent political change in her sphere of influence, for such change came to mean an opportunity for 'communist' expansion. Such an imposition of control over domestic politics, albeit with the consent of the ruling government, constituted a form of imperialism. No change was legitimate unless it had the approval of the United States. Such an involvement amounted to an attempt to control an unstable and inherently dangerous environment in the interests of American security. Security came to mean not simply the creation of a defence capacity and a system of foreign bases designed to confer an advantage on the United States in the event of conflict with the Soviet Union, but also the preservation of the political status quo in the so-called Free World. Containment committed the United States to a wide variety of courses of action — economic, military and political — in an attempt to arrest or control change itself.

Such a policy was justified in ideological as well as security terms. But the central argument and indeed the whole *raison d'être* of global containment was the danger to the United States of an expanding communism, which sought by various means ranging from direct aggression on weak states to the support of 'national liberation movements' and the use of indigenous communist parties to acquire territory in order to dominate the world. Such an expansion struck at the heart of American security, based as it was on the Strategic Air Command and its system of bases encircling the Soviet Union.

On the face of it the power-security hypothesis seems to fit post-war developments in international politics. The new weapon largely depended on air power and this in turn depended upon the satisfaction of geo-political conditions in the form of a worldwide network of bomber bases. Such bases themselves were vulnerable, not so much from Soviet attacks as from the inability of the governments that agreed to the installation of the bases to govern, and so maintain, their contractual obligations. Their weakness was a potential danger to American security that the Soviet Union appeared quick to recognize. The quest for power in the sense of an extension of control and authority over an anarchic environment appeared to stem directly from security competition with the Soviet Union and from the technological requirements of existing weapons. Space and territory were as important to security as in the days of naval power and formal empires. So in spite of the apparent superiority enjoyed by the United States in the immediate post-war years in terms of its capacity to use violence, the conditions necessary for its realization impelled her into the world arena. Whatever her other motives, that of security was the dominant impetus for her involvement in world politics and her attempt at world domination.

Underlying the policy of global containment was a major arms race. It was clear to American planners that the American monopoly of the atom bomb could not be maintained for ever, although opinions varied as to the time it would take the Soviet Union to make the new weapon.[18] In the meantime, it was necessary to create a situation that would give the United States a lasting advantage. The Soviet success in exploding a nuclear device in August 1949 did not reduce the American capability to strike at the Soviet Union with relative impunity. What mattered was the capacity to deliver the weapon. The advent of the thermo-nuclear weapon — the hydrogen bomb — made little difference other than that of increasing the scale of the damage caused by a strike. The Soviets too succeeding in developing this weapon very shortly after the United States.[19]

The British and French, it was pointed out earlier, decided very early on to develop their own nuclear weapons. The Attlee government decided to do this in January 1947 and the Pleven government in 1951. Successful tests followed, for the British in 1952 and the French early in 1960. In spite of their alliance with a state that possessed a monopoly of the new weapon and a superior capacity to deliver it, these states clearly assumed that while their immediate security needs were catered for the future was less certain. In addition to the development of atom bombs, these countries also embarked on the creation of a viable bomber fleet capable of reaching long-range targets. In effect a dual policy was pursued: on the one hand they endorsed the Atlantic Alliance and its dependence on American military superiority, while on the other, as insurance, Britain and

France attempted to create a nuclear capacity independent of the United States.

Such a policy was prescient, if linked to an obsolescent military technology. In October 1957 the Soviet Union demonstrated a capacity to attack targets in the United States with the launching of Sputnik. The significance of the intercontinental ballistic missile (ICBM) for the concept of security can hardly be overestimated. As we have seen, a coincidence of interests existed in the Western Alliance based on the United States' need for bases abroad and on her overwhelming superiority in nuclear capacity. Both these vanished almost overnight. The ICBM did not need to be deployed in a system of relatively vulnerable overseas bases. At one and the same time it released the United States from the political problems in maintaining such bases and exposed her to attack. The ballistic missile base presented a minute target to any attempts to eliminate it by a pre-emptive strike, it was exceedingly difficult to intercept in flight, it could be mass-produced and it needed no elaborate logistical support in terms of men and equipment comparable with that of a strategic airforce. It was a genuine technological change in methods of war and altered completely the relative importance of spatial relations in terms of security. The emphasis in the new arms race shifted from the deployment of nuclear weapons in foreign territories to the problem of protecting the missile launching sites and improving the accuracy of the missiles.

With the advent of the ICBM, the only guarantee of security for the Western allies was the development of the new weapon. Now that their protecting ally had itself become vulnerable to direct attacks from the Soviet Union, the nuclear umbrella hitherto extended over them disappeared. It was unlikely that the United States would expose herself to nuclear attack on behalf of a threatened ally. Moreover, their embryonic strategic airforces that were to become effective in the 1960s were almost at a stroke made redundant. Even before Sputnik, the Macmillan government had realized the radical implications of long-range missiles and had embarked on a British missile programme.[20] So important were these new weapons that when the British programme broke down in 1960 with the abandonment of the Blue Streak project, the utmost pressure was put on the United States to supply Britain with the Polaris missile.[21] The Nassau Agreement of December 1962 in effect gave Britain a new weapon designed to be launched from submarines and so relatively immune from countering attack. Nominally it was deemed part of the NATO force, but in fact it was directly controlled by the British government and constituted what came to be called an independent nuclear deterrent.[22] It was to be deployed in a small fleet of nuclear submarines. Between 1966 and 1970, four of these submarines were produced with the aid of American technology and materials. Each of them carried sixteen Polaris missiles with a range of 2,500 miles. The V bomber force, given a 'low-flying' role in 1964, was phased out in 1969. On the face of it Britain had received unusual help from the United States and had been provided with a *national* guarantee of security inconsistent with that apparently provided by the NATO alliance. Continuing support was given by the United States as ballistic missiles became more sophisticated and as air defences came into being. Multiple independently targeted warheads were fitted and successive governments, both Labour and Conservative, were able to update their missile force with the aid of American technology.

The French were not so fortunate. They were excluded from this happy collaboration between the United States and Britain. After failing to achieve a re-negotiation of the NATO alliance as an adjustment to the new situation,[23] the French government embarked on a protracted attempt to create its own missile force. But while its policy differed from the British in this respect, the reasoning was essentially the same. The protection afforded by the United States was now in doubt. The American government could no longer credibly threaten to attack the Soviet Union on behalf of an endangered ally. If the American monopoly of control over nuclear weapons within the Western alliance was to continue, an ally might well find itself either a nuclear battleground or sacrificed to an enemy. The proliferation of nuclear weapons was the inevitable consequence of this reasoning. Security law in *national* control over a retaliatory nuclear capacity. Whether the new weapon was obtained from an ally or created from prolonged national effort made no difference to the importance of having national control over it.

Deterrence became the basis of the new concept of national security. Essentially, deterrence is a negative concept. What is deterred is a direct attack on national territory. If, hypothetically, a state is able to retaliate after suffering a major nuclear attack, then the prospect of retaliation is considered a sufficient deterrent to inhibit any such attack. Two conditions are necessary: the first is the possession of an invulnerable riposte capacity, and the second is vulnerable territory — the potential targets. The degree of damage that can be inflicted on an attacking state in retaliation need not be total. All that is necessary, according to this argument, is that the damage is sufficient to be unacceptable to the aggressor. Consequently, a deterrent force need not be large. All that is required is that it be certain. If it could be destroyed in the course of an attack then clearly it has no credibility as a deterrent. Equally, if important targets could be protected, then deterrence ceases to prevail. It must be stressed that deterrence is essentially defensive. The only threat posed is in the event of a nuclear attack on the national homeland. Such a threat is responsive and, given a number of states capable of making such a threat, it follows that nuclear war between them is inhibited by the absence of any credible reason for the use or the threat of this scale of violence. National security consists of maintaining the capacity to retaliate. General war is also inhibited for the same reason. The rationale of the use of violence in pursuit of an end disintegrates if no end can be realized other than national suicide in the event of a nuclear war. Conventional war could not be pushed to the point of victory as in the last two world wars if the contenders were also nuclear powers.

There are a number of imponderables in this argument. Clearly what constitutes unacceptable damage cannot be ascertained easily. But making the cost of a nuclear strike as high as possible is a rational policy. It seems a reasonable assumption, for example, that the Soviet Union is unlikely to risk losing her major industrial centres as the price of destroying Britain completely. What would be the purpose of such a move? Equally, Britain is no danger to Soviet security given the same inhibition on a British attack. But rationality is not something that can merely be assumed. Deterrence only holds if it is presumed that statesmen observe its rules. There is no guarantee that they will do so.

Another variable factor is that of technological innovation. For example, if we consider the possibility of territory becoming invulnerable to nuclear attack through the development of an effective defence such as an anti-ballistic missile system, then the state possessing this advantage could make credible threats of violence against other nuclear powers. It would possess what has been called offensive deterrence. But if *two* or more states succeeded in doing this, then they would have achieved the paradoxical effect of rendering nuclear weapons ineffective. The result would be a return to conventional warfare or the development of new weapons. They would face a security dilemma similar to that in the past where the effect of a capacity for violence could not be precisely measured and where political and security conflicts are inextricably mixed. But no state can ignore the possibility of another state achieving an advantage through technological innovation in weapons, and so the competitive element in security provision might well produce an unforeseen and paradoxical result.

Having said this, and accepting that no situation in international politics is immutable, there is evidence that the dangers of an uninhibited arms race have been understood by politicians. The preservation of mutual defensive deterrence through arms control and negotiated agreements has been an objective pursued by the major nuclear powers. The problem of using a capacity for violence in order to achieve a condition of security seems to have found a solution, however temporary, in the concept of deterrence. Such a capacity can be insulated from the pursuit of other objectives as was not the case in the past. National security lies in preserving or creating a defensive deterrent capacity, and a capacity for violence for other purposes can be separated from this. For example, while Britain relies on an independently controlled ballistic missile force to preserve her territorial integrity from aggression, such a force cannot be used for any other purpose. Conceivably it might be used against a non-nuclear power, but such a course of action faces the same difficulties that faced the United States during the period of its nuclear monopoly: it might prove counter-productive. Other threats to British interests cannot be so countered. And so the possibilities of an economic blockade, of internal insurrection or of a threat to external interests have had to be provided for in a 'defence' policy. Hence the armed services have been organized to meet such possibilities. The likelihood of large-scale conventional warfare has been effectively discounted even in the European theatre. And this reflects not so much a paucity of resources, or domestic political expediency, as a radical change in the notion of security.

The point here is that factors such as spatial relations, which formerly played so important a part in defining national security, are subordinate to the technology created in order to subsume them. Geography, and the distribution of differential capacities for violence possessed by nation-states in the past, provided an inducement to adopt policies designed to control an unstable and potentially hostile environment. Spatial relations were important in defining security but only in terms of the current weapons technology. Sea and air forces pose different problems. But ballistic weapons are radically different. Compare, for example, the problem posed by a carrier strike force operating in the Pacific against Japan in the last war with that of countering a missile capable of hitting its target many thousand miles away within half an hour of its launching. The strategic reasoning associated with these two types of weapons is clearly based on very different premises.

Imperialism, in the sense of the acquisition of power and authority over the external world in order to preserve national territorial integrity, is necessary only if the technology of violence requires this. It is a by-product of security competition, but this competition itself arises out of technological innovation in the means of violence. In the past, territory was important for the deployment of an effective defence against potential aggressors. This was because of the technical limitations of existing weapons. But present weapons make this form of imperialism irrelevant. It is no longer necessary to extend national power over other states in order to achieve national security. Such a state of affairs is not of course immutable and further technological changes may radically alter it. But the point here is that, although there may be a relation between imperialism and security, such a relation is contingent and not necessary. It is a historical and not a theoretical association.

The idea of nuclear *balance* thus changed the concept of national security. No longer was security provided by a national capacity for violence superior to that of any potential aggressor and supported by a set of diplomatic and political arrangements designed to act as a constraint upon such a threat. Bases and alliances ceased to be relevant to the problem of national security, whatever any other rationale or political momentum they might possess. The power-security hypothesis asserted the primacy of security fears, which at moments of political crisis, whatever the occasion or the nature of the dispute, brought the issue of national survival into question. This was because the element of threat in any inter-state dispute was determined not by the actual demands and counter-demands made by the contending states but by their respective capacities for violence created on grounds of national security. In a sense, the magnitude of the conflict was determined not by the ostensible issue, but by the existence of this capacity. Political and security questions were thus inextricably interfused. However rational it was to limit the means — threats, diplomacy, violence, etc. — to the ends sought, and thus keep the contest limited, the existence of a general war capacity possessed by the contenders meant there was a tendency to extend the means in order to win and in so doing change the ends sought. Limited wars thus had a tendency to become general wars because of the existence of a so-called defence capacity. Security could not be defined and provided for in such a way as to make a clear distinction between a capacity for violence designed to protect the state and one that was limited to the achievement of lesser objectives.

A distinction between defensive and offensive deterrence could now be made with the new weapons, given their unprecedented accuracy and the precise measurement of their destructive effects. The damage they could inflict in material terms could be measured in a way that was not possible with the tank, the submarine, the bomber and biochemical weapons. Defensive deterrence could be defined in terms of the national possession of an invulnerable retaliatory capacity capable of inflicting an unacceptable level of damage on an aggressor. And with this definition a clear distinction could at last be made between a national capacity for defence — a minimal notion of security — and the capacity to use violence for other more limited ends than the preservation of national territorial integrity. The problem posed by Clausewitz, that war is rational only where the ends are not changed by the means adopted, appears to have been solved. The only rational end that is served by the possession of nuclear weapons is that of national security. They cannot be used rationally in any other context than against non-nuclear opponents.

Now the rationality of deterrence *emerged,* rather than formed the basis of the strategic planning that underpinned the nuclear arms race. In a sense, the conditions for the present nuclear stalemate were created by politicians acting on quite different assumptions and with a different end in view. It was not until the Cuban missiles crisis of 1962 that a full realization of the stalemate appeared, together with a lively sense of the dangers of irrational action. This realization that national restraint was at the basis of deterrence and of security produced a series of negotiations between the major nuclear powers on the question of arms control that continue into the present. In a sense these states are formulating and following rules, either explicitly through treaties and conventions, or implicitly in terms of circumspect foreign policies and restrained actions. They recognized that the chief danger lies in irrational conduct. It was important moreover to try to maintain a stable balance. Those conditions for stability — the recognition and acceptance of rules inhibiting violent courses of action, and the conscious avoidance of technological innovations likely to accelerate the arms race or to create a superiority to be used in a pre-emptive attack — are explicit both in their negotiations and in their conduct. The United States accepted a humiliating failure in the Vietnam War rather than extend the war to China or the Soviet Union. Indeed, the nuclear status of the Soviet Union precluded this as a rational step. At the same time the irrelevance of the war in Vietnam to American security made its prosecution to the point of victory futile. In effect, the spheres of influence policy rejected by the United States at the end of the Second World War has now been adopted and the ideological posturing of the Cold War period abandoned.

There is of course no guarantee that this will continue, or that a nuclear war will not occur between the major powers. The point is that security has come to mean the maintenance of the conditions for mutual defensive deterrence. Whatever else is required from the external world, any move that endangers this is deemed illegitimate and inherently dangerous. Thus the pursuit of power and influence in the world at large on the part of the major nuclear powers is both removed from the question of national security and conducted with caution. Conflicts and competition occur between states, but the security element is irrelevant. This is provided by the possession of a *national* nuclear riposte capacity whose invulnerability is provided through underwater launchers or protected silos on national territory. The logistics of this deployment do not entail a worldwide system of bases or any form of world hegemony. In short, this form of security does not entail imperialism.

If we return to the problem of the explanatory power of the power-security hypothesis, we can see that it postulates a rationale in the form of a dynamic that results in security competition. Such competition has the paradoxical effect of making the state insecure and intensifying the competition. Although statesmen think that they are acting rationally in providing for national defence, in fact they create unwittingly a constant challenge to the integrity of the nation-state. Imperialism is a direct consequence of this dynamic because only through hegemonial control over other states can a state provide a genuine and lasting guarantee of its own security.

Now a 'fit' between this rationale and the policies and actions pursued by the major powers in the inter-war period appears to exist. Such a 'fit' appears to continue until the advent of a radically different weapons technology in the post-war period. But what is the nature of this apparent 'fit' between an interpretative conceptual framework such as the power-security hypothesis and the events it purports to explain? Does it really explain? And if so what kind of explanation does it provide? I said earlier that there were two possibilities in terms of putative explanations derived from this argument. If we accept that the thesis is limited to time, to place and to specific states and statesmen, then the putative explanation is nominally at least historical in character. The security dilemma is finite and temporal in nature. It is a function of contingent factors, such as a particular weapons technology, spatial relations, the existence of sovereign nation-states possessing the material capacities for waging large-scale war, and so on. But these factors are not independent of the reasoning of the individuals who create and respond to them. A historical explanation is not based on a selection of factors deemed relevant by an 'objective' observer, but upon his identification of such factors in terms of the reasoning of the political agents whose actions he is seeking to explain. Otherwise the result is not history but an anachronistic rationalization.

As we have seen earlier, the notion of security is essentially normative, and a definition of it in terms of action lies in the conceptions of historical agents. There is evidence that the solution of the security problem in the pre-nuclear period was seen as inhibiting or controlling a potentially hostile environment. The problem indeed was seen in terms of the existence of differential capacities for violence possessed by states and the inability to produce some system of collective control and thus collective security. Imperialist policies in this sense were pursued by the major states during this period. That Germany, Japan and Italy possessed forms of government inimical to the democracies, only masked the reality of the security struggle. The democracies themselves were imperialist powers and had a vested interest in security too. That they were on the defensive and justified their defence of the status quo in ideological terms, merely concealed the fact that their interests in the world at large were largely the same as the 'aggressive' fascist powers. The case of the Soviet Union, delicately poised in this contest, illustrates sufficiently the fundamental security problem. The United States, although apparently isolated from this contest, in fact took a keen interest in the Pacific and in South America and sought to exclude rivals as well as to accommodate existing interests. In short, the crises of the 1930s and of the immediate post-war period saw a major preoccupation on the part of the contending states with the problem of security and a consequent violent contest followed by an arms race. All of these states sought to gain control over foreign territories and although the proffered reasoning contained ideological and material justification, as well as grounds of security, it was the latter that predominated. After the Second World War, the major states were on a permanent war footing and heavily involved in a nuclear arms race. Thus any consideration of the evidence of reasoning of those agents concerned with inter-state relations and with defence would discover the importance of national security and its definition in terms of the capacities and dispositions of rival states.

A historical explanation then might well assert the paramountcy of national security in the policies and actions of the states during this period. It might stress the importance of extending national control over the external environment as an objective actively pursued by the major powers. But in so doing the link between reasoning and action is established, not in terms of a predetermined rationale but on the basis of the evidence of reasoning available to the historian. A superior reasoning is not imposed on the evidence. As we have seen, the point is not that factors such as weapons technology and spatial relations are contingent and not necessary, so that the alleged 'fit' between the power-security hypothesis and empirical 'reality' breaks down in the nuclear age. If we take the thesis to be historical in nature, then this does not matter. We are concerned only with establishing its explanatory adequacy for a given period.

Is the thesis in fact adequate in this sense? The answer must be no; for instead of examining the relationship between the reasoning of the political agents and their alleged imperialist actions, the former is characterized in terms of an external rationale. So far as this type of explanation is concerned, the power-security hypothesis is a rationalization that depicts imperialism as a consequence of 'power-politics'. The associated phenomena — the creation of a capacity for violence intended to deter or dominate other states, the involvement of the powerful states in the domestic politics of the other states, the aggrandizement of the state through conquest or the creation of external empires, a hegemonial diplomacy, and the exacerbation of international anarchy through these actions and their consequent intensification — all constitute imperialism. If we accept this, then we find ourselves in a circularity in which, regardless of the *intentions* of political agents, their actions fall into this rubric. Their actions are made intelligible through the application of this conceptual framework.

But what justifies the framework? It cannot be justified in terms of the alleged empirical phenomena as described above, for these take on their peculiar meaning and significance from the framework itself. They *constitute* imperialism. The involvement of the state in international politics takes on an imperialist character by definition. There are no criteria of reference independent of the 'explanation' to which we can refer in order to validate it. A historical explanation that is dependent upon evidence of reasoning and so explains actions, giving them their intelligibility and character, clearly has such an independent reference. It is no better than the evidence it adduces to make its case. But a rationalization that makes actions intelligible in terms of a postulated rationale, however plausible, cannot make such a reference. The power-security hypothesis, instead of explaining, simply encapsulates a set of alleged phenomena within its reasoning and presents it as if it were somehow derived from the rationale. Instead of providing an explanation in terms of the actual intentions and policies of the agents, it substitutes a general rationale that relies on pseudo-generalizations about state conduct in an anarchic environment.

Thus the level of empirical reference — the 'facts' — is used to support the generalization through a selection of instances that 'prove' the thesis. But clearly the 'facts' are themselves the product of the argument and are not an independent source of reference or independent of the 'explanation'. If the power-security hypothesis were an adequate historical explanation it would have to show the relation between reasoning and action that brought about a given international situation. This it does not do, for it defines what this relation must be in terms of the rationale of the thesis. A reference to actual events in this context is circular, for they are defined by the thesis in such a way as to preclude any other interpretation. As we shall see in later chapters, the power-security version of imperialism is incommensurable with other versions of imperialism in international politics.

The temptation to impose this sort of rationalization upon international political events stems from the fact that situations of crisis and conflict are very often the unintended consequences of human action. Statesmen do not normally wish to place themselves or their states into jeopardy through their decisions and actions. The prospect of success, even in the negative sense of avoiding defeat, is a postulate of action. But nothing is certain. The rationality of their actions and of their intentions is clearly at odds with the result in many cases. Consequently, the detached observer in looking at the past feels able to pass judgement, drawing attention to the discrepancy between the aim and the achievement. The past is full of lost causes and unfulfilled intentions. But in doing so he implicitly or explicitly links cause and effect. The logic of causation is central to the power-security hypothesis, as we shall see when its theoretical status as an explanation is discussed shortly. In the context of historical argument the temptation is to argue that the violence in international politics, and its associated imperialism, are a necessary consequence of the security policies pursued by statesmen. They do not intend to create a condition of insecurity for their states, but this in fact is what they do. So, whatever their reasons for embarking upon a course of action, the result is in a sense independent of their reasoning.

To say that a state of affairs is unintended is not to say that it is a necessary consequence of a course of action. To argue the latter is to postulate a relationship between cause and effect in terms of human actions and events that is demonstrable in a non-tautological manner. The power-security hypothesis, if it is explanatory rather than concerned with passing normative judgement upon past events, asserts this relationship. And so the question of intention becomes irrelevant. The reasoning of the agents is not germane to the rationale of the thesis. The causes of the state of affairs depicted as imperialism lie in the relationship between factors admittedly created by the agents but beyond their control, exercising a determinant influence upon their subsequent conduct. Such an argument is determinist in nature and, as such, non-historical. It is distinct from an assessment of a state of affairs as at odds with the intentions of those involved in it. Such an assessment is intimately bound up in an appreciation of the nature of the reasoning of the agents whose actions constitute the subject of an explanation. In this context we may talk of success or failure but not of mistakes. For while we can relate aims and intentions to actions in terms of the reasoning of the agents, we cannot go beyond this and talk of *necessary* consequences and of results, as if we were in possession of a superior knowledge of the proper relation between cause and effects. To do this we would need to have a properly grounded theoretical explanation.

This brings me to the question of the power-security hypothesis as a general theoretical explanation. At the beginning of this chapter I said that security was a normative concept whose meaning is derived from a specific historical context of usage. Its content, as it were, is constituted by the meaning it had for political practitioners acting in their subjectively understood international context. An explanation employing the concept *security* is constrained either to justify a usage independent of this context, that is to give it theoretical content, or to elicit its historical meaning. The former possibility is discounted in the power-security argument because of its dependence on the subjective level of fear and the actual empirical phenomena of security policies. So it is to the second major concept, that of power, to which we turn in order to discover the theoretical dynamic that forces states into the form of imperialism alleged to hold by the thesis. What is the nature of the drive to power central to the thesis?

Let me recapitulate the main argument of the power-security hypothesis. It asserts that all nation-states with the requisite resources engage in a form of imperialism. They seek power over other states in order to achieve a position of hegemony. This is not a conscious policy in the sense that statesmen rationally pursue imperialist policies in order to achieve world empire. They are in a sense forced to extend their control over other states because of a basic problem of security. Given that all states have their own preservation as territorial entities as a primary objective, they create a capacity for violence designed to guarantee this. But in so doing, a reciprocal effect occurs in which one state's security becomes another state's insecurity. A multitude of factors affect this relation, most of them emanating from an inherently unstable and anarchic environment. The creation of a *defensive* capacity for violence produces competition. In any case, whatever a state's resources, it cannot hope to provide national security purely through its own domestic efforts. The consequence of this is an exacerbation of international anarchy and a compelling need to control it. The state is induced to extend some form of control over its external environment — other states — in order to guarantee or preserve the conditions for national security. Imperialist policies are thus a necessary consequence of this security dilemma.

Now this process is alleged to be beyond the control of individual statesmen. They are at the mercy of the reciprocal dynamic that makes it apparently rational to control those forces in the external world that are an actual or potential danger to national security. But this rationality is illusory if the result is an intensification of competition and of insecurity. Agreement between states cannot achieve security because the grounds of such agreements are only *ad hoc*. States will always seek relative advantages as a rational policy as circumstances change. Factors such as changes of government, technological innovations in weapons and economic strength introduce variables that alter the nature and status of international agreements. A purely national effort at providing defence induces competition, yet attempts at negotiated agreements between states on security do not provide a lasting solution. The answer to the problem is world hegemony, and until this is achieved by one state a condition of permanent war is the central characteristic of international politics.

Enough has been said earlier of the rationalizing elements in this argument in the context of historical explanation. What of the notion of power and its theoretical implications? It will be recalled that in the early part of this chapter I argued that the concept power had two applications. The first was that of power as a capacity for action and the second was power as an exercise, as action itself. Translating this into more concrete terms, this distinction can be seen as the pursuit of power by the nation-state in its environment in order to achieve security and as the achievement of a state power — imperial power. Both of these notions are implicit in the power-security hypothesis, and, as was argued earlier, difficult to disentangle. But in what sense are these two uses theoretical; do they help us towards an explanation of imperialism in inter-state relations? Clearly a theory is implicit in the conceptual framework, for both these notions of power entail a level of abstraction remote from the empirical level of the reasoning of the political agents. A capacity for action, and a state of affairs characterized as power, are independent of human volition, although they may be the product of human action.

Essentially the thesis states that all nation-states seek to maximize their power in order to survive as states. If we look at the first conceptual usage, that of power as a capacity, we can see that power here is conceived of as an unrealized potential. The state, in embarking on its attempt to control its dangerous environment, creates a capacity for violence as a means to this end. This postulates an attribute — the possession of the means of violence — as a necessary pre-condition for the achievement of an end — power, or the condition of hegemony over other states. If this attribute can be stated as a genuine pre-condition for the successful achievement of an objective — in this case hegemony — then we have a means of stating what the outcome will be depending on its presence or absence, or on which state possesses it. Power in this sense is an unrealized potential that enables predictive statements, or at the least statements of probability.

But if we wish to state a general proposition linking means to ends in this way then we must specify a set of conditions necessary and sufficient to a given action. A causal principle is involved applicable to all 'power situations'. Having attributes does not entail actions. We must establish a general explanatory link between these and action itself. Conceiving power as capacity tells us nothing more than that doing something and being capable of doing something are somehow linked. But, of course, inferring the latter from the former is nothing more than a tautology. If we wish to make non-tautological and non-trivial statements of a theoretical nature using the concept power as capacity, then we must connect capacity — as means — to specific ends, within a testable causal hypothesis. In other words, we must specify the necessary and sufficient conditions, the law-like governing principle and the outcome.

If, then, we wish to treat the power-security hypothesis as a theoretical explanation of imperialism in world politics, these conditions require satisfaction. Power as capacity needs specification if we are to distinguish between means and ends in political action. The pursuit of power is a chimerical notion if we can make no genuine theoretical statement as to what power is in terms of capacity for action. Otherwise any action in international politics on the part of a state can fall into the rubric of the pursuit of power. In this case there is a theoretical vacuity wherever the notion of power as capacity occurs in the argument.

What of the other conceptual usage, that of power as an end in itself? Power here is treated as an absolute form: it consists of world hegemony. It is thus a synonym for dominion. When stated in this ideal form it cannot be related to any particular state of affairs at all. Absolute power is built into the power-security hypothesis as an ultimate goal. It is a logical solution to the problems of national autonomy and providing for its security. In this sense it is an ideal form. As such it can be regarded as an aim or aspiration of the political agents, void of empirical content. It is a goal to be realized. If this is the case, then no theoretical argument is entailed and we fall back on a reconstruction in historical terms of the reasoning of those agents in practice who aspire to this end. The implications of doing this will be considered in a later chapter. In short, if we do this we derive the meaning of power as an end from historical practice and not from the conceptual framework.

If, however, we try to use it in a theoretical context, then the meaning of power is logically derived from the conceptual framework that employs it. In the case of the power-security hypothesis, power is defined as a condition of absolute security in which the nation-state assumes total hegemony over the world at large. It is a logically necessary consequence of the conception of security employed in the argument. The co-existence of sovereign autonomous states constitutes a danger to the state. If this autonomy is removed or limited then this results in a condition of genuine security for the state that succeeds in doing so. This is, of course, exceedingly remote from actual practice, but it is a necessary postulate of the argument and conditions any interpretation of the 'facts' of inter-state relations. That states have not succeeded in achieving this condition of hegemony does not of itself refute the argument that it is this condition to which they aspire or are driven.

But there is no means of stating this ideal condition as a theoretical concept, other than through satisfying the logical and empirical requirements for an adequate theoretical explanation stated earlier. Power remains a mere abstraction if these are not fulfilled. It cannot be translated into an empirical context with any explanatory force. Hence, in the case of the power-security hypothesis, we are left with a generalized and rationalizing argument that seeks to subsume actions and events in international politics within the terms of its conceptual framework. We have no means of formulating or testing empirical propositions that can be derived from the 'theory'.

If we look more closely at the notion of power politics that is central to this thesis, and indeed to the whole 'realist' school of interpretation of international politics, we can see in a clearer perspective some of the problems in using the notion of power in explanations. Power is treated generally as an attribute of states, something that they possess, or as a relationship between states in which one state achieves or exercises power over another. The notion of power is also used to make an argument coherent by presenting a sort of minimal pattern in events. The concept is used to organize facts as a narrative. There are many examples of this kind of usage in historical, as well as in social scientific, literature. Although they appear on the face of it to use the notion of power in a limited context, confined to specific events in time and place, they in fact entail generalization on the level exemplified by the power-security hypothesis. There is a tacit assumption that there is an element — power — over and above the level of human action, that somehow makes the latter meaningful.

But if this is not related to a genuine theoretical explanation, then all that is offered is a form of intelligibility that is empirically vacuous. We are in a position to verify a factual statement in a way we are not with a conceptual one. In this case, power is not simply a redundant concept — another way of talking about potential or capacity for action in the context of international politics; it also weakens an explanation that nominally is historical in character, because factual statements are replaced by conceptual statements that do not add to its explanatory force. Instead of a set of verifiable references, we are offered a level of vague generality. As we have seen, where politicians act upon a particular notion of security, their actions can be made intelligible in the light of the evidence of their reasoning. In this sense we have explained them and, so far as the evidence is good we have an adequate historical explanation. But where these actions are designated and interpreted under the concept of security as defined by the power-security hypothesis, to what do we refer to establish the adequacy of the associated explanation? If the reference is to the conceptual scheme itself then we have a circularity. If such arguments are refined so as to make the definitions tighter, and the conceptual relations consistent, they are even further removed from empirical reference, and their empirical content and reference becomes even more contingent. Historical arguments that eschew any theoretical pretensions are open to the same criticism where they are heavily dependent upon concepts such as power.

Another criticism, again within the context of historical explanation, of the use of the notion of power is that it is inherently anachronistic. The implication of its use is that the historian or the 'observer' of international politics can make evaluatory judgements that would not necessarily be made by the political agents whose actions they seek to explain. This would not be the case where its meaning is derived from the reasoning of the latter. Where it is imposed upon political events, then there is a direct implication that the historian is making an external judgement. In fact he is rationalizing, and the validity of this exercise lies outside the terms of historical argument. A theoretical justification is required on the basis of the satisfaction of those conditions noted earlier. Clearly if this is the case much of this kind of 'history' is of a quasi-theoretical nature.

But my main criticism is directed at the concept itself. There is an inextricable confusion of means and ends in the use of this concept. Power is conceived, as we have seen, as a capacity, that is, a means to an end, a latent force, an unrealized potential. But it is also treated as an entity, a state or condition, an end in itself, a characteristic mode of behaviour, a relationship and a goal-directed activity. All of these involve some notion of the achievement of objectives. For example, to have successfully accomplished an objective in the face of opposition can be construed as having been powerful. A statement of the reasons why success and not failure resulted can be projected into a statement of capacity for power. Success may mean that power has been exercised or achieved. A run of successes may be conceived of as an indication that a state is, and will continue to be, powerful, and so on. All these constructions work back from the ends to the means in such a way as to confuse the conditions for success with success itself.

If we argue that the possession of power is in some way established by success in achieving objectives, then we are supposing that a distinction can be made between it and the objective itself. Power here becomes some undefinable entity existing in any political situation. This is to give it some notion of essence. Power can be gained, lost or exercised. We have here both an entity and an activity, but always unrelated and open-ended in empirical terms. To what do we refer it to give it substance? If it is revealed in the achievement of objectives then power is as power does, that is to say that we can only make retrospective statements, descriptive in nature, about relative successes and failures in international relations. These would seem to be normative judgements. From the recent past we can indeed make projections into our immediate future, but this is a practical judgement and void of any explanatory basis.

If power really is as power does, then it cannot be considered more of an aim than the aim itself. We are really talking about success and not power. A distinction between the achievement of power and the achievement of a specified objective cannot be made, because in the absence of a means of identifying the essential nature of power and thus isolating it the two are identical. We cannot argue that the primal national interest is the pursuit of power because in this sense it is a necessary pre-condition for the achievement of anything. In other words it is tautological to use the concept power in this way: achievement *is* power and power is achievement. We add nothing to the statement that X was gained or lost by saying that a state or a particular politician had the power (or not) to achieve it, or that achieving it made it or him powerful. We must specify the objectives and in doing this we do not need the concept power.

Similarly, we must specify the conditions and the reasoning, and the concept power is unhelpful here too. Our commonsense judgement about the relative power of states are based upon past achievement, combined with a rough notion that there must be some relationship between capacity and objectives if the latter are to have some chance of fulfilment. But of course the problem for those who wish to make *explanatory* statements using the concept of power is specifying what this relationship is, either within a given historical context or as a basis for generalization.

We can see from all this that the power-security explanation of imperialism in world politics is inadequate on a number of grounds. It is essentially a conceptual scheme, although not a very rigorous or well worked out one. In comparison with other models of imperialism, notably that of economic imperialism, it is diffuse, ambiguous and very general. This is inevitable, for it is a world picture and not an empirical explanation, and in this sense provides us with an understanding of world politics. But such an understanding, as well as being incommensurate with that provided by other such schemes, is not subject to any further judgement. If we accept it we do so on purely subjective grounds.

Where we question it, the problem becomes one of coherence not of empirical reference. If a conceptual category, such as that of power, is ambivalent or ambiguous, the solution is not to alter any particular empirical reference — to the actual events of world politics — but to redefine it in terms of other conceptual categories within the scheme. And such an adjustment is really a semantic or logical exercise. The kinds of empirical reference it makes are little more than self-evident or a matter of definition. The interpretation of world events it provides is in a sense not an *empirical* derivation from a theory but a logical one from a conceptual framework. It is impossible to use the scheme to *explain* facts for these are merely contingent upon the conceptual categories.

If we apply historical criteria to it and treat it as a putative historical explanation, we find it does not refer to any evidence of reasoning. It is a rationalization and not a reason-giving explanation. And if we treat it as a putative theoretical explanation, it fails to satisfy the criteria appropriate to this mode too. If my argument is accepted, then it must be concluded that the form of imperialism postulated by the power-security hypothesis is tautological. It is a logical and not an empirical necessity of the alleged processes at work in inter-state politics. Yet, in spite of these criticisms, in one guise or another the idea that international politics is power politics has had a long life. It continues to retain its attractions as a generalized view of the world, but an explanation of that is beyond my brief.

NOTES AND REFERENCES

1　For example, see Hans J. Morgenthau *Politics among Nations* (New York, Alfred A. Knopf, 1951), *Dilemmas of Politics* (Chicago, University of Chicago Press, 1958); Charles A. Beard *The Idea of National Interest* (New York, Macmillan, 1934); E. H. Carr *The Twenty Years Crisis 1919-1939* (London, Macmillan, 1940); Raymond Aron *The Century of Total War* (New York, Doubleday, 1954); L. J. Halle *The Cold War as History* (London, Chatto and Windus, 1970); G. Schwartzenberger *Power Politics* (London, Stevens and Sons, 1964, 3rd edn);

Arnold Wolfers *Discord and Collaboration* (Baltimore, Johns Hopkins, 1962).

2 The power-security hypothesis is a composite that synthesizes the arguments of the realist school of interpreters of inter-state relations. Its origins lie in conceptions of the world of states as inherently anarchic and owes much to the writings of Hobbes, Bodin, Machievelli and Rousseau.

3 In the inter-war period Hitler consciously created a military capacity designed to achieve limited political objectives by threat and the exercise of force. The post-war nuclear programmes pursued by the major powers eventually came to be limited to defensive deterrence and designed to avoid war, rather than to use nuclear power as a rational instrument. Similarly, small neutral states such as Switzerland and Sweden adopted defensive measures designed to deter an invasion by making it costly for the invader.

4 Or, to be more precise, 'War is not merely a political act, but also a real political instrument, a continuation of political commerce, a carrying out of the same by other means' (Carl von Clausewitz *On War,* trans. Col. J. J. Graham, ed. Col. F. N. Maude, London, Routledge and Kegan Paul, 1949, Book 1, Chapter 1, p. 23; first published in 1908).

5 An extreme example of this approach is Lewis Richardson *Arms and Insecurity* (ed. N. Rachevsky and E. Trucco, Chicago, Boxwood Press, 1968).

6 This was actually the case during the Vietnam War when President Johnson was faced with a demand in 1968 from his military commander for an additional 200,000 men. Only by breaking the constraints that limited the scale of the war and related the use of violence to what were conceived of as attainable goals, could it be won in the military sense of victory. But to do this meant changing these ends and so losing control over the war and perhaps putting other policy objectives in jeopardy, President Johnson refused to accept this demand and in effect accepted that he could not win the war in the political sense without changing its nature and changing his goals.

7 This remark was made by the Mexican delegate to the San Francisco Conference.

8 The first genuine 'strategic' long-range bomber was the B 29 developed by the United States at the end of the war. The first Soviet long-range bomber — the Bear — appeared in 1954.

9 See Chamberlain speeches made in the Commons, 25 May 1938, and at Kettering, 2 July 1938, in *In Search of Peace. Speeches 1937-38* (ed. A. Bryant, London, Hutchinson, 1939).

10 See F. P. Walters *A History of the League of Nations* (London, Oxford University Press, 1960) pp. 500-16.

11 In this year Hitler embarked on a rearmament programme, and on 12 May 1936 initiated a Four Year Plan designed to put Germany in an economic position insulated from outside intervention.

12 The French had wanted a draconic peace treaty to be imposed on Germany but were persuaded out of this position by the offer of a joint British and American guarantee of the new French frontiers. The failure of the US Senate to ratify the peace settlement saw the demise of this guarantee.

13 Hitler demanded the incorporation of Danzig within the Reich, and road and rail links connecting East and West Prussia across the 'Polish corridor'.

14 This was a short-lived peace treaty concluded between Britain and Napoleon in 1802.

15 See Lord Avon *The Eden Memoirs: The Reckoning* (London, Cassells, 1965) pp. 271-303.

16 The famous percentage agreement between Churchill and Stalin of October 1944 excluded Poland.

17 Dulles had assumed responsibility for the negotiation of a peace treaty with Japan, which was signed in September 1951. He also negotiated the South-East Asia Collective Defence Treaty signed on 8 September 1954.
18 See Margaret Truman *Harry S. Truman* (London, Hamish Hamilton 1973) pp. 415-19.
19 The USSR exploded its H bomb in August 1953.
20 The Defence White Paper, Cmnd 124 (London, HMSO, 1957).
21 See Richard Meustadt *Alliance Politics* (New York, Columbia University Press, 1970) pp. 50-6.
22 See Andrew Pierre *Nuclear Politics: The British Experience with an Independent Strategic Force 1939-70* (London, Oxford University Press, 1972).
23 See Arthur Schlesinger *A Thousand Days* (London, Mayflower-Dell, 1967) pp. 316-17.

3

Economic Imperialism

Any discussion on economic theories of imperialism inevitably revolves around Marxism. It should be said at once that there is no Marxist theory of imperialism as such. Strictly speaking there can be no *Marxist* theory of economic imperialism, for Marxist theory concerns itself with structural relations of production and society and hence subsumes the political within the economic and social. If it is anything, it is a theory of capitalist society in the particular, and a theory of society and social development in the general. What is conceived of as imperialism within the Marxist framework is something that is not purely economic, but represents a stage in the development of capitalist society. But of course the underlying structure that produces the phenomenon of imperialism is conceived of in economic terms. Imperialism is a label both for the total complex of capitalist development, and for a set of empirical phenomena that are to be explained through an analysis of their economic provenance. As we shall see, there is considerable ambiguity between the *descriptive* level of Marxist analysis of imperialism as a product of capitalism, and the *theoretical* level of the analysis of the dynamics of economic forces within a society. It is never clear whether the argument is concerned with describing the actual relations of economic and sociopolitical phenomena as a kind of descriptive model, or whether it is explaining such phenomena in terms of a theory of economic development atemporal in nature.

The expression 'theory' is used a good deal in Marxist argument and one of the problems with which this study is concerned is its status in explanatory terms. Does 'theory' imply a general explanation that expresses a causal connection between precedent necessary and sufficient conditions and a given and predictable result, governed by a law specific to that class of events? In this case the phenomena to be explained, i.e. the effects, *qua* imperialism are logically independent of the explanation *qua* theory of imperialism. The adequacy of such a 'theory' lies in its reference to empirical phenomena through a test.

Prediction and retrodiction are thus made possible. Or, alternatively, does 'theory' simply connote a 'world view' in which the empirical phenomena that puzzle us — in this case, economic activities of one kind or another, political relations between states, exchange relations, wars, the acquisition of colonies, economic development, and so on — are all subsumed within a conceptual framework that enables us to make a coherent and intelligible picture of these complex and various 'facts'? If this last is the case and this is really what the Marxist argument amounts to, then in what sense do we have an *explanation* of imperialism and in what sense is it adequate or preferable to the other 'explanations' of imperialism considered in this study? These questions will be considered in the context of relations between the developed and the underdeveloped countries and the status and role of multinational corporations.

For the moment I am concerned with elucidating a model of economic imperialism. In projecting such a model it should be stressed that there is considerable diversity amongst those who claim to have derived their inspiration from Marx. And there are a number of writers, most notably J. A. Hobson, who have contributed to the debate and who could not be described as Marxist. An exegeticist would be hard pressed to give a coherent account acceptable to Marxists, firstly, because no two Marxists seem to agree on what constitutes orthodox Marxism and, secondly, because such an account itself would have to be Marxist, i.e. formulated within a Marxist framework. (For only then would it be truly 'objective'; all other accounts are tainted by bourgeois ideologies.) However, I think that in spite of the sometimes petty distinctions made by those writing in the Marxist tradition, there is sufficient family resemblance between them to justify treating their arguments as representations of a model. Where there are substantive differences I shall try to make these clear.

Marx himself never mentioned the word imperialism. But he provided the conceptual framework, however modified and perhaps distorted it became, for the idea of economic imperialism. It can be expressed quite simply: political, social, cultural and intellectual activities are all explicable in terms of some economic dynamic or process in human relations. In one form or another, in a mechanistic, determinist or possibilist vein, these theories assert the primacy of economic forces in explanations of human actions and experience. Of course, this view is not confined to Marxists nor do they have a monopoly of historicist or teleological arguments, as is made clear in this study, but the idea of contradiction and conflict emanating from the capitalist mode of production is essentially Marxist and it is at the core of economic imperialism.

So while extant Marxist theories vary in their focuses — some are primarily concerned to explain the nature of capitalism with its innate drive to maximize profits by expanding investment opportunities beyond its national base; some are concerned to explain the actual acquisition of territories and the creation of formal empires, some to explain wars and the inevitable crisis and collapse of capitalism through the intense competition generated by competing imperialism, or through its own inner contradiction; some concentrate on the phenomenon of unequal development and the effects of a dominant capitalist system on developing countries; and some seek to encompass all these 'phenomena' within a general theoretical explanation — all share common features and all assert the primacy of economic forces. And, as I shall argue, in terms of their explanatory capacity they all belong to the same category of argument as well as deriving from the same conceptual framework.

At the core of economic theories of imperialism is the notion of unequal exchange arising out of an inherent contradiction in the capitalist mode of production. According to the later Marxists the propensity of capitalism to expand beyond the national economy arises out of the inability of that economy to absorb its own surplus capital. Marx himself conceived of a capitalist dynamic that forced the capitalist to seek to accumulate profit. This was done through technological development and the expansion of production continually converting the surplus value of labour into capital. All this was within the locus of a *national* economy. The contradictions arising out of unemployment and underconsumption — the discrepancy between production and consumption — led to a fall in the rate of profit and to frequent crises and distortions in capitalist development. Further technological innovation and reorganization of industrial capital through the creation of monopolies and cartels only staved off the inevitable collapse of the capitalist system. For Marx there was no answer to the problem of unequal exchange within the capitalist system other than through revolution and the elimination both of capitalists and of free labour. A communist society achieved equilibrium, and *inter alia* the elimination of exploitation, by destroying the relationship between capitalists and free labour that constituted the rationale of capitalism.

Nowhere does Marx, explicitly at least, argue that a partial solution to the actual falling rate of profit and the dynamic of pressure for its increase inherent in the system lay in the acquisition of empires or in 'economic territory' beyond the nation-state. The expansionist aspect of capitalism for him lay in the historic process that operated in all societies, however primitive, and that induced a progression from primitive accumulation to the kind of economic stage he termed capitalism.[1] Such developments could be induced outside the existing capitalist states by the promotion of industrialization and through entrepreneurial activities. Colonies, he believed, could develop capitalism given the involvement of *capitalist* metropolitan rulers. Where the colonial relationship was between a non-capitalist state and primitive societies, as in the Tsarist Empire, then no such development was likely.[2] But in any case such colonial expansion and consequent exploitation were not necessitated by the capitalist system. In short, it was not the expansion of capitalism from capitalist societies that was fundamental to capitalism, but the development *within* extant societies of capitalist forms. This constituted a form of modernization that produced in all societies, albeit unequally and differentially, the dissassociation between capital and free labour, and its contradictions, characteristic of capitalism.

Having said this, it could be argued that Marx viewed trade as a temporary expedient to offset declining profits. The importation of cheaper raw materials and food countered this fall by taking surplus value from extra-national sources. As we shall see, this aspect forms one of the arguments of later neo-Marxist writers on economic imperialism. But as Winslow points out,[3] this hardly forms a basis for *trade* given its inbuilt inequality in exchange terms. The exporting country, given this argument, suffers a net loss of surplus value. Such an exchange in the long run is possible only if it is forced by the importer and, of course, this forcible expropriation is the nub of neo-Marxist views of economic imperialism.

Although Marx himself did not conceive of any inevitable necessity of capitalism to expand beyond the nation-state in which it flourished, he provided the basic conceptual framework for later exponents of economic imperialism. His notion of surplus capital[4] and its transfer as capital from labour, together with the constant pressure on capitalists to increase the rate of 'accumulation', the contradictions within the capitalist system by which this rate tended to fall, the reorganization of capital into more concentrated monopolistic forms, were all picked out of the central Marxist argument and employed with other notions to form more or less coherent accounts of economic imperialism.

Rosa Luxemburg, for example, sought to explain how the contradiction in capital accumulation is resolved by arguing that 'it is the invasion of primitive economies by capitalism which keeps the system alive'.[5] The domestic imbalance between consumption and production and the consequent crisis arising out of underconsumption are offset by the development of markets abroad and investment in natural resources. Here we have, as we do not in Marx's own argument, a direct link between capitalism and economic imperialism.

Surplus value was 'realized' by creating markets in non-capitalist societies in order to create necessary investment outlets that could not exist in a closed 'underconsumptionist' capitalist society. As she put it,

> It becomes necessary for capitalism progressively to dispose ever more fully of the whole globe, to acquire an unlimited choice of means of production, with regard to both quality and quantity, so as to find productive employment for the surplus value it has realised.[6]

Hence the process of capital accumulation requires external outlets for investment, which in turn accelerates it. Such investment utilizes and needs an ever-expanding supply of labour, which the domestic source cannot provide, in order to realize its surplus value. Capitalism, through its drive to accumulate capital, has an innate dynamic to expand its activities beyond the national capitalist system.

The two major effects of this necessity are on the one hand, the acquisition of an external economic 'empire' and, on the other, competition between the major capitalist countries in achieving this. 'Imperialism', she argued, 'is the political expression of the accumulation of capital in its competitive struggle for what remains still open of the non-capitalist environment.'[7] But since this area is finite, as soon as capitalism has expanded to its limits it destroys itself through the fundamental inability to resolve the problem of capital accumulation and the contradictions of effective demand and falling profit rates. In her view, imperialism was the highest and final stage of capitalism.

Its associated phenomena were cartels and monopoly organizations, heavy external investment in the non-capitalist world and its progressive industrialization, and wars between the competing capitalist countries. The root cause was the insoluble problem of realizing surplus value from a finite labour supply, initially nationally located and subsequently globally located. Although she accepted Marx's labour theory of value, in her view Marx had limited himself to the problem of primitive accumulation in explaining the phenomenon of capitalism. Her own argument took the thesis further. Nevertheless her conclusion echoed that of Marx, namely that the inherent contradiction of imperialism would bring about its collapse.[8]

Lenin took the argument in a different direction, although again within the general Marxist framework. While Luxemburg wrote before the First World War, Lenin was concerned in his *Imperialism, the Highest Stage of Capitalism*[9] to place the war in its proper theoretical context. He believed the war to be a direct product of competition between the major capitalist powers. There is much that is common ground between these two Marxist writers: the emphasis on investment in the non-capitalist world, the emergence and growth of capitalism in this area, the monopolistic nature of capital investment, the importance of external sources of raw materials and food, and the existence of surplus capital requiring an outlet, for example. But his argument is much less analytic and departs from her emphasis on the theory of capital accumulation and the problem of a closed economic system. There is little analysis of the actual processes of capitalism and his focus is mainly on their asserted effects in terms of empirical phenomena.

He asserts as the main dynamic the appearance of a new form of capital — finance capital — and a new 'social organisation',[10] that of the national cartel. The main characteristic of cartels is their attempt to divide the markets and profits and to exert control over competition. This leads to what Lenin called 'the socialisation of production'. Having effectively done this within the national economy, the same drive urges them to do the same in the world at large. The national cartel is impelled to pursue 'the highest socialisation of production'. 'It drags, as it were, the capitalists against their will and understanding, into some new social order, which is transitional leading from complete freedom of competition to complete socialisation.'[11] So the drive for capitalist expansion derives from finance capital organized into monopolies.

Although he refers to the inability of national capitalist economies to absorb surplus capital and relates this to underconsumption following J. A. Hobson,[12] in no way does he consider this to be the central dynamic nor does he devote much of his argument to it. He is far more concerned with the external *effects* of capitalism — the phenomenon he termed imperialism. He takes for granted the alleged fact that national monopolies seek to transform themselves into super-monopolies and that this entails a process of exporting capital in order to effect control over 'economic territory'. The reasons for imperialist expansion he sees as the need to guarantee sources of raw materials, to provide an outlet for surplus capital, to create a source of profits from investment and to guarantee markets. But these 'reasons' all stem from the appearance of finance capital and monopoly conditions within capitalist states. In a sense they are supernumerary to the central reason — the nature of monopoly. In a way it is an organization theory that begs the question as to the nature of the processes that created the asserted monopolies in the first place, and then goes on to use them as instruments.

Lenin conceived of 'economic territory' as constituting not merely the formal empires of the period, but also the area described by Luxemburg as the primitive economies of the world. These included nominally sovereign independent states, as much as 'unclaimed' peoples and territories.[13] They were brought under the control of the major capitalist states. Such control was exercised through a 'net of financial and diplomatic dependence'. Colonies coexist with dependent states as part of the economic territory of the growing national monopoly. An essential feature of the 'new' imperialism, according to Lenin, is competition between the advanced capitalist societies. He considered, as did Marx, the state and capitalism to be synonymous. The state *was* capitalism. And this competition was necessary in terms not only of perceived relative advantage but also in the denial of opportunities. As he put it, 'an essential feature of imperialism is the rivalry between a number of great powers in striving for hegemony, i.e. for the seizure of territory, not so much for their own direct advantage as to weaken the adversary and undermine *his* hegemony.'[14] Wars were inevitable, for no other means existed to resolve this fundamental conflict between national monopolies. He argued,

> the question arises is there *under capitalism* any means of eliminating the disparity between the development of productive forces and the accumulation of capital on the one side, and the partition of colonies and 'spheres of influence' by finance capital on the other side — other than by war.[15]

Lenin was silent on the question of the expansion of capitalism as such. He said little on the subject of its development in the economic territory acquired by the capitalist state. From what he did say it appears that he conceived of no independent capitalist development; rather the world was divided into two categories: the major capitalist powers and the exploited dependent areas of economic territory. The industrial proletariat in the former lived at the expense of the proletariat in the latter. The national bourgeoisie were still further isolated from production, and the capitalist country lived in a state of parasitism on the exploitation of the labour of several overseas countries and colonies. 'Imperialism', he said, 'has the tendency to create privileged sections even among the workers and to separate them from the main proletarian masses.'[16] It seems from this that these last had no prospect of escape from the consequences of their dependency through the workings out of their own capitalist development. As we shall see, this aspect of Lenin's argument, itself a departure from Marx, is taken up and developed by later Marxist writers on economic imperialism.

Finally, in this necessarily brief review of what might be called the dogmatic model of economic imperialism, we have Bukharin's contribution. Written before Lenin's pamphlet, it received Lenin's endorsement.[17] Drawing heavily upon Hilferding's notion of finance capital,[18] Bukharin conceived imperialism to be a necessary stage of capitalism. Like Lenin he concentrated on the 'external' effects of imperialism rather than embarking on an analysis of the internal workings of the capitalist system. Capitalism in his view was expansionist in nature, creating a world market economy in which national economies are enmeshed in a network of interdependent relations. The trust or cartel is the means of regulating and organizing this system. The world is divided into two categories of states: 'a few consolidated organised economic bodies on the one hand and a periphery of underdeveloped countries with a semi-agrarian or agrarian system on the other.'[19] These underdeveloped countries constitute economic territory for the developed states.

Two new classes make their appearance — the international bourgeoisie and the international proletariat. They reflect the drive of capital to expand in the world beyond the nation-state. The dynamic of expansion is seen as being the crisis of overproduction and the consequent need to expand the market. Capital, in seeking the highest rate of profit, is invested abroad. But capitalism does not succeed in creating either unity or equilibrium in the world at large. Bukharin argued that the separate capitalist economies engage in a struggle for control over economic territory. Internally, a military—industrial complex makes its appearance combined with a militaristic ideology while, externally, war is the inevitable result.

In spite of differences, these arguments all stress the same thing: they assert that imperialism is a form of capitalism necessitated by capitalist development. The nexus of relations that makes imperialism is forced upon capitalist society through the operation of an economic dynamic that it is not in the power of capitalists to change or to control. I shall take up this point after discussion of the later neo-Marxist variations of imperialism. But it is this point that enables a distinction to be made between these writers and the voluntaristic notions of economic imperialism propounded by Hobson, Hilferding and possibly Kautsky.[20] These writers conceived of imperialism as a conscious policy pursued by capitalists seeking to maximize their profits, and, in so doing, manipulating governments to serve their ends. Their concern in investing abroad lies not simply in maximizing profits that could not be made for one reason or another within the domestic economy, but in exercising control over markets and raw materials. Their primary interest is to safeguard their investments and to create as favourable a climate for investment return as could be achieved using the resources of their home states. Such a policy is reversible.

Hobson, for example, urged the adoption of a welfare programme designed to increase the capacity to consume.[21] This would solve the problem of underconsumption and surplus capital caused solely by the manipulations of sectional capitalist interests acting in collusion with the government. A political change could thus induce a change in an economic structure.

For Hilferding the structural changes in the organization of capital produced a type of entrepreneur who dealt in money rather than in commodities. The banker replaced the producer as the pivot of the capitalist system. Cartels were the product of financial institutions, which through their central position in the system encouraged mergers and discouraged competition, so keeping prices and profits artificially high. He coupled this to imperialism by insisting that the export of capital via the agency of monopolies was necessary in order to transfer surplus to the exporting country. The latter retained control over the ownership of capital. The characteristics of monopoly are transferred to the importing area. The exclusive control exercised by the capital exporting country constitutes imperialism and its typical features are broadly those described by the dogmatic school, namely colonial annexation, the economic dominance of the capitalist country over the non-capitalist area of exploitation, competition, often violent, between the capital exporting countries, and so on.

But although Hilferding used some of the Marxist categories — surplus value, the concentration of capital, cartels, etc. — and, like Marx, was concerned with the problems of disequilibrium and effective demand within capitalism, he believed that imperialism as such was not a state or stage of capitalism, and that it was not a necessary expedient for resolving capitalist contradictions. Finance capitalists, albeit acting out the rationale of high finance and its dictates, were in a position to choose. Given this voluntarism it is clear that Hilferding, like Hobson, was neither a determinist nor applying a purely mechanistic model of economic imperialism with an inbuilt dynamic of expansion beyond human control. The monopoly condition induced by the financial institutions was a reflection of their desire for equilibrium and regulation. While it is true that beyond the state the familiar phenomena of imperialist conflicts and rivalry produced instability, such competition was not necessary to the survival of capitalism. Imperialism was thus epiphenomenal to capitalism and *contra* Lenin and his followers, not a necessary or higher stage. In short, the voluntaristic notion of imperialism, however much it overlaps the dogmatic model in terms of concepts and phenomena, is of a quite different mode of explanation. It belongs to the historical rather than to the theoretical mode, and a critique of its explanatory power would concentrate upon evidence of the reasoning of those engaged in financial and entrepreneurial activities in states pursuing 'imperialist' policies.

The dogmatic model is of a different order, for it purports to offer a truly *general* explanation of human activities. The imperialism with which it is concerned is of a totally different nature, despite the apparent similarities. Let me summarize its salient features. The proponents of the dogmatic model all agree that imperialism constitutes the activities of capitalist states in the non-capitalist areas of the world. Colonies are merely one aspect of this. Investment in these areas in the form of loans made for public utilities, investment in mining and the extraction of raw materials and in plantation and primary commodities, the expansion of trade to these areas, a general participation in their industrialization and the necessary transport and communications infrastructure, are all aspects of this involvement. These phenomena are complemented on the political side by diplomacy, coups, wars, revolutions and direct intervention in the non-capitalist area.

Within the capitalist states a new form of capital makes its appearance — bank and industrial capital merge to become finance capital. This is accompanied by the creation of national monopolies that, after eliminating domestic competition, look beyond the state for further expansion. The national bourgeoisie are transformed into an international bourgeoisie and so, with the related development of an international proletariat, duplicate the pattern of capitalist development within the state in the world at large.

All these alleged phenomena are explained by an economic dynamic or process that simultaneously creates cartels and exports the drive to create surplus capital from the state to the entire world. This drive in turn is explained by the basic contradictions of capitalism stemming from the problem of realizing an increasing rate of profit from a finite pool of labour, the propensity of this rate to fall and the exhaustion of expedients that include the creation of monopolies and the reorganization of capital. Capitalism is thus forced to expand. Such expansion is competitive, for all advanced capitalist states are in this position. The consequence is thus a prolonged struggle between them, in which economic territory is sought not merely for the tangible return or investment opportunities that exist, but in order to create monopoly conditions by denying opportunity to competitors. Direct exploitation occurs side by side with pre-emptive seizures of 'economic territory'.

I want now to turn to more contemporary neo-Marxist revisions of what I have termed the dogmatic model of economic imperialism before looking at its empirical application. The Marxist—Leninist model of imperialism, for all the diversity of views within the basic argument, conceived of capitalism as evolutionary in nature. The structural development of capitalism produced a drive for expansion into economic territory, widening the base of the capitalist system and, through its own contradictions (specifically the appearance of conflict between labour and capital), it created the conditions for a world revolution. Capitalism produced an imperialism that was national capitalism become world wide. The national proletariat became international labour. The necessity of ever-increasing profits, and all the phenomena attributed to the last stage of capitalism, created an imperialism that brought capitalism to its final struggle out of which a true revolution could emerge. But this last dying struggle is to be explained solely in terms of the nature of capitalism itself, and not in terms of relations between it and the economic territory it sought to exploit. Essentially, this theory of imperialism is based on a theory of capitalism.

In total contrast is the notion of imperialism that looks at the condition of the economic territory itself and is concerned with the position of the underdeveloped countries. Marx had expected that national capitalism would be exported through the aegis of empires, provided that the metropolitan powers were capitalist. Lenin lumped colonies in with nominally independent but underdeveloped countries and termed them economic territory. Yet his notion of imperialism was nationally based. The struggle for world monopoly between competing capitalist states and the drive to acquire sole control of all economic territory blurred the distinction between national capitalism and world capitalism. His monopolies were national in character. So an expansion of a nationally based capitalism, in competition with others, constituted imperialism. It was compelled to expand for the reasons given earlier. Economic development was not a problem in his view, for the advanced industrial nations *constituted* capitalism.

The neocolonial model of imperialism, however, stresses not the structure of a modern capitalism as the core of a theory of imperialism, but a relationship between the world capitalist system and the underdeveloped countries. I want to outline the main features of this model before contrasting it with the earlier Marxist—Leninist notion of economic imperialism. In essence this variant conceives of capitalism as having broken away from its domestic locus. It has become an international or transnational system in which the several domestic sources of capitalism — the major industrialized countries — are merged within a complex set of interrelationships dominated by a number of super-monopolies. Imperialism is a form of dependency between capitalist forms and an exploited labour. It is not confined to developed countries and their relations with the underdeveloped world, but is to be found within the former as capitalist manifestations are to be found in the latter. What characterizes capitalism is the process of extracting surplus value in a chain of processes that ultimately ends at the highest level of capitalist development — the major financial institutions and monopolies of the United States. Although the United States is conceived of as the locus of the new capitalism, it is important to stress that this is an *economic* system and not a political one. Within the United States, as in other advanced countries, it is argued, dependent relations of an imperialist nature exist between capitalist and labour sections. Some sections of the proletariat are privileged, while others constitute exploited labour. The government, of course, is merely an instrument of the highest capitalist forms — the giant monopolies.

The state as such is no longer the source of capitalism, for capitalism has become an inter- and intra-national system. There are differences in emphasis between the exponents of this thesis of immanent imperialism, but they are generally agreed that the monopoly stage of capitalism has broken away from the state. The apparent dominance of the United States in world politics in the post-war years simply reflected the fact that the greatest capitalist monopolies operated from an American base. They used the state as an instrument in exactly the same way as Lenin argued monopoly capital used the European states in the First World War.

Much of this argument is concerned with the effects of capitalism in the same way as the earlier model, that is, with an analysis of the alleged phenomena of imperialism and, in particular with the problem of development. The notion of surplus value is central to the thesis, as is of course the case for the earlier argument. The new monopolies seek to appropriate this surplus from the underdeveloped world through the usual media of investment and control over commodity and other markets. They do this through the creation of metropolis—satellite relationships that institutionalize a pattern of development trying the latter economies firmly within a system of exploitation. A chain of economic transactions occurs connecting all producers, however small, to a network of dependent relations. For example, as one of the main exponents of this argument, Andre Gunder-Frank, put it in relation to Brazil,

> we get a whole chain of metropolises and satellites which runs from the world metropolis down to the hacienda or rural merchant who are satellites of the local commercial metropolitan center but who in turn have peasants as their satellites . . . [No part of this chain enjoys autonomy for] the international and national metropolis—satellite structure of capitalism is inescapably intertwined.[22]

This network of interdependent relations, directed and dominated by the great international corporations, creates a special condition of dependency in the underdeveloped world. The ruling elite in effect acts both as a channel by which surplus value is realized by the giant monopoly and as a recipient itself of part of this value; it thus acts as a capitalist form as well as a satellite of capitalism. No genuine development can take place, given this dependent relation, without emancipation from the super-monopolies on the one hand and the local metropolis on the other. The economic and social structure of an underdeveloped country is what it is because of an inbuilt distortion introduced by the paramount need of the capitalist system to realize surplus value by drawing off profits from the underdeveloped sector. Its ruling elite benefits from this by sharing in the profit and so continues to act as an agent of capitalism. And this is the case all down the chain of capitalist relations. At the bottom and supporting the whole system is the 'free labour' of the underdeveloped world, which acts as an international proletariat exploited by, and dependent on, the international capitalist system. As Gunder-Frank argues in the case of Brazil,

> To adopt a substantially different pattern of import substitution and to avoid this fate by beginning with heavy producer goods industry and intermediate equipment manufacturing instead of light consumer goods industry as the Soviet Union did, Brazil would have to have an income distribution and therefore pattern of consumer demand other than that of a satellite capitalist country and/or a distribution of political power and the consequent ability to allocate investment in response to criteria other than immediate consumer demand.[23]

Thus free of the constraints of management capitalist control, the underdeveloped economy would be able to pursue an autonomous pattern of economic development that would not be capitalist in nature. It would have a genuine and not a spurious independence.

It will be apparent from this that a theory of non-capitalist economic development is implicit in the argument. What this would entail is left unanswered, for the theory concerns itself mainly with the alleged relations of dependency and with the concomitant conflict of interest. Nor is the capitalist dynamic discussed in any detail. The actual workings of capitalism at the metropolis level are not analysed. Contrary to Marx, the theory does not conceive of modern capitalism as a stage of growth — of economic development possible in the non-capitalist area. And, contrary to Lenin, it conceives of the capitalist *state* system as fundamentally non-competitive. The only element that is clearly Marxist in inspiration in this view of economic imperialism is that of the labour cost theory of value and the consequent conflict between capital and labour. Even this is modified into a conflict between the city and the peasant rather than between capital and an urban industrialized proletariat, who are seen as themselves exploiters as well as exploited.

From Lenin are taken the notions of super-monopoly and the necessity of economic territory for its sustenance and growth. The underdeveloped world constitutes the area of economic territory necessary to monopoly capitalism. The nexus of relations between the two areas and the condition of the under-developed countries constitute imperialism. The most fundamental contradiction of capitalism in this view is the way in which the underdevelopment of economic territory is a condition of the continued development of capitalism. The capitalist system is thus parasitic on the under-developed world. This is the neocolonialist argument in essence, for while it urges the importance of economic territory to modern capitalism, it is far more concerned with the alleged exploitative *effects* of relations between capitalist countries and the under-developed world. Its focus is a form of dependent relationship and not the economic dynamics of capitalism itself. Political independence is only nominal, given the penetration and control exercised through the chain of metropolis—satellite relations.

While the alleged effects of this dependency are detailed in the argument (constituting an arrested and distorted economic development), the causes of this relationship are not. They are assumed to stem from the innate drive to expand characteristic of monopoly capitalism. Nor is much consideration given to the question of the ultimate collapse of capitalism. Given the emphasis on the problem of underdevelopment, the prescriptive aspects of the theory are central. The overthrow of the ruling elites in the underdeveloped countries and the severance of all economic ties with the capitalist world, together with the eradication of internal capitalist elements — the local metropolis—satellite structure — and the institution of a planned socialist economy, are the solution to the problem of economic development. Revolt and not revolution seems to be the panacea urged. And autarky is the appropriate economic condition to be achieved.

So far as the classic model is concerned, imperialism is a particular (and final) stage of capitalism in which its innate expansionist tendencies are accelerated by its own inner contradictions, which stem from the problem of realizing surplus value. It is to be understood in terms of its own internal processes and not from its effects, which are 'explained' by reference to the analysis of the capitalist economic stage itself *in situ,* so to speak. Its demise is through wars between the major capitalist states and the ensuing revolution as the proletariat repudiates the system and its leaders. The revised model conceives of imperialism as a pervasive system, directed by the non-national giant monopolies manipulating all states, including their own home countries, that, *inter alia,* distorts the natural pattern of economic development. This system operates at all levels, within states as well as between them. Instead of wars between the capitalist countries, imperialist violence takes the form of intervention of governments repressing forces inimical to capitalist interests within their own states and in the underdeveloped world. The capitalist world is assumed to be united or at least controlled by the giant corporations. Salvation will only come through genuine national liberation movements, in the form of a revolt against the metropolis, the ruling elite and the city.

There are close similarities between this argument and what I previously termed the voluntaristic model of economic imperialism urged by Hobson and others. It does not emphasize any inevitable or necessary aspects of capitalist development. In placing the emphasis upon the evil effects of capitalism on the developing economies and drawing conclusions for practice, it strongly suggests that this form of imperialism can be eliminated. Men can take their fate in their own hands and defeat monopoly capitalism. Capitalism will fail not because of its own inner contradictions but through the rebellion of the exploited against their exploiters. The consequences for capitalism of the alienation of economic territory from the capitalist orbit are not examined, but clearly without it capitalism is itself in peril. This, combined with the existence of the socialist planned economies (an area both challenging and denied to capitalism), affords the best prospect of an end to economic imperialism. Capitalism can be defeated in the underdeveloped world.

Such an argument appears to be far removed from the dogmatic model with its innate determinism. The reason for this would appear to be, firstly, the concentration of the argument upon the *effects* of capitalism on the underdeveloped world. The importance of the latter to the capitalist countries is not denied but neither is it stressed as it is in the dogmatic model. Consequently, with less emphasis on the dynamics of capitalism, there is a theoretical lacuna for we do not know why capitalism seeks to maintain the alleged dependent relationship with the underdeveloped world. The phenomena of imperialism described in the argument — foreign investment, control over markets, government loans, aid, exploitation and control over extractive industries and primary commodity production, political intervention and control — are considered as evil effects without any analysis of their basic causes. Hence the notion of causation is not treated theoretically and we are left with a rationalization rather than with a theory of imperialism. Secondly, an emphasis is placed on action and the argument is concerned with practical prescriptions. A voluntaristic element thus enters into the analysis. There is an ethical basis to the argument directly related to the reform of an intolerable situation. Given this, it follows that references to necessary conditions, or the inevitability of the situation, are out of harmony with the model. Imperialism in this view is the product of policies consciously formulated and pursued by capitalists supported by conniving governments.

We can see from this that there is a considerable variety of interpretations within the Marxist framework. Imperialism is seen by some as the nexus of relations between *national* monopolies arising out of a new stage of capitalist development and resulting in violent international competition for economic territory. For others it is the appearance of super-monopolies that transcend the extant nation-states and seek world monopoly. For yet others it is the creation of dependent relations between a united capitalist world and the underdeveloped countries. The capitalist world is sometimes seen as a more or less cohesive set of monopolies dominated by those domiciled in the United States, and sometimes as a set of economic relations between metropolis and satellite, permeating both developed and underdeveloped countries alike. The emphasis here is placed upon what might be called the worm's eye view, that of the underdeveloped countries and their problems of economic development.

Broadly there is a contrast between a state centrist view of economic imperialism and a view that sees the state as absorbed within a super-riding economic system. There might be some measures of agreement between these views, particularly on the associated phenomena of imperialism (wars, military intervention, economic penetration, exploitation and dependent relations, etc.), and both agree on the state acting as an instrument of capitalism, but the relationship between capitalism and the state is very different in these analyses. If we are concerned with imperialism as consisting of relations between nations in which some direct or control others, that is with a set of *political* relationships, whether or not we offer an economic explanation for this phenomenon we cannot simply use imperialism as a synonym for capitalism and still be concerned with explaining political actions and relations.

If imperialism simply means capitalism, and this in turn consists of a set of *economic* relations *per se,* then the questions of the role of the nation-state and the problem of relations between states are begged. We may concede that the political consists of epiphenomena, to be explained by underlying economic processes, so that capitalism explains imperialism or perhaps constitutes it, but the conflation of the two relegates the political to the irrelevant, either as a subject for explanation or as part of an explanation. As we shall see, much of the argument about economic imperialism is dependent upon non-economic concepts that are ethical or political in nature. The point here is that the relations between economic activities and the state, and between these and inter-state relations, are crucial to any account of imperialism. Whether the state is deemed to be only an instrument of capitalism or is 'explained', together with its activities beyond its frontiers, by an economic hypothesis, the case has to be made and not merely assumed. Theories of imperialism that are really theories of capitalism largely avoid the problem of explaining political relationships that nominally at least are imperialistic. The role of the state requires explanation whether it is as an agent or a product of economic processes.

Now in what sense do these arguments offer a coherent explanation of imperialism? I intend to approach this question in two stages, firstly by examining an empirical example — the multinational corporation in the context of capitalist development and relations between the developed and the underdeveloped countries — and, secondly, by examining theoretical and analytic problems arising out of the conceptual framework of theories of economic imperialism. The reason I take the multinational corporation as an empirical case by means of which these arguments can be tested is not because I make any assumption about its significance but because monopoly is a central concept in all Marxist writings about imperialism. If we have an adequate explanation of the multinationals and of their role as agents of imperialism, then we have a key to an explanation of capitalist development and world politics. If we do not, then not only do Marxist arguments concerning these bodies break down but the whole economic imperialist argument collapses, given the centrality of the notion of monopoly and financial organization. In short, it is a test-case not simply for latter-day exponents of Marxism but for the whole Marxist theory of imperialism with all its variants.

Now the way in which this example is used as a test-case begs the question as to the relation of an empirical test to arguments formulated within a conceptual framework of this type. Empirical references can be made to bend as well as to fit a thesis. A correspondence between theory and 'facts' depends on the identity and autonomy of the two categories of reference — theory and facts. It could be argued that this relation requires explanation and that what might appear to be disconfirming or confirming 'facts' to a non-Marxist are based on criteria that are non-Marxist in character. 'Facts' do not speak for themselves, nor are they neutral. All depends upon the conceptual framework in which they are located. So, while I think that one test of explanatory adequacy is whether the phenomena asserted to be the subject of explanation are in fact explained, and that this in turn depends upon the prior identification of the alleged phenomena, we must also look at the assumptions of criteria for explanatory adequacy contained in the argument.

In short, without begging the questions as to what multinationals *are,* i.e. their nature and significance, there is a sense in which as phenomena they can be identified, and so distinguished from their explanation, without circularity. An 'explanation' that cannot logically separate the thing explained from the explanation is no explanation. So it is legitimate to ask of phenomena that in principle should be explained by the argument whether they do in fact fit the purported explanation. To anticipate later discussion, if the argument in question postulates the existence of cartels as a pre-condition for a state engaging in imperialist activities, we are entitled, firstly, to ask whether there are in fact cartels in existence and, secondly, to examine the postulated relation (or non-relation) between cartels and imperialism. And this does not entail basing a critique of a theoretical argument upon a concealed and equally suspect counter-hypothesis. While a Marxist conceptual framework is stipulative, in that concepts such as cartels or investment take on a specific meaning, if they have an empirical reference at all then there must be some measure of common ground for Marxist and non-Marxist alike to refer to empirical conditions or 'facts' that constitute in a verifiable manner cartels and investment.

To return to the case of the multinationals, we are not concerned with elucidating their character as monopolies as such, rather we are concerned with the proposition that they *control* the activities of states, either as agents of one category of states or in their own right. It is the postulated relationship between economies and politics that is at the core of economic imperialism. From this, the second proposition that multinationals are essentially competitive and engage in *conflict,* using states as their instruments in order to gain a super-monopoly, is a further subject for investigation. Clearly this entails a measure of conceptual analysis (what is meant by control, or monopoly for that matter?) and this will constitute the second part of this study.

On the face of it the multinational corporations could be subsumed within the Leninist view that economic development in the capitalist world had produced a level of monopolistic organization that he termed cartels. Capital itself, as we saw earlier, was transformed into finance capital. At the national level, finance capital and cartels had emerged as a response to the problem of capital accumulation and the quest for an increasing return on capital in a relatively closed economic system. Monopolies appeared as a result, but the problem of resolving surplus value remained since the environment in which they operated was limited in opportunity, and so national monopolies were forced to expand beyond the nation-state. Capital had to become international. The vehicle was a new kind of monopoly — the cartel.

Lenin did not conceive of the cartel itself becoming disassociated from its national base, but saw the world as composed of competing *states,* each dominated and controlled by its cartels and seeking to establish a world monopoly. Such a view is little different from the power-security model of imperialism considered earlier in terms of the phenomena of power politics. But the *cause* of these epiphenomena is radically different. Capitalism through its inner contradictions produced inter-state conflict, but a conflict whose basic aim was to secure as much economic territory as possible. Imperialism was an inevitable result of this new phase of capitalism. The state was directed by capitalists and so a basic economic necessity dictated the political initiatives that its government took. Wars and colonial adventures became endemic as more and more nations entered into this highest stage of capitalism. World anarchy was the product of the new industrial state, driven by economic forces it did not control.

Now the neo-Marxist school after Lenin were faced with phenomena, the multinational firm for example, that did not fit easily into the Marxist—Leninist model. As Lenin was forced to place the First World War into a Marxist framework, if only to give direction to his followers, so later Marxists faced the same problem of making a changing world intelligible to those who were as much concerned with practice as with theory. In particular, as we have already seen, a number of neo-Marxists became preoccupied with the problem of economic development and the question of dependent relations between the developed and the underdeveloped countries.[24] Moreover, these relations occurred in a world that included, as it had not done for Lenin, a number of 'socialist' states. The 'capitalist' states themselves were engaged in a military alliance. A high degree of regulation and cooperation existed both in the political and in the economic spheres, and this was reflected in formal treaties and in a growing number of international agencies and institutions. On the face of it, capitalism appeared to have achieved a measure of unity inconceivable to Lenin. If wars between the capitalist states were an inevitable necessity, how could this cooperation, together with the absence of any major conflict, be explained? The political and diplomatic apparatus set up by the victor powers after the Second World War was extended to include the defeated, but notably excluded one of the victor powers, the only non-capitalist state, the Soviet Union. On the Marxist argument, these political epiphenomena should be explained through underlying economic causes. While they apparently contradict Lenin's version of economic imperialism, they should nonetheless be explicable in Marxist terms. The multinational corporation seems to provide an answer to this difficulty.

The multinational corporations are phenomena whose explanation is claimed by both the voluntaristic and the dogmatic versions of economic imperialism. The logic of monopolistic control of the market in order to offset wasteful competition and to maximize profits was realized initially by the major financial institutions, and then carried on in a sort of economic momentum by the multinationals themselves generating their own finance. On this argument they are monopolies directed and controlled by a new kind of capitalist and their activities are conducted within the framework of a variety of market conditions only nominally regulated by sovereign states. Whether they constitute a form of imperialism is a difficult question for the voluntaristic view since in a sense they operate outside the nation-state yet under licence. But an explanation of their activities lies in the reasoning of those who direct their activities within a framework of reference that is understood by them as well as by the expositor.

For the dogmatic argument, these phenomena are further confirmation of the arrival of the super-monopoly envisaged by Lenin, albeit only imperfectly understood by him. Where the earlier 'classic' model of economic imperialism and the later concern for a Marxist model that encompassed the phenomenon of under-development come into direct contact is in the conception of monopoly. Both theorists, like Baran and Sweezy,[25] who are concerned with adapting the classic model to changing circumstances, and those who, like Gunder-Frank, are absorbed by the problem of economic development agree on the multinational enterprise as being the major instrument of imperialism.

There are two hypotheses that will be examined here. The main one is the Marxist or neo-Marxist argument that the multinational corporation has replaced the state as the agent of imperialism. On the assumption that capitalism needs an expanding labour pool, the new international firms seek

> a new division of the world . . . less on national lines than through agreement between them on an international framework of institutions, to replace those established at Bretton Woods. Such a framework will only contain the rivalry between the transnational companies as a cartel contains the conflicting interests of its members. The super-states — the U.S.A., the E.E.C. [*sic*] and Japan — will still be required by the giant firms based in them to take action to protect the development of the main areas within their power to assimilate.[26]

The second and related argument is that the multinational

corporation is independent of the state. Within the Marxist or dogmatic model of imperialism, this second hypothesis is a necessary condition of the first, but the voluntaristic model conceives of the multinationals as having some measure of autonomy without this being a necessary consequence of super-riding economic forces. So, if we wish to adopt the dogmatic argument as being adequate as an explanation, some general theoretical explanation is needed that reveals the causes of the super-monopoly and explains its autonomy, and not a description of operations that are alleged to be conceived, and conducted, independently of governments. We need to know not simply what this 'independence' consists of, but what the economic forces and conditions are that determine it. Otherwise we are engaged in a semantic exercise in which terms such as 'independence' and 'the state' are open-ended and have no precise correspondence with any empirical state of affairs. With the voluntaristic model we need to know whether the alleged rationale of the international firm corresponds to the actual reasoning of those involved in the formulation and prosecution of their activities. In a sense all 'private' economic activities are independent of the public sector, and, in another, are part and parcel of what we conceive to be the state. So in the case of the dogmatic model we are looking for a theory and in the case of the voluntaristic model we are looking for an adequate historical account. The two should not be confused or referred to inappropriate criteria of adequacy.

The neo-Marxist view of the multinational corporation is that it is a form of monopoly that gradually emerged from within the advanced capitalist state. Having removed competition from within the state, it now continually seeks to create a 'world-wide productive system'. It creates what are termed 'export processing zones',[27] that is, through establishing subsidiaries in other countries, it rationalizes production in terms of cost by breaking it down into product components and then manufacturing and assembling products at different points according to relative cost advantages. Marketing is similarly conceived of in worldwide terms. Multinationals concerned with manufacturing thus conduct their operations, not in the context of a single state's economy, but in terms of a global strategy of investment, production and marketing. In particular, they create a set of host countries directly tied to this global strategy. The two main consequences of this for the host country, it is argued, are, firstly, that it has no direct control over the activities of the multinational operating within it and, secondly, that its own economy is distorted by the presence of an unintegrated operation whose rationale lies outside the economic policies of the host. The first is held to be generally true for all host countries, including the developed capitalist countries, but the second point is particularly the case for the underdeveloped countries, which often find themselves supporting a highly sophisticated production operation only very remotely related to the rest of their economy and with no control over it. This development is most marked in the case of those multinational corporations engaged in manufacturing. But the marketing and investment policies of the other multinationals are similarly organized on a global basis and ignore the particular interests both of the home and the host countries in which they operate. The process seeks to amalgamate states into regional economic groups as a preliminary to a final attempt to create a genuine world monopoly. Thus the EEC is seen as a response of the European multinationals wanting to expand their activities as super-monopolies and to counter the competitive effect of American capital similarly engaged.

We can see some familiar features in this view of the imperialist role of the multinationals. The drive to monopoly, although not analysed in any depth, is conceived of as stemming from the need to maximize profits within a context of limited opportunity. Eliminating competition is only a partial solution within the domestic economy, and so capital is forced to expand beyond the nation-state. The novelty lies in the dissassociation of capital from its home base. The multinational sees the world as its area of opportunity and the home state takes its place with other states as an instrument for the realization of these opportunities and as part of a global strategy. The political concomitant of this is not necessarily inter-state rivalry, although this is present, but the possibility of a super-state or group of states acting as the vehicle for capitalist expansion. The end of this process is not discussed in any detail. The concern of the neo-Marxist analysis is with the effects of this new form of capitalism.

The problem of economic development is seen as central, although there is diversity of argument. There are those[28] who envisage the demise of the nation-state as an autonomous capitalist system and with it the loss of its sovereignty and political power. Systemic relations thus exist between capitalist development and exploited regions, without any political basis. Within the nation-state, areas of development and underdevelopment coexist. The so-called developed nations are as much part of the system of monopoly capitalism and its exploitation as are the underdeveloped countries. The alleged identification of monopoly capitalism with the United States (or with any state) is only contingent, for capital is free to exploit wherever it sees the opportunity. The present pattern of economic—political relations is thus fortuitous and temporary.

On the other hand, there are those[29] who insist that this extant pattern of dominant capitalist states exploiting the underdeveloped regions is the paradigm case of imperialism. The state takes a subordinate place, acting as an instrument of capitalism, but is nevertheless the basis for the new imperialism. These differences are not so much theoretical or analytic in nature, but arise from the practical aspects of the argument. If the opponent is capitalism at source, then breaking the power of the monopolies by striking at their roots in the most advanced industrial societies assumes primacy in the prescriptive aspects of the argument. Economic nationalism fits rather uneasily with this view for, in principle, there is no way for the underdeveloped country to break its dependency other than by destroying it at source. But, for those who do not accept this argument, an autarkic or independent form of economic development is possible. The necessary condition for its fulfilment is not breaking monopoly capital but severing ties with capitalist *countries*. Both views can coincide with an empirical interpretation of the activities of the multinationals and their alleged distortions of the under-developed economies, while fundamentally disagreeing on the link between the multinationals and the capitalist states.

Now what can be said of this argument is empirical terms? In what sense do multinational corporations and their activities constitute a form of economic imperialism? All commentators are agreed that they constitute a new phenomenon and there has been considerable discussion concerning their alleged independence of national political control.[30] This has not been confined to Marxists. For our purposes what we need to establish is whether the Marxist view that they are a form of monopoly capitalism that overrides the state and that controls and exploits economic territory using states as its instruments is borne out by the evidence. The key concept here is a *political* one, that of control. The alleged existence of a chain of dependent relations directed and controlled by multinational corporations, or, in the alternative view, by their home countries, is the nub of this thesis of economic imperialism.

Multinational corporations are rather loosely defined as firms that engage in productive and extractive activities in a number of different countries. There are considerable differences between these large firms, which should indicate the difficulties in making simple generalizations about them. Generally possessing a 'home' base, they are involved in a number of operations, ranging from mining, the production of raw materials and primary commodities, to manufac-turing. Those engaged in extractive industries operate mainly in the underdeveloped area. Their activities in general are linked to the consumption needs of manufacturing and production requirements of the major industrial countries, including their own home states. The oil companies, which are something of a special case, are similarly related to the energy needs and the petro-chemical industries of the developed world. The second category of multinationals, and by far the most important in terms of direct foreign investment, are those concerned with manufacturing and, in particular, products that entail a high-cost technology combined with a low, or relatively low, labour cost. These operate mainly in the developed areas, although there is an increasing tendency to expand the zone of their activities into the developing countries. Finally, there are those multinational corporations concerned with cash crops and primary commodities produced in the underdeveloped countries. Many of these multinationals have pursued a policy of diversification and are both horizontally and vertically integrated in a number of different fields of production.[31]

The relative importance in terms of their home countries varies — with the United States acting as the home base for the majority,[32] although this is qualified by the fact that European multinationals have been growing at a faster rate over the last ten years. Japan, at the other extreme, has hardly ventured into this field nor is direct foreign investment important to its economy; although, here again, this should be qualified by the fact that of late there has been a tendency to expand investment in a number of neighbouring Asian countries.[33] The United States has the greatest share of total foreign investment, followed by the UK, France, Germany and Switzerland. The bulk of this investment is in the developed area and a considerable amount of cross-involvement and cross-investment takes place. Paradoxically the United States is not only the biggest investor in this sector but is also the second biggest recipient of investment, exceeded only by Canada.[34] The multinationals concerned in this investment are mainly engaged in manufacturing, and the domestic market of the home state constitutes an important part of their total operations. But foreign earnings as a proportion of total earnings of these countries have risen dramatically in the post-war period.[35]

It is generally acknowledged that the main sphere of multinational activities is in the developed area and that their principal focus is in manufacturing industries. The relationship between them and their host governments has been described in the following terms:

> To these giant capital accumulating companies, national governments, even quite powerful governments of developed countries which once had imperial power — are but client states, granted concessions of capital investment only as conditions of good behaviour e.g. tax allowances, state aid, credit guarantees, trade union laws and so on . . . These companies are the new Empires.[36]

A transfer of sovereignty has thus taken place with the multinational companies assuming a political role. They are both autonomous and supra-national.

Let us look more closely at the argument that a new 'ruling elite' has emerged under the aegis of the multinational corporation, which exercises a hegemonial sway over *capitalist* countries. Since the last world war, governmental intervention in the sphere of economic activities in the developed countries has been the rule rather than the exception. Both the domestic economy and external economic exchanges have been to a greater or lesser extent controlled by legislation. Of course, if we take the state-centrist version of economic imperialism, this is entirely consistent with the notion of the state as the basic instrument of capitalism. But it is inconsistent with the idea of super-monopoly imperialism. One argument that seeks to explain the phenomenon of the multinational enterprise is that it came into existence because of regional trade agreements and tariffs. Entering into manufacturing via national subsidiaries is one way of countering market restrictions imposed by governments or regional trade associations.[37] Indeed, the major growth area of the multinationals has been in manufacturing in the advanced industrial countries. There has been a relative decline in raw materials production and in investment in this area.[38] The direction of investment has been largely in the developed area.

Now, regardless of the purely *economic* effects of this development, it can be argued that it would not have occurred at all without, firstly, the existence of state-imposed regulations on trade and, secondly, their consent to such investment taking place. Such consent is neither automatic nor imposed on governments by multinationals, and there are a number of cases[39] of state intervention to stop projected investment of foreign capital where it was thought to create an excessive concentration of foreign capital in one section of industry or where it was deemed detrimental to defence or security interests. Certain industries, such as those concerned with computers and data processing, have been protected from this form of domestic competition. The major industrial countries maintain independent civil and military aviation industries on criteria that are non-economic in character.

Although the industrialized countries have not entered directly into manufacturing, which is mainly a private sector enterprise, certain industries have been nationalized and others subsidized in the interests of maintaining employment levels or of a balanced economy. Again there has been public investment in certain industries deemed important to economic growth.[40] A movement towards a 'mixed' economic structure, with state involvement combined with private enterprise, has been the norm in most European countries since the war. Again, this does not affect the state-centrist view of economic imperialism but it refutes the argument that the multinational corporation is the dominant economic form and that it directly controls capitalist states.

A further point against this last argument is that a number of multinational companies are actually owned by governments[41] and are competitive with 'private' multinationals. Any fundamental division between the state and multinationals is thus difficult to maintain. While the argument that multinationals are preoccupied with a global strategy in seeking to optimize their production and profits, and that this concern is separable from their host's domestic economic policies, is perhaps true, it by no means follows that the two are in conflict or that the latter is subordinated to the former. A government is free to intervene should it consider it to be in the national interest to do so, or alternatively it can cooperate with other governments to regulate the activities of multinationals operating in their zones of cooperation. This admixture of regulation, involvement in competition and 'free' enterprise makes any generalization about the relation of multinationals to governments difficult. Certainly the assertion that governments are 'controlled' by these giant enterprises is untenable. The point is not that measures taken by governments to regulate the activities of multinationals are effective or subordinate them to national control, or that multinationals completely evade any regulation, but that such measures indicate a context of bargaining between governments and multinational corporations. Limits are set tacitly or explicitly to their operations both by governments and by the context in which they operate making their independence more apparent than real.

If we look at the oil multinationals, we can perhaps see a clearer picture of the functional role of these corporations and of the reality of their 'independence'. From acting as instruments of the major consumers — as, for example, during the last war when output and price fixing were determined by the USA and the UK, or during Suez when the United States prevented Standard Oil from supplying the belligerents from Venezuela — the oil multinationals are now dominated very largely by OPEC. A measure of nationalization of oil companies has occurred in the oil-producing countries. Since 1974, prices and marketing have been influenced by the oil-producing countries rather than by the multinationals, whose role has been reduced to processing the raw materials and acting as an agent of exchange.[42] In a sense they are go-betweens performing a necessary function. Their existence and role are largely due to need on the part of both consumers and producers of oil to avoid competition — a competition that would have adverse consequences, both economic and political, if it should get out of hand.[43] They perform a function that cannot be exercised by direct inter-state negotiation in a situation where the interests of consumers and producers of oil are delicately balanced.

Again, an explanation of this relation is found in a study of bargaining rather than in a thesis of super-monopoly or state-centric economic imperialism. What has been termed the obsolescing bargain[44] seems a feature of investment relations of this type. Put simply, the attraction of large amounts of foreign capital is linked to guarantees offered by the recipient designed to reduce the risks of investment and to make the returns attractive to the investor. Once the capital is committed and operations placed on a long-term basis, the terms of the bargain are altered by the host government in order to offset the disadvantages of the original contract. And so a further period of bargaining ensues. The threat of expropriation exists as an extreme case, just as the alienation of further foreign investment is a possibility, but within these extremes the bargain eventually struck reflects the strengths and weaknesses of both sides. The argument that there is a fundamental conflict of interest between the multinational company and the host government is not supported in practice, given the existence of this bargaining process and its compromises.

The case of the Anglo-Iranian oil company and the history of relations between the Iranian government and Western oil interests is illustrative of this point. In 1951 the Iranian government expropriated the Anglo-Iranian oil company. The response from *governments* was a concerted boycott of Iranian oil with disastrous results for the Iranian economy. Nevertheless, the eventual bargain was one that was much more favourable to Iran than the original terms of the Anglo-Iranian oil company. Yet the British government, which was a major shareholder in the company, actually contemplated military intervention in Iran to safeguard its assets. But the problems associated with this, given that the government of the day was both socialist and facing an election, together with the probable costs of such a venture and its uncertainty, were such as to preclude it. The apparent solidarity between the United States and Britain masked the attempt of American oil companies to secure a share of Iranian oil production. The crisis itself had arisen through the differential royalties paid by the major oil companies to the producers and the unilateral nature of such payments. Buying into a market by offering a higher share of the profits was a means of inducing an oil producer to break the near monopoly of its existing contracts.[45] This competitive element between the oil multinationals provided an opportunity for the oil producer to obtain relative advantages in the subsequent bargaining. At the same time the home countries were unable to effect control over them so as to assert an overall monopolistic condition on the producers. Under pressure, the oil multinationals moved to safeguard their position *vis-à-vis* the producers rather than their home base consumers. And so in 1974 Royal Dutch Shell cut United Kingdom oil supplies by 10—15 per cent in spite of demands from its government owners. Petrofina and ten other oil companies boycotted Belgium in order to force higher prices, and both French and American oil companies refused to give preferential treatment to their home countries. France actually got better treatment from US-based firms than from her own.

Thus, looking at the position of the oil multinationals, there seems little in terms of empirical evidence to support the thesis either of super-monopoly or of state-centric imperialism. At times a measure of independence has been shown by the oil companies; at other times they have obeyed the behest both of their home base and of their hosts. In some cases, as in Nigeria in 1979, the host country has expropriated the assets of oil multinationals; in others the obsolescing bargain process has occurred.[46] As circumstances, both political and economic, alter in the world context, the position of the multinationals and of home and host countries alters, and the result is a complex bargaining relationship. If a particular situation is taken as a test of a generalization, as for example the Anglo-Iranian crisis, then the resultant 'confrontation' between a super-monopoly backed by, or using, its home-based capitalist state and a helpless underdeveloped country is as suspect as a selected contrary instance — the Nigerian case for example — used to support a countering generalization.

An explanation of the multinational corporations in the world economy that relies on a reference between a model and a set of empirical instances is almost always circular, as we shall see later in this study. In this case there are as many contrary as confirming instances for the argument that the multinational enjoys an autonomy and is primarily concerned with exploiting its economic territory in competition, resolving this competition by using its capitalist state base to promote its interests. My point here is that what empirical evidence exists in the case of the oil multinationals indicates that *bargaining* with governments, both home and host, is the chief characteristic of their relationship, not control. This does not mean, of course, that such bargaining is void of conflict, political pressure and perhaps, in some instances, corrupt practices and coercive elements, but this is true of all negotiations and is by no means a special feature of economic exchanges. The relegation of the 'political' to mere epiphenomena by the neo-Marxist is a misunderstanding of the nature of politics as a resolution of conflict through various means, which of course include the use of violence. The political repertoire is a large one. Hence any relationship, including those between firms and governments, contains an element of the political where a conflict of interests exists, however 'economic' these may appear to be.

If the activities of the multinationals within the developed area, and in the field of oil production, do not provide much empirical evidence to support the thesis of economic imperialism, what of their activities in the underdeveloped countries? Relations between the multinationals and the underdeveloped world seem to fit the economic imperialist argument rather better. And indeed, as has been stressed earlier in this study, much of the neo-Marxist argument has concentrated on the problem of economic development. Admittedly the major sphere of operations of the multinationals is in manufacturing in the developed countries and, as we have seen, cannot be described either as identifying with the state or as independent of the state. But what of their relations with non-capitalist developing countries?

The essence of imperialism is the control exercised over people who are not constituted into politically autonomous units by those who are. Although the thesis of economic imperialism asserts that the *raison d'être* of such control lies in economic forces, which in one version transcend the state and in another are identified with it, it is the relation between these economic forces and the political phenomenon of control that is at the core of imperialism. As I have argued earlier, economic imperialism is not simply a synonym for capitalism. The essence of the argument is an explanation of epiphenomenal political forms by reference to their underlying economic causes. Whatever is asserted in terms of these economic structures and processes, it is the relation between them and political phenomena that has to be proved.

The economic imperialist argument proceeds by extension. Given that investment is related to risk, it is argued that investors seek to minimize this risk by controlling the internal conditions of the host country. This is done in a variety of different ways: by giving its ruling elite a share of the profits and so involving them in the enterprise; more subtly, by penetration of the economy so that any attempt to break the ties with external investment would lead to a massive and counter-productive redistribution within the national economy; by using the government and the military resources of the home country to maintain a favourable investment climate; through political ties, aid and trade credits; or alternatively, should this be threatened, by direct intervention; and finally by direct colonial rule. Ultimately, the only safe condition for foreign investment is control over the state. Given the necessity for such investment on the part of capitalist states then such control is exercised in these various ways.

Now all these seem reasonable if we assume that the elimination of risk depends on control over the risk factors and that these include the attitude of host governments towards foreign investment. But of course there are other ways of safeguarding investment than taking these draconic precautions. There is no *necessary* conflict of interest between the investor and the recipient unless the basic Marxist thesis of class conflict is assumed. In both Hobson and Lenin's argument this conflict is postulated, although on very different reasoning. For Hobson, the capitalist, in pursuing his selfish interests, was exploiting not only colonial peoples but his own society, by maintaining a forced underconsumption at home. For Lenin, the worker in a capitalist state was being bribed by the capitalist at the expense of the exploited classes in the economic territory. The later neo-Marxists argue that the ruling elite connives at the exploitation of their own people in return for a share of the profits, and so on. If we accept this, then clearly there is a conspiracy between capitalists and governments against the interests of the masses. There is indeed a conflict of interest here. My point is that this is a necessary assumption in order to sustain the notion of risk and the primary conditions for eliminating it.

If we do not make this assumption, then it is far from clear that investment abroad is accompanied by the assertion of power and influence on the part of the investor over the territory in which he invests. In fact, of course, it is true that in many cases attempts have been made to protect investments through coercion, force and bribery.[47] There are many examples in contemporary inter-state relations where such interventions have occurred. The principle of automatic retaliation enshrined in the Hickenlooper and Gonzalez amendments to the Foreign Assistance Acts reflects the attitude that government should protect foreign investment. Yet the former has been applied only once[48] and the latter never. There have been as many cases where attempts at intervention have failed as where they have succeeded. And there have been many cases where the terms of the contract have been altered unilaterally by the government of the underdeveloped country without any form of retaliation.[49]

The ultimate sanction for an investor is not to make an investment where there is no guarantee that basic conditions will be met by the recipient. In systems of credit a consistent defaulter loses the capacity to incur further debt. And a government that expropriates foreign investment is unlikely to receive any more. The crude rationalization that direct control is the only means an investor can have as an absolute safeguard for his investment ignores not only the real world but the nature of investment itself. There is some reciprocity between the investor and the recipient in which the terms of the bargain will vary from case to case, and where the relative advantages to both will similarly vary. The assumption of an absolute inequality in terms of return is as absurd as that of an absolute parity. Clearly, the economic imperialist argument must assume the former as a consequence of the basic thesis of class conflict.

But if we do not accept this argument then, while some bargains appear to be more equitable than others (depending on our notions of equity), the transaction is purely commercial, unless governments intervene, either by extending direct credit or guarantees to the investory or by providing political or economic inducements to the recipient. A good many of such transactions are indeed conditioned by political agreements between states, but it is arguable whether the 'economic' dictates the political. For example, the major recipients of American economic assistance and government-supported investment in the post-war years were Israel, Yugoslavia, Formosa and South Korea. It would be very hard to argue that the motive for this involvement was economic necessity on the part of the United States, seeking either important markets or sources of raw materials. The same is true of American involvement in Indo-China, where the massive costs of intervention in Vietnam cannot be connected to any obvious economic motivation. The retort that in such cases the United States was seeking to contain the spread of socialism and so to protect the area of capitalist opportunity begs the question of motivation. Of course, the Marxist argument has to do this for it follows from the conceptual scheme that capitalist countries behave in this manner — it is in their nature.

However, attention has focused on the *multinationals* as the major agents of capitalism and not on the *states,* and this reflects, as will be argued later, an adaptation of the Marxist argument to the changed condition of inter-state politics arising out of detente and the lapse of Cold War politics. In any case it would be difficult to argue in the cases mentioned above that the United States was promoting the interests of its multinational corporations in such interventions.

Returning to the relations between multinationals and the underdeveloped countries, the issue is not the relative imbalance in bargaining power between investors and recipients, or the alleged economic distortions arising out of the presence in a relatively unsophisticated economy of operations that are designed to fit into the global strategy of a foreign enterprise, but the question of control. What is at stake here is the involuntary nature of the relation between multinationals and underdeveloped countries. In what sense are they forced to accept both investment and subsequent control?

It does not logically follow from the argument of unequal benefit that the bargain is enforced or that the party receiving less, however this is assessed or measured, is impotent to change its terms. Mention has been made of the obsolescing bargain in which the original terms of direct foreign investment are subsequently modified after its commitment by the host government.[50] Economic inducements offered to private investors and political inducements offered to governmental investors are a common phenomenon in the under-developed area. There is little evidence to suggest that commitments on either side are mandatory or that subsequent manoeuvring on the question of relative advantage is precluded by the imposition of external control by the investor.

Parallel with contracts of this kind, with their more or less 'free' bargaining aspects, is the development of producers' cartels and of organizations designed to create collective bargaining strength as an answer to the superior capacity of multinationals to manipulate marketing and production in certain raw materials and commodities.[51] In the case of oil this has been extremely successful, and oil-producing countries, with one or two exceptions, have been able to combine to fix both oil prices and production levels. This of course has not always been the case nor will it necessarily hold for the future. The point is that it is possible and so refutes the contention of the economic imperialist that the operations of multinationals constitute the imposition of a supra-national authority over nation-states. OPEC is a conspicuous success for the oil-producing countries, but other commodities and extractive industries have been organized by the underdeveloped producers, although perhaps less successfully. In general, however, the fact that there has been some organization, and that both expropriation and hard bargaining have been characteristics of the relationship between multinationals and these countries, is further evidence against the simplicities of the economic imperialist thesis.

Relations between the multinationals and host governments in the underdeveloped area have been concerned in the main with raw materials and extractive industries.[52] Investment in these has declined, relatively, over the last decade. But recent growth has been in manufacturing related to markets in the developed countries. This economic relationship between 'export processing areas' in the underdeveloped world and markets in the developed countries poses potential conflicts of interest. It is true that production and investment of this kind in the underdeveloped countries tie them into a global plan, formulated by the multinationals, over which they have little influence, and relate them to a market and to market forces that they do not control. The same is true for the developed home countries, which are affected by the decision of their multinationals to produce abroad and so, it is argued, exporting jobs. But, as has been argued earlier, the opportunities for multinationals to do this can be severely restricted by both home and host governments. The rationale of such operations places the multinationals at risk for, once committed, any concerted action on the part of home and host governments could seriously affect their operations. They depend on the continued acquiescence of governments. There is little evidence that this acquiescence can be enforced on a permanent basis.

To return to the question of controls; this is central to the thesis of economic imperialism. It is not simply a question of economic leverage — the use of an economic connection to obtain a political *quid pro quo,* or vice-versa. Politics, *inter alia,* consists of negotiating and bargaining in situations where interests are competing, if potentially compatible. Relative advantage depends on the strengths and weaknesses of the contenders and the outcome must be mutually acceptable if any bargain is possible. If this sort of political activity is replaced by the exercise of power through coercion, force or direct control, then a very different relationship is postulated. What is at stake is the involuntary nature of such a relationship, not its comparative inequality, however this is assessed. Imperialism is fundamentally about rule.

The question is, therefore, whether host governments (or home governments for that matter) are *compelled* to act as instruments of multinational corporations. The mere existence of inducements to investment such as tax concessions, long-term leases, freedom to export profits, favourable labour legislation or lack of it, and all the other aspects of bargains between a 'ruling elite' and a multinational enterprise, only indicates the terms of a bargain. Are they imposed by the multinational? Can they be maintained once they are agreed? Can the multinational insist unilaterally on their maintenance? The economic imperialist thesis asserts that this is the case. It is not simply that this alleged state of affairs corresponds to reality but that it is a necessary consequence of capitalism. Unequal relationships are built into the theory. And so it is not the rationale of large-scale enterprise that matters — the level of reasoning of those who direct the multinationals — but the inbuilt necessity to act in this way. Men may change their minds but not their natures. And if they are capitalists they have no choice but to act as they do. The theoretical implications of this argument will be considered later; the point here is that what constitutes empirical evidence for or against the thesis is in a sense irrelevant.

Evidence that direct control by the multinationals, of either their home or host governments, is less than convincing does not therefore matter to the economic imperialist thesis. As formal empires are replaced by invisible empires, so direct is replaced by indirect control. By this is meant that constraints on governments are imposed by the existence of foreign investment. The freedom of action of a government is restricted by the need to cater for the requirements of such investment. But this is true of all contractual obligations whatever their character. The sanction imposed by breaking the contract is two-fold: firstly, the loss of present or short-term advantages that inspired the initial bargain, and, secondly, the inhibition imposed on any future negotiations by such a default. As I argued earlier, all commercial or financial transactions are conditioned by such penalties. Governments are free in principle to make or break contracts with other governments or with institutions such as multinational corporations. They are free to balance questions of relative advantage against existing or future contractual obligations and to act accordingly. Merely pointing out the possibilities of sanctions does not impair this freedom.

The imperialist argument comes in, firstly, in the assertion that this freedom does not, and indeed cannot, exist and that governments are compelled to enter into unequal contracts and are bound by them, and, secondly, in the assertion that through such transactions they have lost sovereignty, or political autonomy, and are simply annexes of capitalism — whether of the capitalist state or of the multinational corporation makes little difference in this respect. Power is exercised by the capitalist agent over such an annex. The relationship is involuntary both in its inception and in its continuation.

Now, merely indicating that governments are not 'free' to break such relationships without incurring some sort of penalty is not to say that governments are not free. And to argue that all contractual relationships between capitalism and underdeveloped states impair the independence of the latter is to postulate not an economic but a *political* theory of sovereignty. Few states, in historical terms, can be said to be independent in the sense that they enjoy a condition of absolute power. Questions of relative advantage, and a rational perception of losses and gain in economic and political relationships, are of the essence of practical politics. What political system is postulated in which absolute sovereignty is regarded as the touchstone for assessing such relationships? Clearly, in Marxist terms no political system composed of sovereign states has any reality, for all politics consist of epiphenomena, merely representations determined by economic processes.

This is to say that concepts such as dependency[53] cannot be related to *political* phenomena in the economic imperialist thesis. In the dogmatic version of it at least, an independent political status is a theoretical impossibility. What is meant by a dependent relationship, therefore, is an economic condition imposed by monopoly capital on a network of economic transactions designed to extract profit from the exploited area. This is not so much a limitation on sovereignty as a denial of its existence. All states, capitalist and underdeveloped, are enmeshed in this network and the world of international politics is only an appearance and not a reality. If an explanation is sought it is found in a characterization of capitalism. In short, if we seek empirical confirmation of the explanatory force of concepts such as control, dependency, domination, exploitation, and so on, we cannot, on the Marxist argument, appeal to a countering political theory in which these terms have meaning and significance and produce evidence of relative independence in inter-state politics. Such an appeal is invalid, since the political is subsumed within the economic argument. There is no contradiction between the apparent freedom of states to conduct their affairs and the thesis of their subordination to an economic system that controls them. The reference in the state-centric version of economic imperialism is not to the actions of the capitalist state seeking to create as large a zone of economic territory as possible, in competition with other such states, but to the economic drive that forces it to do so.

There is considerable ambiguity between the state-centric and the super-monopoly versions of economic imperialism. In the case of the former, imperialism consists of the capitalist *state* acting as an instrument of its controlling monopolies in competition with other capitalist states. The identity of the state is merged with that of the capitalist system. Consequently, all external activities of the state can be interpreted, where they are relevant, as the defence or the promotion of capitalism. Its diplomacy and external relations are all directed by the need for capitalist expansion and are imperialist in nature. The acquisition and control of economic territory (whether consisting of other states or of colonies, is immaterial) is its central task. A translation of this version of economic imperialism into political terms is relatively easy, if unnecessary. The state is capitalism personified and its ostensibly political actions are aspects of its economic system. The world of empires, wars, colonial adventures, arms races and competitive politics is fundamentally a world of *economic* conflict.

But the non-state view has some problems in accommodating the traditional notion of power politics to an economic thesis. This is not merely because the struggle for power between the major states seems to have abated in the nuclear age, but because the central imperialist agent is seen as the super-monopoly — the multinational corporation. Capital, in becoming international, has lost its national locus. The capitalist *state* as such has ceased to exist and it is as much 'economic territory' for the super-monopoly as formerly the underdeveloped areas were for it. Taken to the extreme of Franks' notion of an interlocking system of metropolis—satellite relations within, as well as between, states, the political aspects of imperialism seem to have been abandoned. Imperialism seems to have lost its competitive element in terms of states, and becomes instead a system of exploitation pervading all states and transcending all political divisions. So the state-centric version of economic imperialism in effect subsumes, and *inter alia* explains, the ostensibly political phenomena of world power politics, while the super-monopoly view deems this either irrelevant or mere appearance, favouring a pervasive capitalist system in which the basic contradiction and conflict are between the exploiter and the exploited. Both metropolis and satellites lack a *political* focus. Clearly both views are incommensurable. And, more to the point, their empirical references would also seem to be completely different. What empirical evidence would 'prove' the state-centric view to be true? And, equally, to what do we refer to establish the truth of the super-monopoly view?

To return to the central thesis of economic imperialism; if an empirical focus or test is difficult to establish, there is common ground in the notion that capitalism is innately expansionist. The actual forms of this expansionism may vary but its cause is the same. At the core of the Marxist argument is the idea that the problem of equilibrium between production and consumption within the domestic economy and the contradictions between labour and capital are temporarily solved by the export of capital and the extension of capitalism beyond the nation-state. This is not a matter of policy; it is a necessity stemming from the very nature of capitalism. Surplus capital appears within the economy because of more sophisticated means of production utilizing less labour; given the labour-cost theory of value, a declining rate of profit ensues. Added to this is the notion of underconsumption, in which the consumer — the masses — cannot respond to overproduction and so there is a problem of effective demand. The answer is economic imperialism — a drive to find outlets for surplus capital.

This, then, is the theoretical core of economic imperialism. Its status as a theory will be examined shortly. When it is applied to the facts of economic exchange it appears less than adequate as an explanation. The significance, pattern, direction and volume of direct foreign investment of the major capitalist countries do not 'fit' the theory. There is considerable variety in the relative importance to the national economy of external exchanges, trade and investment between these countries. Measured as a net contribution to GNP, there is a significant difference between France and the United

Kingdom for example.[54] The United States, the biggest net exporter of capital in this century, makes a smaller contribution to its GNP through external economic exchange than Japan or Britain. Most foreign direct investment is cross-investment within the developed area. And this investment is not in raw materials or in the extractive industries, but in manufacturing, which has seen the biggest growth in the post-war period. Investment in the allegedly exploited areas of the underdeveloped world is less than a third of the total amount of direct foreign investment[55] and again reveals a relative decline in extractive industries and an increase in manufacturing, much of which is directed towards the export of manufactured goods back to the developed countries. If there is a problem of underconsumption this does not appear to support it.

All this does not deny the importance of investment in the developing countries, or the existence of unequal bargains between the investor and the recipient. But on the economic imperialist argument the capitalist states should, of necessity, be deeply involved in exporting capital into, and controlling, 'economic territory', and not in fact concentrating most of this capital in cross-investment in each other's economies. The underdeveloped areas are important in terms of investment opportunities, markets and trade, but their relations with the developed countries — or with capitalist institutions such as the multinational corporations — do not reflect those postulated by economic imperialism; they are not central to the preoccupations of modern capitalism. Only by selected instances can the imperialist argument be maintained. And given both that the theory is atemporal, that is, it is a *general* theory of capitalist development, and that this form of capital export is central to it, contrary instances are crucial.

Nor do the notions of underconsumption and super-monopoly fare much better in terms of evidence. Far from there being a critical condition of underconsumption in the capitalist countries, there has been a boom in the post-war years. Even in the developing countries there has been a slow increase in living standards. In some of them a radical improvement has occurred.[56] Rising disposable incomes and welfare policies have been common features rather than the permanently depressed levels of consumption postulated by the neo-Marxists. Again it is stressed that this argument has nothing to do with the distribution of income, or with the disparities in living standards between societies; it is concerned with the alleged cause of economic imperialism stemming from underconsumption. There is no evidence that a depressed level of consumption in the developed economies is either a cause, or a function, of declining profit rates, or indeed exists as a general phenomenon.

I said earlier that the multinational corporation and its activities constituted a test-case for the theory of economic imperialism. The notion of monopoly is central to the argument. But, instead of acting as agents of imperialism competing for economic territory, we find that their main zone of operations lies in the developed countries and that they are chiefly investing in manufacturing. Their involvement in extractive industries and raw materials production in the developing countries is much smaller, and is in any case declining. In spite of their oligopolistic character, they appear to be less agents of imperialism than institutions dependent upon conditions that they do not control and that serve as their *raison d'être*. They operate in an environment largely created by governments and their freedom is illusory. Changes in this environment — induced by governments that are either producers or consumers — force them to adapt. They are not substitutes for the body-politic in spite of their apparent autonomy; rather they are parasites upon it, or have at least a symbiotic relationship with it. There is little evidence that they control governments, although here again argument by selected instance is often used to support this thesis,[57] or that they are independent of governments and act as the main agents of imperialism.

Of course multinationals can, and do, play the system by taking advantage of cleavages between developing and developed countries, and seeking to use the power and influence of their home states[58] to drive better bargains or to maintain a dominant position. They have benefited from the lack of cohesion among producing and consuming countries in terms of the production and marketing of raw materials. The multinationals in manufacturing seek to invest and produce in terms of the optimal advantages to them, regardless of their effects on national economies. Investment in extractive industries also reflects this optimalizing policy. But equally there have been countering responses to this on the part of governments, both developed and underdeveloped. A variety of relationships exist between multi-nationals and their host and home governments.

The factors that encouraged the growth of multinationals, both economic and political — differentials in relative costs of production, market growth and size, technological innovation, the existence of competitors, labour skills and union organization, stable governments, permissive legislation, tax laws, tariffs and trade policies — are all largely within the control of governments. Should it be more in their interest to curtail the apparent independence of the multinationals, they have the means to do so. There is a move in this direction on the part of both developed and underdeveloped countries. As with all relations that involve competing interests, the question of relative advantage is paramount. The rationalization of such a competition into an absolute conflict of interests in which either the government or the multinational enjoys a condition of power is, like most such rationalizations, empirically false, or at best unprovable. Neither the state nor the multinational is 'free' in the sense that it possesses an autonomy or sovereignty that is absolute. Only a state that enjoyed complete autarky would be in that position. And this would merely be a negative freedom, without any implications for the exercise of power over other states.

A model of interdependent economic relations between states, in which relative advantage is sought without radical change in the system of negotiation, seems to fit the facts better than the postulate of innate violent conflict made by economic imperialism. Violence there certainly is between states, but it is not explained by the thesis of economic imperialism except tautologically as the product of 'capitalism'. Bargaining between states and between states and institutions such as large firms is not apolitical and an element of coercion and threat may well be present. The military resources of the state may well be a factor in certain cases, but this does not axiomatically follow from the evidence of such bargaining. The doctrine of the sanctity of contracts, however unequal, has been accompanied by tame acquiescence in unilateral revision or abrogation by a dissatisfied partner.[59] An explanation of violence used in such transactions, or of violence in general in world politics, does not emanate from an analysis of capitalism in the Marxist tradition. It has to be shown that imperialism — that is, the control exercised over other people and other states beyond the capitalist state — is *caused* by economic conditions within that state. A concern with the alleged ill-effects of capitalism in underdeveloped countries, with its alleged manifestations in the form of giant multinational corporations, with selected instances of the use of violence in pursuit of economic interests, or with a characterization of capitalism as an all-embracing system subsuming all of these phenomena, begs the question of this relationship between cause and effect.

This brings me to the second aspect of this examination of economic imperialism as an *explanation* of the international political economy. In what sense do these related arguments explain anything at all? What criteria do they need to satisfy in oder to fulfil a claim to explanatory adequacy? This aspect involves more than an attempt to match the 'facts' with the theory. As we have seen, an empirical focus or reference for these arguments presents some difficulties, for in a sense they *constitute* the phenomena of imperialism. In their characterization of concrete empirical situations, such as that of certain Latin American economies and their relationship to the

major developed economies,[60] we are forced to accept a description
of phenomena presented through a given conceptual framework.
And similarly with descriptions of multinational institutions we are
constrained to accept them as imperialist agents if we also accept the
language of the analysis. Capitalism is imperialism and imperialism is
capitalism. This is indeed a hermeneutic circle! The conceptual
framework determines the nature of the phenomena it purports to
'explain', and it also determines what is empirically relevant. It is true
that some consensus on facts exists between Marxists and non-
Marxists, (those relating to investment patterns, for example), but the
capacity to revise the framework to accommodate changing
conditions appears to be infinite.[61] What then is its status in terms of
its explanatory capacity?

Throughout this study I have used the expressions *dogmatic* and
voluntaristic to characterize the considerable variety of arguments in
the field of economic imperialism. The basis of this distinction
depends on whether an account appeals to a process at work in
human affairs that determines their outcome, or whether the appeal
is to specific human reasoning. In the case of the former, a general
theory is postulated, either explicitly or implicitly, that stipulates
certain conditions that when satisfied produce certain phenomena.
The asserted link between the two provides an explanation that *inter
alia* tells us what such phenomena really are. The latter, however
general its categories and concepts, seeks to specify the reasoning of
particular groups of people — capitalists and politicians — whose
activities constitute imperialism. Both types of account formulate a
rationale for imperialism, but in the case of the former it is derived
from the conceptual framework, and in the latter from the rationality
of individuals.[62]

If this distinction is accepted, the question of the adequacy of the
explanation will be answered quite differently for each argument:
that of the dogmatic model of imperialism depends upon a reference
to an empirical test of its general propositions; that of the voluntaristic
model will depend upon adequate evidence of the actual reasoning of
individuals in a given historical context. The point is not that one
supersedes the other or is superior in any way, but that they are
fundamentally different in character. Of course those who maintain
the former argument will assert that the latter is subsumed within
their theory. There is no room for individual reasoning entering into a
theory based upon the ineluctable nature of economic processes. It is
either irrelevant or subsumed. I do not want to enter into the
epistemological implications of this claim, for they are complex and
beyond the scope of this study.[63] My point here is that the truth or
adequacy of a theoretical argument depends upon whether explicit

criteria of evaluation quite independent of the argument have been satisfied. And the same is true for a historical argument. There is a difference between criteria appropriate to a *generalizing* explanatory account and those relevant to a *particularizing* explanatory account.

In the context of economic imperialism we are offered two different types of argument that are apparently about the same phenomenon. The former offers a general explanation of imperialist phenomena based upon economic categories and concepts formulated into a theory of capitalism atemporal in nature. The latter offers an explanation linked directly to the motivations of individuals and to specific circumstances of time, place, decision and action. Superficially they might seem to be about the same thing — the activities of the multinational corporations concerned with manufacturing, extractive industries and raw materials production in the underdeveloped countries, for example — but the nature and significance of the phenomena under examination are very different. This difference is obscured if attention is concentrated by the critic on the empirical aspects of these arguments. Non-Marxist historians have sought to refute certain aspects of the Marxist thesis on empirical grounds,[64] but of course they implicitly reject the Marxist framwork that is at the basis of empirical interpretation. And it is this that requires critical scrutiny, not selected empirical instances that on the face of it seem to run counter to it. For example, monopoly in the context of Marxist and neo-Marxist argument has a different meaning and associated explanation from that in a voluntaristic account. For Lenin, monopolies were the logical consequences of economic processes and were impersonal in nature. This is the case, of course, for any economic theory since it is dealing with abstractions. But for Hobson they were the rational goals of a small section of people actively concerned with benefiting themselves at the expense of others. Lenin believed the processes and the monopolies they created were inevitable and beyond the control of those involved in their activities. Hobson believed the contrary. Who was right? On my thesis, both types of argument are incommensurable and their truth depends upon different criteria. An appeal to the actual reasoning of Morgan or Rockefeller[65] would confirm or refute Hobson, but the truth of Lenin's thesis depends upon whether his general propositions can be confirmed through empirical instances in the form of a rigorous test.

If, then, we take the dogmatic model, the central problem in considering its explanatory status lies in determining the adequacy of the postulated theory. The picture of imperialism that emerges from the later Marxists is akin to that produced for capitalism by Marx himself, that is, it constitutes a system of relationships between concepts that purports to be a general explanation. There is no causal process that can be isolated from the phenomena it produces; rather, the system can only be viewed as a whole. Marx conceived of capitalism as evolving from sets of pre-conditions that were necessary for the later stage to develop. Once this last stage had been reached, the process had fulfilled itself. A description of capitalism corresponding to the phenomena of mid-Victorian industrial society was then made. All empirical phenomena could be subsumed one way or another within the rubric *capitalism*. His concern was to elucidate the interaction of relations within this condition of capitalism, not to explain how this nexus came into being. The 'historic process'[66] at work was not analysed as a chain of causation, with clearly stated necessary and sufficient pre-conditions for subsequent effects, but as a system of related factors and influences.

Similarly, the model of imperialism developed by Lenin and his followers was a holistic one, subsuming empirical phenomena unknown in Marx's day, such as worldwide, successful revolutions, competition between global alliances systems, socialist states, economic development, economic institutions such as regional trade associations, the multinational corporation and so on, all phenomena 'beyond' the capitalist state. The notion of a causal process was subordinate to the attempt to incorporate such phenomena within the conceptual framework of capitalism. As was pointed out earlier, the compelling need to provide theoretical guidance for practical action often pre-empted a concern for theoretical rigour. Now, in spite of considerable differences in interpretation between Marxist writers on imperialism and the many revisions of Marx's own theory of capitalism that have appeared over the last 100 years, I want to argue that in substance they are concerned with the same kind of theory.

Before examining this argument more closely, let me clarify what in this context is meant by theory. As we have seen throughout this study, it is a vague and ambiguous term. By theory I mean a form of explanation that explains by subsuming a class of phenomena within the framework of a set of propositions organized in a deductive argument, from which are deduced general statements that assert that, given specific conditions and relationships, specific conclusions will follow. The explanation is logically independent of the phenomenon explained, that is, it is not circular. Putting it more simply, the theory consists of a conceptual framework non-empirical in character, that is, an abstract piece of reasoning. From it are derived hypotheses that seek to make true propositions about the occurrence of phenomena. These are exposed to test by observation and experiment and, where the predictive statements are not falsified by the rest, the associated set of reasoning — the statement of necessary and sufficient conditions and the covering law — is said to be adequate in terms of its explanatory value.[67] Such an explanation is not true in any absolute sense, for correspondence between the covering law theory and the empirical phenomenon that 'confirms' it cannot be established as holding in perpetuity. Each such 'confirmation' merely stands as a ground for holding to the theory, and so is of a conventional character. The point is that, however abstract the general theoretical framework, it must be capable of this form of test through hypotheses that have an empirical reference. Non-failure is the ground on which the explanation is deemed to be adequate. Without such a reference to an empirical test we would have merely a conceptual framework — the 'theory' *tout court*. We can see from this that if we can predict the behaviour and occurrence of phenomena through a statement of necessary and sufficient conditions, a covering law and a technique of testing, either through observation or experiment, then the incidence of such phenomena can be brought about under controlled conditions. Not only can predictions be made and tested, but the whole process can be induced, and so a practical application is possible. A sequence of events can be identified and examined as stages of a process in which causes and effects are distinct.

Now, turning back to the claim of Marxist and neo-Marxist writers that their theory is a general explanation of human behaviour, we can ask the question: does it explain in this way? If the systemic relations of capitalism assert that one set of conditions is determined by another — those relating to the need to realize surplus value and the consequent necessity of expansion, for example — then we have, implicitly at least, an assertion of causation. The logical entailments of this postulated relationship need to be fulfilled, together with that of an empirical test, if it is claimed that it is an *explanation*. If the weaker argument is offered, namely that one set is found in 'association' with another set, we have the problem of deciding whether this 'association' is conceptual or empirical. To put it another way, the assertion that the inability to absorb or accumulate capital in a particular economy results in its export, and that this export in turn results in an extended form of capitalism termed imperialism, could in its *logical* implications be making a causal connection between the alleged phenomenon of surplus capital and the alleged phenomenon of a necessary capital export. As we have seen, the necessity for capital export in the economic imperialist argument is linked to the drive for profit maximization within a domestic framework of diminishing returns on investment and limited investment opportunities.

But what is the nature of this 'necessity' to export capital? And in what sense are these assertions conceptual or empirical? The point is not that their truth lies in whether they can be backed up by reference to facts, that is, that in a given time, place and set of activities there is evidence that capital was exported because of a limited capacity for absorption in the domestic economy; or that the rate of investment abroad increased over a period of time in conjunction with an enhanced interest in colonization and involvement in world politics. What is at stake is the explanatory basis of these statements and this involves the postulated link between phenomena as causes and as effects. A generalization is entailed, not a postulated historical coincidence. And since capitalism is seen as a *system,* we need to know what constitutes systemic relations in a dynamic sense if we are to have more than an abstract conceptual scheme whose alleged relationships are merely illustrated, and not demonstrated, by the empirical evidence. This involves an elucidation of the processes allegedly at work that, from certain conditions, proceed to induce a further state of affairs called imperialism. If this is not provided in a form that is empirically testable, then all we have is a method of describing or re-describing phenomena and not an explanation. In short, a testable causal theory is entailed by this kind of argument.

A number of Marxists have tried to repudiate the charge of determinism imputed to this theory.[68] In so doing they emphatically reject the notion of a theory that explains in terms of causes. Yet at the same time they wish to retain the notion of economic force or process operating in some sense independently of human volition. They also wish to retain the authority associated with an 'objective' and 'scientific' account that has the sole claim to truth. A good deal of Jesuitical analysis has been undertaken over the knotty problem of 'consciousness' in Marxist argument.

If we take the example of the phenomenon of the multinational firm discussed earlier, the neo-Marxist argument has it that its activities constitute a new form of capitalism — imperialist in nature. Its existence is explained by the necessity of capitalism to seek more effective ways of capital accumulation. This is an impersonal force derived from basic assumptions about the nature of capitalism. Whether or not the multinationals actually behave in the way they are supposed to, that is channelling their activities so as to command an ever-expanding pool of labour, it is this theoretical necessity that is at the core of the thesis. It is clearly independent of any reasoning on the part of those who, nominally at least, direct them. Their 'consciousness' is determined by the rationale of the economic forces that created them. Or, to put it another way, their reasoning is subsumed within the thesis — they cannot reason any other way since they are constrained by capitalist necessities.

But what constitutes a test of such a hypothesis? Clearly not a reference to the actual (or postulated) activities of the multinational corporation, since this would be circular. How can the driving force of capitalism be separated from what capitalism is presumed to be in terms of its phenomena, so as to constitute a theoretical explanation in which the explanation is logically independent of the thing explained? Capitalism must be explained in terms of capitalism. There is no way of breaking out of this circle so as to test it. The phenomenon is 'explained' by definition within the conceptual framework, and so we must take it or leave it on that basis.

If we turn to the voluntaristic model of economic imperialism, we find that although apparently referring to the same empirical phenomena it is a very different type of argument *qua* explanation. A rationale is advanced based on certain assumptions about the nature of economic activity within a given context. Inspired by the desire for profit, and operating within a limited market economy, the capitalist is forced to look elsewhere for investment opportunities. The assumptions here are, firstly, that the maximization of profit is the sole motivating force for a capitalist and, secondly, that his opportunities for this are restricted within the domestic economy. Accepting this, it is reasonable to suppose that he seeks to expand his activities beyond the nation-state. If all capitalists are inspired by this motivation and influenced by the same conditions, then international competition occurs. A third assumption is made to the effect that the capitalists effectively control their sociopolitical systems so that governments act as their agents. It then follows that this competition takes a political form in which the resources of the state for conquest and violence are put at the disposal of the capitalist.

In this very simplified version of Hobson's argument we can see that what is really being offered is a conspiratorial theory of inter-state politics. Imperialism is a policy pursued by the state in the interests of its own capitalists. Yet in spite of its simplicity it is a more likely candidate as an explanatory form than the dogmatic model, for such an explanation can in principle be tested by reference to the actual reasoning of those involved — both capitalists and politicians. If it can be shown that they accepted the rationale of profit-seeking and that imperialist policies were consciously pursued, then we have a means of relating their actions — the phenomena of imperialism — to their reasons, which would include the conceptual framework that they accepted as their world view. Such an explanation would clearly be limited to the time, place and set of activities that constituted the form of imperialism we seek to explain. The adequacy of the explanation would depend upon the quality of the evidence of reasoning that is adduced in support of the argument.

Having said this, it is unfortunately the case that, instead of the actual reasoning of the agents of imperialism, we are actually offered a rationalization based on certain categorical assumptions about the reality of economic life in a given historical context. There is no alleged necessity about the rationale of imperialism, unlike the dogmatic model, but neither is there any evidence that those whose actions are depicted as imperialistic actually accepted it. It is this link that is missing. And so the plausibility of the alleged motivation of capitalists becomes a subjective matter.

It should be apparent from this that an assessment of these two types of argument proceeds on different grounds. The difference is that the conceptual framework employed in the voluntaristic model has a direct relationship to the reasoning of the agents. The nature of this relationship is left imprecise, and this certainly constitutes a criticism, but the appeal is to *reasons* and not the ineluctable purpose of an abstract economic system. In a sense, the conceptual framework of this model is a form of understanding shared, if only partially, by both observer and the participants. The conceptual framework of the dogmatic model *is* the theory. The forces and processes of the economic system operate in such a way as to exclude the understanding of those who act as its agents. Whether they are aware or not, they are compelled to act out the dictates of the system. The question here is not the relationship of the rationale of the system to the reasoning of the agent, but the relationship of the theory to its logical structure and to an empirical test that establishes the theory as an adequate explanation. As in the case of the voluntaristic model, it fails to fulfil its conditions of adequacy.

Finally, let us look at economic imperialism as a conceptual framework and examine some of its aspects. I want to argue that the use and meaning of its concepts — monopoly, underconsumption, surplus value, profits, investment, dependency, imperialism, and so on — depend upon an implicit range of empirical knowledge that acts as a field of reference but that is not itself explained by the conceptual scheme. Putting this more simply, the conceptual usage appeals to a level of knowledge that pre-exists the theory, but that is organized and made 'intelligible' by the concepts. As this level of knowledge changes, so the conceptual framework is adapted and revised. Trade, for example, between a developed and an underdeveloped country is not what it nominally appears to be, that is, an exchange of goods, money and services, but exploitation and proof of a condition of dependency. The 'facts' as such, that is, the statistical information at our disposal concerning these transactions, are interpreted through the application of such concepts as development, exploitation and dependency. Changes are not anticipated or predicted so much as interpreted. For example, the abandonment of formal empires after the Second World War by the major colonial powers was in no way explained by neo-Marxist theories of economic imperialism. Rather this phenomenon, together with the unanticipated unity and cooperation between the advanced capitalist countries, was explained away in terms of a monolithic capitalism directed by the United States and the creation of an 'informal' empire.

There are many such revisions or adaptations of the theory in response to changing circumstances in inter-state relations. Sometimes anomalous 'facts' are interpreted so as to make them consistent with the theory, and sometimes new concepts are introduced into the general theoretical framework so as to encompass change. For example, confronted with the fact that much of American foreign investment is made in other capitalist countries and not in the underdeveloped area, one commentator asserts that investment in the latter area is pivotal to the United States' economy.[69] In other words, while it is smaller it has a special significance in terms of the dependence of the economy on that area. Similar sophistries occur in the attempt to link United States' involvement in Vietnam in the 1960s to an economic necessity. Confronted with the lack of evidence of any American economic interest in Indo-China, the argument turns on unexploited potential, on the creation of future investment opportunities, on the denial of these to competitors and finally, or rather ultimately, on the defence of the capitalist system against the socialist challenge. The truth of these assertions lies not in any direct evidence of motivation but in the characterization of capitalism contained in the conceptual framework. Capitalism of its nature behaves in this way. So all activities of capitalist states constitute the workings of the capitalist system. It is difficult to break out of such circularity.

The progressive shift in the theory of economic imperialism away from a concern with competition between the capitalist states, or between the super-monopolies, to the problem of underdevelopment in the so-called Third World indicates both an adaptation to changing phenomena and also a change in the conceptual framework. What has been called dependency theory[70] has tended to dominate the literature and attempts to relate more classical Marxist views to modern circumstances have lapsed. And so a concern for surplus value, the labour-cost theory of value and similar concepts dealing with the phenomenon of capitalism takes a subordinate place to concepts such as development, dependency, exploitation, and so on, that are primarily concerned with the *effects* of capitalism on the underdeveloped countries. This change of emphasis is perhaps explained more by the practical or prescriptive aspects of this type of theoretical argument than by a concern for theory for theory's sake. World revolution may lurk in the background but an immediate salvation can be sought in the promotion of national liberation movements in Third World countries.

Throughout this study I have emphasized that theories of economic imperialism are political in nature in spite of the dismissal of political phenomena as epiphenomena. The economic system characterized as capitalism is a system of production and exchange, and as such is made intelligible by the assertion of dynamic principles such as the accumulation of wealth, realization of surplus value, profit-seeking, and so on. But its locus is depicted as state-based. The economic system in the earlier versions of economic imperialism corresponds to the capitalist state. But there is an ambivalence in the application of economic concepts such as value, growth and development, labour, capital, etc. to geographical, political and spatial concepts such as territory, the state, control and power.

On the empirical level, political phenomena are deemed either irrelevant or subordinate to the economic analysis. But on the conceptual level, political concepts are extremely important. Imperialism is fundamentally a system of power and this underlies the economic reasoning. The geo-political is also written into the theory: territory is space, and the capitalist system is conceived of in spatial terms, corresponding to the extant nations and their empires and spheres of influence. Yet the essential element in the earlier version is the existence of labour or potential labour open to capitalist exploitation. Hence population and not space would appear to be the crucial element. Instead of territory, one would expect population distribution and favourable economic conditions for development to be the important factors for a *Marxist* theory of imperialism. The point is that the economic model, with its emphasis on economic activities and transactions, constitutes a system of relationships between *economic* categories — capital, labour, profit, and so on — and does not correspond to a political model based on the nation-state and its external activities. The latter is assumed to be explicable in terms of the former but this stands as an assumption without any link with an analysis of political processes. The argument that capitalism has an inbuilt tendency to expand out of the framework of the domestic economy begs the question of what is meant by expansion. Is the expansion into space—territory — or is it the proliferation of economic activities associated with capitalism? If the former, then it is hard to see any economic justification, not even the weak one of acquiring space in order to preclude competition from other capitalists. If the latter, then it is an economic system that is expanding, and the state as such is irrelevant, except perhaps contingently in specific links with capitalist enterprises, where these use the resources of particular states to achieve their ends.

Lenin's version of imperialism postulates the arrival of monopoly capitalism, which seeks to create a world monopoly. But he skated over the problem of relating *international* capitalism to national loci. The new monopolies emerged from capitalist nation-states and their *raison d'être* stemmed from the finite labour resources of the domestic economy. Having outgrown their origins, as it were, these monopolies enter into competition with one another in order to achieve a super-monopoly. The nation-states are drawn into this competition as agents of monopoly capitalism. But no longer can they serve as the *economic* basis of capitalism, given their limitations, which forced capitalist expansion in the first place.

And, as we have seen, this problem is not resolved in later neo-Marxist versions of economic imperialism, which assert that the multinational enterprise is the locus of modern capitalism. This dissassociation between the states and capitalism begs the question of power and control. If modern capitalism is an all-pervasive system that subsumes all states, developed and underdeveloped alike, then what is the *imperial* relationship? Do multinationals control states? Do states have a genuine existence? And if dependent relations are the focus does not this imply a form of economic nationalism in which, it is postulated, genuine independence can be achieved by breaking this relationship?

In my view these ambiguities exist in theories of economic imperialism because their lack of theoretical and explanatory rigour stems from an attempt to relate them to practice. Such theories are intended to persuade or to prescribe a course of action or an attitude, and they have an ethical basis. This link with political practice is deemed essential by Marxist theorists for they do not merely wish to explain the world, they wish also to change it. A 'correct' analysis of a current situation is one that falls within the theoretical rubric and is so defined and explained as to indicate the 'correct' solution to the problem. It interprets the world.

It was important to Lenin to characterize the war as a phenomenon of capitalism in order to give a basis to opposition. A general ground for this opposition was necessary. Similarly with his successors, changes in the post-war world had to be placed within a general conceptual framework with a view to prescribing practical *action*. The encouragement of revolution in the Third World and the severance of all economic ties with capitalist countries were the only ways to achieve a genuine economic development. Rebellion against the corrupt regimes that operated under licence from their capitalist masters was the only way in which to free the underdeveloped states from permanent exploitation and the socially divisive distortions of their economies created by the capitalist connection.

Even the voluntaristic model of economic imperialism is directed towards practical action and not towards establishing an adequate historical explanation for its own sake. Welfare policies and reform were the practical necessities for the solution of the problem of underconsumption and the exploitation of the state and its economy by sectional interests. Again an ethical dimension enters into the economic analysis. Essentially what is being provided is a justification for action.

The point is that practical considerations enter into the argument so as to determine its nature. The 'theory' is a constant adjustment to practice and a means of deciding on appropriate action. Both theory and practice — the conceptual framework and the phenomena of the 'real' world — are so interwoven and subject to interpretation and reinterpretation as to preclude any form of explanation in which the explanation is logically independent of the phenomena explained. Economic imperialism is a world view that 'explains' by making 'real' phenomena intelligible and so enables action to become rational in terms of the postulates of the analysis. It is an encapsulated rationality. And so the theory has to be both general — encompassing *all* aspects of the 'real' world, whether emphasizing some as central to the thesis or relegating others as mere epiphenomena — and flexible, so as to enable revision and adaptation as circumstances change.

But clearly men can do nothing to arrest the inevitable process of capitalist dissolution. At best they can take stock and ally themselves with the enlightened and await its death throes. A knowledge of the economic forces of imperialism cannot be falsified by an attempt to reverse them. A practice made authoritative by a theory whose adequacy is attested is of a wholly different character from one based upon ethical or ideological precepts. An applied science follows from science itself. A genuine explanatory theory would allow legitimate prescriptions to guide action. Its relation to practice would be established through its capacity to predict. And the phenomena of the 'real' world would be explained in terms of their occurrence through the explanatory adequacy of the theory, which in turn would be established through rigorous empirical testing. None of this is the case for theories of economic imperialism.

A theory of economic imperialism that cannot explain changes in the world market economy or in the structure of production and investment, or the process of economic growth and development, other than by *ex post facto* rationalization is not a theoretical explanation. Marxist and neo-Marxist theories of imperialism do not provide us with any reference to an appropriate test that would determine their explanatory adequacy. Acceptance of their arguments is simply an acceptance void of all standards. The diversity of opinion in Marxist argument about economic imperialism over the nature and significance of changes in capitalist development in this century is an indication of the explanatory weakness of the Marxist conceptual framework. There can be no genuine agreement or disagreement between rival exponents without clear criteria of evaluation that allow the identification of good as opposed to bad arguments. The constant revision and reinterpretation in the literature, which stem from unforeseen, or rather unpredicted, changes in the 'capitalist' system, tell us that we are dealing not with a mode of explanation but with a world view or an ideology.

NOTES AND REFERENCES

1 See, for example, Karl Marx *Pre-Capitalist Economic Formations* (ed. E. J. Hobsbawm, London, Lawrence and Wishart, 1964).
2 See S. Avineri (ed.) *Karl Marx on Colonialism and Modernization* (New York, Anchor Books and Doubleday, 1968) p. 63.
3 see E. M. Winslow *The Pattern of Imperialism* (New York, Octagon Books, 1972) p. 137. Originally published by Columbia University Press in 1948.
4 see Karl Marx *Capital* Vol. III (Moscow, Foreign Languages Publishing House, 1966) and I. I. Rubin *Essays on Marx's Theory of Value* (Detroit, Black and Red, 1972) pp. 63-75.
5 Rosa Luxemburg *The Accumulation of Capital* (trans. A. F. Schwarzchild, London, Routledge and Kegan Paul, 1951) p. 26. First published in 1913.
6 *ibid.,* p. 358.
7 *ibid.,* p. 446.
8 *ibid.,* p. 417.
9 V. I. Lenin *Imperialism, the Highest Stage of Capitalism* (Moscow, Progress Publishers, 1966, 13th edn). First published in 1917.
10 *ibid.,* p. 25.
11 *ibid.,* p. 25.
12 J. A. Hobson *Imperialism: a Study* (London, Allen and Unwin, 1968). First published in 1902. Lenin acknowledged his debt to Hobson in *op. cit.* Preface to the Russian edition, p. 7.
13 Lenin, *op. cit.,* p. 75.
14 *ibid.,* p. 83.
15 *ibid.,* p. 89.
16 *ibid.,* p. 96.
17 N. Bukharin *Imperialism and World Economy* (London, Merlin Press, 1972). Introduction by V. I. Lenin. First published in 1917.
18 R. Hilferding *Das Finanzkapital* (Vienna, 1910).
19 Bukharin, *op. cit.,* p. 74.
20 for Kautsky, see translation of his article published in *Die Neue Zeit* (September 1914) in *New Left Review* 59, January—February 1970.

21 Hobson, *op. cit.,* pp. 81-93.
22 Andre Gunder-Frank *Capitalism and Underdevelopment in Latin America* (New York, Monthly Review Press) pp. 146-50.
23 *ibid.,* p. 207.
24 See, for example, S. Amin *Neocolonialism in West Africa* (Harmondsworth, Penguin, 1973), and *Imperialism and Unequal Development* (Brighton, Harvester Press, 1978); F. H. Cardoso and E. Faletto *Dependency and Development in Latin America* 1977); T. Dos Santos 'The crisis of development theory and the problems of dependence in Latin America' in H. Bernstein (ed.) *Underdevelopment and Development* (Harmondsworth, Penguin, 1973); A. Emmanuel *Unequal Exchange: a study of the Imperialism of Trade* (London, New Left Books, 1972); A. Gunder-Frank *Latin America: underdevelopment or revolution* (London and New York, Monthly Review Press, 1969); R. I. Rhodes (ed.) *Imperialism and Underdevelopment* (New York, Monthly Review Press, 1970).
25 See Paul A. Baran *The Political Economy of Growth* (revised edn, New York, Monthly Review Press, 1962); Paul A. Baran and Paul M. Sweezy *Monopoly Capital* (New York, Monthly Review Press, 1966); Paul M. Sweezy and H. Magdoff 'Notes on the multinational corporation' *Monthly Review* 21, no. 5, pt. 1, pp. 1-13 and no. 6, pt. 11, pp. 1-13.
26 M. Barratt Brown *The Economics of Imperialism* (Harmondsworth, Penguin Books, 1974) p. 281.
27 See Gyorgy Adam 'Multinational corporations and worldwide economy' in Hugo Radice (ed.) *International Firms and Modern Imkperialism* (Harmondsworth, Penguin, 1975), p. 98.
28 For example, Barratt Brown *op. cit.:* 'Thus as the British economy became more integrated into a global capitalism over which the British state had no control it became increasingly vulnerable internationally and the potential benefits to big capital of a straightforwardly aggressive nationalist development have dwindled accordingly' (p. 175).
29 See, for example, H. Magdoff *The Age of Imperialism* (New York and London, Monthly Review Press, 1969) esp. pp. 115-71 and 173-202.
30 For example, M. R. Hahlo, J. G. Smith and R. W. Wright *Nationalism and the Multinational Enterprise* Leiden, A. W. Sijthoff, 1973); Raymond Vernon *Sovereignty at Bay* (New York, Basic Books, 1971); R. J. Barnet and R. E. Muller *Global Reach; the Power of the Multinational Corporations* (New York, Simon and Schuster, 1974).
31 See, for example, Lawrence G. Franko *The European Multinationals* (London, Harper and Row, 1976) pp. 75-104.
32 The United States in 1971 had some 52 per cent of all direct foreign investment made by the market economies. See C. Fred Bergsten, T. Horst and T. H. Moran *American Multinationals and American Interests* (Washington, Brookings, 1978) Table 1-5, p. 15.
33 See *ibid.,* pp. 37-8.
34 *ibid.,* p. 14.
35 *ibid.,* Table 1-4, pp. 11-13.
36 M. Barratt Brown *Essays on Imperialism* (Nottingham, Spokesman Books, 1972) p. 76.
37 See Franko, *op. cit.,* pp. 134-60.
38 See S. Lall and P. Streeten *Foreign Investment: Transnationals and Developing Countries* (London, Macmillan, 1977) p. 6.
39 For example, the British government promoted the merger of its computer industries in 1968 (ICL) so as to restrict IBM's share of the British market. See

Michael Hodges *Multinational Corporations and National Governments; case study UK, 1964-70* (London, Saxon House, 1974).

40 For example, British investment in ship-building, steel, car manufacturing and North Sea oil, and projected investment in the micro-chip industry.

41 British Petroleum is an obvious example. See Chart 1 in Franko, *op. cit.*, pp. 4-6.

42 See Bergsten *et al.*, *op. cit.*, p. 36.

43 *ibid.:* 'Only the ability of the large oil companies, European as well as American, to keep themselves immune from the demands of the governments where they marketed their products, to play the detested role of being accountable to no-one but themselves, kept the conflict among the E.E.C. countries from growing to unmanageable proportions' (p. 417). This role was in effect forced on them by the OPEC countries and they had very little control over pricing. Theirs was the invidious role of organizing a system of rationing.

44 *ibid.*, pp. 130-3.

45 As early as 1949 US oil companies 'bought into' Saudi Arabia offering larger tax payments than the established oil concessionaries. In the case of Iran, the US government insisted that eight American oil companies be included in the new agreement with the Iranian government thus breaking the British monopoly.

46 Peru, for example, expropriated Standard Oil in 1968. But General Motors withdrew in 1970 because it refused to comply with the demands for 70 per cent local content, the elimination of engine imports within a three-year period and the sale of 51 per cent of the company's shares to Peruvian nationals within one year. See Bergsten *et al.*, *op. cit.*, p. 379.

47 For example, the support given to the opponents of Dr Castro over the period 1959-61 and the continued boycott of Cuban goods by the United States government. The earlier cases of intervention in support of the United Fruit Company in Guatamala in 1954. Much of the American food aid programme has been attached to economic and political conditions related to US interests. There have been numerous examples of European states intervening in Africa — the British and the French, for example, in the Congo in 1960-2, and the British involvement in the Nigerian civil war.

48 The Hickenlooper Amendment was introduced at the instigation of the president of one of the multinationals, ITT, whose assets in Brazil and Argentina were under threat. See Bergsten *et al.*, *op. cit.*, p. 389. Significantly, ITT has subsequently moved out of utilities and into manufacturing.

49 For example, Chile nationalized Anaconda in 1969 and, in spite of the fall of Allende, the succeeding regime continued his policies in this respect. It offered to Anaconda and Kennecott only a fraction of the book value of their investments as compensation.

50 An example cited by Bergsten *et al.*, *op. cit.*, p. 139, illustrates this. In 1966 the US government offered Chile a forty-year, ten million dollar AID loan at less than 1 per cent, providing that the Chilean government allowed the sale of Anaconda copper at the domestic producers' price of 36 cents to the pound. This was very much lower than the price on the London Metals Exchange. The Chilean government accepted this but once the loan was negotiated then insisted on any further sales being paid for at the higher rate.

51 OPEC is the most conspicuous example, although its power was not evident until 1973 in connection with the Arab—Israeli conflict. There are other producers' cartels: the Intergovernmental Council of Copper Exporters (CIPEC): the International Bauxite Association (IBA); and the Association of Iron Exporting Countries (AIEC), all created in the late 1960s and early 1970s. Of course, producers' cartels are dependent upon the cohesion of their members and

relative advantages may be sought by one or more of them, thus breaking the agreement. Moreover, the effects of control over prices and their high levels may result in import substitution on the part of the consuming countries, and changes in consumption in the long run may offset the advantages of producers' oligopoly. But although their effectiveness as cartels clearly depends upon a number of variable factors, the fact that they exist at all is an indication of the *political* nature of the bargaining relation between multinationals and the developing countries.

52 See Franko, *op. cit.,* pp. 94 and 104.
53 As an example of this genre, see Gabriel Palma 'Dependency: a formal theory of underdevelopment or a methodology for the analysis of concrete situations of underdevelopment' in *World Development,* Vol. 6 (Oxford, Pergamon Press, 1978) pp. 88-912.
54 Expressed as a ratio of foreign trade to GDP in 1968 the figures were: UK 19, France 12, West Germany 19, Japan 10 and USA only 4.
55 See Lall and Streeten, *op. cit.,* p. 6.
56 The annual growth rate over the period 1965-1973 in per capita income, for example, was for Brazil 6%, Nigeria 8%, Indonesia 4.5%, but for India only 1.5%, Venezuela 1.3% and Ghana 0.8%. In contrast, increases in the developed countries over the same period were: UK 2.3%, West Germany 4%, France 5%, USA 2.5% and Japan 9.6%.
57 See, for example, A. Sampson *The Sovereign State* (London, Coronet Books, 1974).
58 ITT and the Hickenlooper Amendment for example.
59 For example, in 1974 Jamaica related the price of bauxite to the price of aluminium imports into the USA and so achieved a six-fold rise in revenue. In July 1979 Nigeria nationalized BP.
60 See Gunder-Frank, *Capitalism, op. cit.,* in his case studies of Chile and Brazil.
61 The historiography of Marxist interpretation of actual economic and political conditions shows a lag between theory and practice. Change is rarely anticipated, and subsequent interpretation inevitably becomes revisionist. Compare, for example, Lenin and Magdoff, *op. cit.*
62 While I think this distinction both important and tenable, I do not want to suggest that all arguments in this field fall readily into these two categories. There are considerable ambiguities in the literature and many arguments are hybrids combining abstract reasoning with highly detailed empirical 'case studies', so that a level of generalization coexists with specific historical references. The two, however, are never combined into a testable theory in the sense used in this study.
63 There is a growing literature on the philosophy of the social sciences and the best introduction to it is probably through the philosophy of the natural sciences. See, for example, Ernst Nagel *The Structure of Science* (London, Routledge and Kegan Paul, 1968).
64 For example, see D. K. Fieldhouse 'The new imperialism: the Hobson—Lenin thesis revised' in G. H. Nadel and P. Curtis (eds) *Imperialism and Colonialism* (London, Macmillan, 1964) pp. 74-97.
65 Hobson, *op. cit.:* 'It was Messrs. Rockefeller, Pierpont, Morgan and their associates, who needed Imperialism and who fastened it upon the shoulders of the great Republic of the West' (p. 77).
66 See Karl Marx and Freidrich Engels *The German Ideology* (London, Lawrence and Wishart, 1965) p. 50. First published in 1845-6.
67 See Carl G. Hempel 'Studies in the logic of expanation' in *Aspects of Scientific Explanation* (New York, Free Press, 1965) pp. 245-96.

68 See Hobsbawm in Marx *Pre-Capitalist Economic Formations, op. cit.*, pp. 9-65, esp. p. 60.
69 See Magdoff, *op. cit.,* p. 38 and p. 177.
70 See, for example, Palma, *op. cit.*

4

Imperialism and Ideology

In considering the relation between the *phenomenon* of imperialism and ideology it is important to stress that this relationship is historical and contingent in nature. Imperialism is not a necessary consequence of nationalism or of any other set of ideological beliefs. Yet it is impossible to discuss the former without also considering the latter if we wish to explain, since the political locus of imperialist policies is the nation-state.[1] Consequently in an enquiry we are faced with a mixture of *ex post facto* justification, rationalization, political argument and rhetoric, as well as evidence of reasoning associated with the actual decisions and actions of political agents. A distinction needs to be made between political argument designed to fulfil objectives other than that concerned with the nominal policy in hand. Few statements made by politicians are solely concerned with the immediate issue or made *in vacuo*. Hyperbole and rhetoric are devices designed to create solidarity among adherents and to emphasize differences from other competing beliefs. They are accentuations that should not be taken literally. The nominal content of such arguments might be far less important than the eliciting of support for the politicians making them. Their context is the arena of political debate within the state, with its factions, opposition and the need for continuity of support for the regime in power. The existence of a wider context in the world of inter-state relations also constitutes a conditioning factor on such argument. Interviews with the press, public speeches and so on, are all conducted in relation to the tactics and constraints of diplomacy. This is especially true of political statements made in the context of ideological debate or where the political agent subscribes to an ideology.

But while recognizing that this should introduce caution into any interpretation of political statements in terms of explaining action, my concern is not with the contextual aspect of ideology or its relation to the achievement or maintenance of power, but with the derivation of imperialist policies from a more or less developed system of beliefs and ideas held by political agents. In this sense I am concerned with imperialism as a 'logical' consequence of the system. I hasten to say that this does not necessitate any level or kind of action at all.[2] As we shall see, the relation between ideology and action is ambiguous and the kind of evidence that links the two, together with the nature of the link, is difficult to determine and rarely conclusive. But while a belief system can be examined as analytically independent of its historical context — as a set of propositions and connected ideas about a world rather than as a product of its social and political milieus — it is the latter that is important in explaining action and decision.

My concern here is not with the question why a particular belief system came to be held in any sociological or psychological sense, but with the relation between action and the belief system, as the belief system is represented in the reasoning of the agent. It seems to me that, firstly, these are two quite distinct exercises and, secondly, the former requires the postulates of a theory that 'explains' the belief. What such a theory would be is beyond the scope of this study. In short, where the ideology forms part of the reasoning of historical agents then it provides, in part at least, an explanation of their actions. But such an explanation is not ideological, that is, it does not make the same appeal as an ideologue to an authentic level of argument that justifies it.

Nor am I concerned with the question of the rationality of actions in relation to the belief system, or with the rationality of the belief system. Rather my concern is with what I take to be the historical question of the actual reference to the ideology and the actual relation of the action to it, in terms of the agent, time and place. This is not to deny that the belief system in itself might present analytical problems or that, in the realm of practice, normative arguments might be relevant in terms of prescriptions and choices. The larger question of the relation between theory and practice may be part of a critique of the former. In the sense that I am concerned with the *explanatory* significance of an ideology in terms of the phenomenon or the idea of imperialism, then questions of this sort are clearly relevant. But in the context of the example I have chosen, that of national socialism, the question of its rationality resolves itself into one of the consistency or otherwise of Hitler's actions and decisions with his beliefs. The problem is one of their nature and relevance; whether they were systematically held or coherent are clearly important if subordinate questions.

It must be accepted, then, that an enquiry into the ideological basis of imperialism does not provide an empirical explanation of imperialist acts. No causal propositions linking thought to action can be elicited from such an enquiry. What links ideology and action is a process of reasoning in which the ideological content renders the action intelligible to the observer. By appealing to the belief system of the actor, the decisions and actions he undertakes are understood as being what they really are. They are explained. This is not to say that they are entailed by the belief system in any way. Believing that some given state of affairs is desirable does not necessitate its fulfilment or any attempt to fulfil it. An aim is not necessarily a purpose or an intention. In so far as a reference to ideology provides an account of the reasoning of the agent in connection with his decisions and actions, then we have advanced an empirical explanation of these and these alone.

Ideologies, if they direct at all, direct not actions but choices. Out of the range of what appears possible, a belief system directs that choice which in its terms appears better than another. Its appropriateness and justification is seen in terms of the ideology. It postulates, firstly, an ideal objective — an aim — and, secondly, in the world of practice, a proper choice, which albeit falling short of the ideal nevertheless reflects it. Alternatively, the range of choices open to an ideologically committed agent may be defined in terms of his ideology. Some possible courses of action may be either not considered or deemed counter to the ideology. None of this, of course, imposes any necessity on an actor to conform to an ideological dictate nor does it preclude any action being deemed ideologically appropriate given the necessary justification. As we have seen in the case of economic imperialism, the ideological argument is sufficiently flexible to allow revision, and general enough to subsume a variety of courses of action. What is of concern to us is the extent to which the belief system entered into the reasoning of agents *prior* to their taking decisions and making choices, and whether there was any consistency both in the actions and in the associated reasoning that suggests the primacy of ideological considerations.

But what is the link between belief and an action in terms of an explanation, if it is not causal, rational or normative? How can we establish a reference from an action or series of actions to a specific belief system? There are a number of problems here, some of which are conceptual and some empirical. Taking the first, it could be argued that, while things do not change, conceptions of them do. If we wish to establish the significance of an action in ideological terms, how can we ensure that this connexion is not itself interpreted ideologically by the interposition of our own beliefs. Or, alternatively, the agent himself may be indulging in *ex post facto* reasoning, which makes his past actions intelligible and coherent with respect to his ideology. The historian and the agent may both interpolate into their interpretations of actions beliefs that change their significance. Indeed the agent, if he is ideologically committed, is virtually constrained to do so, for his view of the past is innately ideological. This is particularly true of the example considered in this study — national socialism. Hence, while the action may be performed for extraneous reasons, it is difficult to discover this where the agent has an interest in making it ideologically coherent. If the historian substitutes his own reasoning in order to create a consistent narrative, then he is imposing his own belief system or rationality, introducing anachronistic assumptions that the agent could not be shown to hold on that evidence.

How then can an explanation of the action be advanced where reason and justification are apparently so inextricably mixed? In what sense can an appeal to a belief system be deemed to be a reason that preceded the action and hence 'explains' it? In the case of Hitler's expressed reasoning there is, as we shall see, a plethora of justification, rhetoric, suasion and special pleading, all designed to show the supreme rationality of his policies and to reinforce his authority to make them. The elements of contingency, accident and circumstance are suppressed in order to demonstrate the superior view of the Führer and to elicit from his followers and his generals an unquestioning obedience to his orders. Privately he might concede the importance of the unforeseen — the weather, for example,[3] or unpredictable events[4] that adversely affected his plans — but factors of this kind were not allowable as points of discussion in the fabrication of his plans. The only contingencies admitted as variables in Hitler's judgement were the movement of global forces conceived of as the interplay of nation-states whose geopolitical manoeuvrings only Hitler was permitted to assess and judge.

Actions, however, are always contingent, dependent upon the play of circumstances as well as on the reasoning of the agent. The problem is not how can we relate theory to practice and remove the merely contingent (that is a problem for the practitioner or the theorist), but rather how can an appeal to 'theory' *explain* practice? This brings me to the problem of evidence; what I conceive of as an empirical problem. If, for example, we succeed in relating the decision to invade the Soviet Union in 1941 to a series of reasons for which we have adequate evidence, we have the problem of deciding which of these reasons were instrumental in making the decision. Some of these relate to practical matters and some to a wider purpose. This example will be discussed at length later, but the difficulty in terms of evidence is that we have a number of apparently contradictory reasons given by Hitler at different times. They support a number of competing hypotheses. We might say that some of these relate to the timing of the invasion and to the relative priority given to that choice of action rather than another. Some of them might be eliminated as having reference to different purposes in persuading his associates about the wisdom of his proposed actions, and so inducing them to make the appropriate preparations. The point here is that explaining the circumstances of the decision does not explain its nature. At one level, in producing the reasons for timing for example, we have 'explained' the invasion of the Soviet Union. But this leaves the wider question of what this might be apart from its nominal meaning. We need to relate the 'logic of the situation' to a context of purpose and aim. In my view, this entails an appeal to Hitler's ideology. Clearly this case must be made and not merely assumed. I intend to argue that the invasion of the Soviet Union in 1941 was not simply an attempt to eliminate a power competitor, and thus explicable in terms of opportunism or of assumptions about the mechanics of power politics, but is to be explained as an act of imperialism, whose intent and significance are clarified only through an understanding of Hitler's wider purposes. In short, this particular decision and consequent actions need to be placed within the context of Hitler's system of thought for them to be made completely intelligible. Reference to the immediate context of reasoning will not provide a complete explanation.

There is certainly a problem, both in eliciting evidence of this thought and in justifying an appeal to it, that is, treating it as relevant evidence in an explanation of this action. The former is in a sense practical and contingent and depends on what has survived, but the latter is of wider significance. What counts as evidence is determined by the use to which it is put by a historian. In this case it depends on accepting the notion of an explanation as consisting of the reasoning of the agent. It is this form of explanation that throughout this study I have termed 'historical'. It does not entail treating reasons as causes, or human actions as events, which find their explanation by an appeal to factors and forces beyond human reasoning. But what are *reasons*?

An appeal to an ideology made either by the agent or by the historian explains everything, which is to say that it explains nothing. And similarly reference to the immediate context of reasoning surrounding a particular decision or action provides only a partial explanation. It does not tell us the meaning the action had for this agent. This is to be found in the notion of aim. Hitler himself made a revealing remark in *Mein Kampf* when he said, 'The theoretician of a movement must lay down its goal, the politician strive for its fulfilment. The thinking of the one, therefore, will be determined by eternal truth, the actions of the other more by the practical reality of the moment.'[5] In his view, while these are distinct, the latter must always be guided by the former regardless of the short-term deviations borne of expediency that he recognized as being an essential part of politics. And of course Hitler became both the ideological and the political leader of his country.

If, then, we focus on the *phenomenon* of imperialism without any consideration of the reasoning of its agents, we are engaged in an ahistorical argument in which the nature of the phenomenon is either decided deductively or begged. This study, on the other hand, is concerned to relate the agent's system of thought to his decisions and actions in order to determine whether an imperialist ideology explains imperialist policies. There are serious problems associated with the relation of theory to practice, as we have seen in the discussion of economic imperialism. Relating aims and intentions to practice presents similar difficulties.

Taking the nominal view of imperialism, Hitler's imperialism has been regarded as a later flowering of the European imperialism of the nineteenth century in which the implicit right to govern beyond the nation-state was vested in an assumption of cultural superiority, linked to military capacity and technological achievements. The right to rule was conferred on a state not simply by force of arms but by its civilizing mission. Certainly there are traces of this in Hitler's programme,[6] although the notion of the promotion of the general welfare, barely apparent in the other European empires, was conspicuously absent. However, over the inter-war period the growth of nationalism and the rising costs of colonial administration encouraged a liberal attitude on the part of the metropolitan powers to the political and economic 'rights' of the people they ruled. By the end of the 1930s the ability of the imperial powers to govern and administer millions of subject peoples, which Hitler so much admired, was seriously in question. But he recognized that these empires were not acquired or maintained through persuasion or the consent of the colonial peoples.[7] And equally for the 'old' empires, the rise of Japanese and Italian imperialism in the thirties was seen as more important than a relaxation of imperial rule.

But to consider German imperialism as a continuation of nineteenth-century ideas of imperialism is to ignore the novel features in it. It is true there are parallels, in the notion of the economic utility of empire, for example, and in the racialism implicit in the 'white man's burden'. The peculiarities in Hitler's imperialism lay more in its systematically developed conception of race and politics and in its extension to white peoples. This was bringing imperialism home with a vengeance. What was acceptable in the colonies did not appear, to liberals at least, acceptable in Europe. While self-determination had, nominally at least, been accepted as a principle in deciding government and nations in post-war Europe, it certainly had not been accepted as applying to the empires. Hitler's reversal of the principle, in seeking to apply 'imperial' rule in Europe as it had been applied outside Europe, was deemed to be not merely a threat to European security but immoral.

However, the claim that national—socialism is an imperialist ideology should be examined before turning to the question of its relation to practice and to practitioners. I should at this juncture stress that I am primarily concerned with Hitler's thought rather than with the antecedents and development of national—socialism as a set of ideas. The NSDAP had its own party ideologue, Alfred Rosenberg, and Hitler was indebted to a number of writers for his views.[8] But Hitler explicitly rejected any external authority:

> I must insist that Rosenberg's 'The Myth of the Twentieth Century' is not to be regarded as an expression of the official doctrine of the Party. The moment the book appeared, I deliberately refrained from recognising it as any such thing . . . I have myself merely glanced cursorily at it.[9]

Although he was undoubtedly influenced by a number of writers, national—socialist thought was largely his own creation. Hitler conceived of national—socialism as an ideology of action uniting theory and practice in his own person. Hence his own version is more directly relevant to a study of the relation between ideology and practice than the general body of ideas associated with national—socialist and fascist thought. Moreover, it is not only the rare position of Hitler as a political leader possessed of an all-embracing political ideology, both capable and willing to put certain of his ideas into practice, that fixes our attention on Hitler the thinker, but also the fact that while many of his ideas are derivative the synthesis is peculiarly his own. He drew them together from a number of sources and conceived of them as both a set of principles and a programme for action.

There are three main strands in Hitler's thought that are directly related to imperialism—blood, the nation and space.[10] His notion of race was based on an elemental component — a blood type — which could be mixed or adulterated but never completely lost through miscegenation. In spite of centuries of interbreeding between races, if the innate blood was present, selective breeding and exposure to the appropriate environmental stimuli could eradicate inferior admixtures. For Hitler believed in a hierarchy of blood types. Hence, for example, it was possible to 'germanize' Czechs or even some Poles, providing they possessed a trace of the superior Aryan blood type. The presence or absence of this precious element was indicated by the behaviour of the individual. But race was not determined by cultural or social conditions. Exposure to the 'right' conditioning could not compensate for the lack of Aryan blood. However, given this blood type, an appropriate conditioning could make it realize its potential and assume its rightful place as the dominant race.

The Jew occupied a special position in this racial theory. Unlike the other races, which possessed some measure of autonomy albeit subject to the dictates of order and degree imposed by the racial hierarchy, the Jewish race had unique characteristics. It was parasitic on other races. The Slav was born to be a slave but a slave in his place. Given appropriate relations with the master race, the Slav could fulfil his destiny and, in a sense, be fulfilled receiving protection and material well-being from his Aryan overlords. The Jew, however, could not exist as a race apart or fit into the hierarchical order. He was destined to prey on superior blood. The biological conception of racial types, each with its innate characteristics represented in differing responses to their physical environment, is modified in the case of the Jew, who was seen as a catalyst for the destruction of other races. He is depicted as a disease preying on other races, dependent on them yet contributing to their degeneration. The Jew is a microbe, a bacillus, a tuberculosis and so on.[11]

Internationalism and the subordination of individual talents and creative effort to the political doctrine of the domination of the masses through socialism and Bolshevism were peculiarly the contribution of the Jew to political life. In reducing the authority of the blood community, and in stifling or reducing the contribution of individuals as leaders in political, scientific, technological and cultural fields, the Jew was a countering force to the realization of the destiny of the Aryan race. This was not simply a matter of a hostile ideology as represented by Bolshevism or by the machinations of international finance, but constituted a *biological* menace. Mixing the blood through miscegenation endangered the race by reducing its chances for survival. What prevented the *Herrenvolk* from fulfilling their manifest destiny through their racial superiority was the corruption of the blood by the Jews. The failures of the past, the 'defeat' of the world war, the wrong directions taken in foreign policy, the humiliations of the Weimar Republic, mass unemployment, the failure to achieve German unity, and so on, were all attributed to this corruption and to the presence of Jews in other states.

Hitler in the last year of his life came to see the Jew not as a biologically constituted race but as a 'race of the mind'.[12] In this way he explained the tenacity of the Jewish race. Confronting the successes of the Russians (possessed of a Jewish ideology and dominated by Jews) and at the same time having purged Germany of its own Jews, Hitler was caught up in his own ambiguities. The ambiguity of the notion of race was deliberate and not simply a product of undisciplined thought. On the level of practice, it allowed both an easy recognition of 'racist' phenomena and an opportunistic policy. As a concept, the notion of the Jew and the general idea of race was invaluable in legitimizing any course of action. It acted as a unifying principle without compromising or constraining his leadership. The inherent ambiguity of the idea of race, and its place in national—socialist ideology, were a necessary adjoint to practice. An ideologue who was also a political leader would find his freedom of action seriously constrained by a logically worked out system that, in a sense, was in the public domain. Hitler did not intend that he should be a prisoner of his own ideology or subject to scrutiny and criticism from other ideologues, and so he discouraged his own party from ideological expression while making his ideological pronouncements sufficiently Delphic to maximize support without commitment to a specific course of action. The notion of 'the Jew' was invaluable to Hitler in achieving blind loyalty to his cause and to his person.

Hitler's special targets — social democracy, the Catholic Church, liberal economics, international finance, the Jews, Bolshevism, pacifism, and politically conscious art and music, and so on — although each had its own special dangers to the national—socialist state, all had one thing in common, they promoted internationalist ideas and values at the expense of German national consciousness. They all contributed in their individual way to the weakening of nationalist sentiment and ultimately to the destruction of the German race. They were un-German. Social democracy was attacked because of its emphasis on parliamentary government, which Hitler regarded generally as the rejection of true national leadership, and because, in the form of the Weimar Republic, it constituted a weakness in the face of the enemies of Germany. The Catholic Church was not a *German* church and was an alternative authority that challenged the attempts of national—socialist thought to be a transcendent ideology for the German people. Liberal economics and international exchange relationships challenged the independence of the German economy and enmeshed it in a system of constraints and inducements that limited the authority of the German government. The Jews were the agents of such a system and through their involvement in capitalism and their manipulation of its apparent rival system — that of Bolshevism — they similarly threatened the racial and political integrity of Germany. And pacifists, Jehovahs Witnesses, artists, etc., promoted values antagonistic to nationalism or refused to lend a hand to German revival and so constituted sources of weakness. The more weakened the German state became through these inimical elements, the more exposed it was to decadence through the enhancement of respect for the individual over the interests of the race. Given the challenge of rival states, Hitler concluded, following the analogy of the later Roman Empire, that the barbarians had an advantage in competing with 'civilized' states. Hence it was necessary to restore the balance through a policy of racial purity in the creation of a 'blood-state'. Elements that impeded this policy or were positively harmful had to be destroyed.

Hitler's conception of nation was not territorial, cultural or political, but racial.[13] The actual boundaries or frontiers of a state were merely contingent,[14] in the final analysis reflecting the fortunes of the race at any given time. The nation constituted a biological entity, more or less pure, depending on the admixture of races through its history. A racial or blood-state was the nation purged of its alien blood. Its primary concern was survival in the face of attacks designed to weaken its racial purity. Such attacks reduced the nation's chances of survival in a world of competing nations. A racial state represented not a political unit but a human species. The state was the means to the end of racial survival, and the preservation of the race was a primal necessity. Recognition of this through a form of government capable of promoting the ends of the race and keeping it free from contamination was a first charge upon the state. All other national goals were secondary. This required leadership, a recognition of the significance of its task and a programme designed to eradicate inimical influences upon its racial identity.[15] This was a more fundamental view than the use of the Jew as a national scapegoat or as a means to obtain political support.

Thus far the idea of a racial hierarchy and the need to free the Aryan race from its racial contamination can be seen as a justification of racial policies in Germany itself. The creation of a genuine racial state by purging it of undesirable elements and by uniting all Germans within one nation-state can be seen as a non-imperialistic nationalism. The assertion of a racial hierarchy in which the Aryan assumed supremacy had no necessary concomitant of an aggressive imperialism in which racial inferiors were enslaved. The racial theories espoused by Hitler could be seen as a programme of reform designed to create a strong government with himself at its head.

However, in conjunction with two other strands of Hitler's thought — the nation as a political entity, and space — race assumes a different character. In Hitler's early years in power, anti-Semitism and appeals to German nationalism through calls for the self-determination of ethnic German minorities in Europe concealed his aspirations to empire and their racial basis. Most Germans and many foreigners could agree with certain aspects of Hitler's demands for the incorporation of 'German' territories within the Reich. Racism and the persecution of the Jews was solely a domestic matter. And the demands for territory were carefully orchestrated to meet both the fears of the major opponents — the other European powers — and also those of allies: no demands were made for the return of Alsace, the Alto-Adige, 'German' Switzerland or the 'German' Baltic. The consolidation of the German Reich was less a cause for alarm than the rearmament and the unscrupulous tactics devised to achieve it.

But of course the very notion of supremacy implicit in the racial theory justified a German hegemony over other races. That Hitler tended to underplay this aspect in his early years in power is understandable in view of his problems of securing himself as Führer and in outmanoeuvring the other European states in order to destroy the Versailles and Locarno treaties and to create a greater German Reich. But it was present nonetheless, and became explicitly linked to a policy of territorial expansion in Europe. The racial state needed space.[16] Hitler linked the notion of inalienable blood types to a kind of social Darwinism in which the nation-state was engaged in a permanent struggle. He conceived of the world of states as an anarchy, in which political existence depended on success in the struggle of all against all. In his view, politics was primarily concerned with guaranteeing the survival of the racial state and this was achieved by measures designed to purify the race within the state and by an aggressive policy towards other states. No racial state could adopt a purely defensive policy without lapsing into degeneracy.[17] And no contractual obligation or agreement between states was anything other than a move in a perpetual contest, nor was it binding once the advantages it had bought had passed away.[18] Force was the determinant of success, the final arbiter and the ultimate justification. War was inherent in politics both as a means of purifying the race and so guaranteeing its survival, and also, following Clausewitz, as policy by other means. Appeals to justice or to the conventions of a world order — the spirit of the League of Nations — were empty, for what determined the proper or just conduct of states and the very rulers themselves was the sword.[19] It was not by accident or by just means that the great European empires had come into existence. As Hitler never tired of pointing out, Britain had gained her empire by force and brutality. Not that this was reprehensible, for he argued 'I know full well that no other empire has come into being in any other way, and that in the final resort it is not so much the methods that are taken into account in history as success and not the success of the methods as such but rather the general good which the methods yield'.[20] Victory meant the survival of the fittest and to the fittest went the spoils.

Empire was thus a necessity for the racial state. It was a necessity:

space was a pre-condition for, as well as a consequence of, survival. Hitler's reasoning here was based on his view of the world as an anarchy in which survival depended on fitness; this in turn depended on possessing resources. The possession of adequate territory was an indication of this fitness and also its guarantee. The effect of the peace treaties, he argued, was to arrest a 'natural' development and to confine Germany to an inadequate living-space. He believed that population increase in Germany was outstripping resources and instead of strengthening the state constituted a source of weakness.[21] In answer to the argument that birth control or more intensive exploitation of existing resources could mitigate the problem, he asserted characteristically that the imposition of human limits weakened the state. Human, as opposed to natural, control did not produce the struggle of all against all that ensured that the fittest survived. The individual was exalted over the race.[22] The process of natural selection operating through war produced the fittest race and so to the victor the spoils. If Germany adopted effete methods of controlling its population, it would in the course of time be swamped by those races that, although more barbaric, freely exposed themselves to nature's controls. Living-space was not simply a necessity for survival; it also had to be fought for. Fighting was a virtue in itself, for it toughened the race.

Central to this argument was the notion that autarky was an essential condition for the survival of the racial state.[23] Hitler argued that the state should be economically autonomous, eschewing dependence on trade and foreign investment and involvement in an interdependent multilateral international economy. He was aware that interdependent economic relations between industrialized states were not only beyond the control of any one state, as the world economic depression of the thirties had shown, but were also beyond the control of a dictatorial ruler and constituted a weakening of his authority. Moreover, they inhibited the creation of a capacity for, and the use of, force in the national interest, since they provided both a countering rationale to war as well as a means of manipulation and pressure on the part of foreign powers. Trading and business interests within Germany might well become disaffected should national policies have an adverse effect on their activities abroad. More fundamentally, all sources of raw materials and food should be under the direct control of the state. It followed that if Germany did not possess such control then it had to be created through the internal development of import substitutes, governmental control over investment and the acquisition of resources through conquest. What Germany lacked was to be obtained through force. If autarky could not be achieved with domestic resources, then it had to be created by territorial expansion. An autarkic policy entailed a policy of expansionism, which meant war with those states that sought to deny the Aryan race its legitimate space.[24] Such legitimacy was justified by successful violence.

The basic premise of the racial superiority of the Aryan justified the assertion of imperial domination over those races deemed inferior and subject. Yet it was also empirically open-ended, for this superiority depended ultimately on success in the struggle of all against all. In a sense it was a hypothesis to be tested. The 'failure' of Germany in the First World War and its subsequent ignominy in the years after could be 'explained' by the 'stab in the back' argument based on the thesis of racial contamination.[25] Once the race had been purged of its impurities it was free to fulfil its destiny. Theoretically, success was guaranteed because of its innate superiority. Slavs and those races, albeit of Aryan stock, that were contaminated by Jews, would by their unfitness either fall victim to the master race or fail to impede its triumphant progress. But the only proof of this was in war itself. National—socialism, or rather Hitler's version of it, was essentially an imperialist ideology. The racial state was of its nature compelled to acquire its own living-space and in so doing dominate the anarchic world that endangered it.

Of course this apocalyptic view of world politics as a struggle for survival, in which the factor of 'blood' determined that the fittest survived, need have no necessary consequences for political action. Many other politicians shared this view including one who was to become Hitler's inveterate opponent, Winston Churchill. True he did not share the pseudo-scientific absurdities of Hitler's racism, but he had both a patrician attitude and a 'realist' view of international relations. Force was the final argument, empires were got by the same means that kept them. The point about Hitler's beliefs is that they were orientated to a programme. They were the basis not of a vague world view but of prescriptions. Action was a necessary concomitant of the ideology. Clearly the prescriptions of *Mein Kampf* were, to say the least, remote from any prospect of implementation given Hitler's political impotence at the time. Hitler clearly recognized this; he argued:

> . . . if the art of the politician is really the art of the possible, the theoretician is one of those of whom it can be said that they are pleasing to the gods only if they demand and want the impossible. He will almost always have to renounce the recognition of the present but in return, provided his ideas are immortal, will harvest the fame of posterity.[26]

Moreover, when he came to power circumstances had altered both within Germany and outside it. The world economic depression had affected all major international powers and weakened their will and capacity to engage in armed interventions designed to frustrate those states who wished to upset the status quo. Other states besides Germany were unsatisfied with their lot, and Japan and Italy had shown an aggressive and successful imperialism in the face of weak opposition from the other major powers. The full extent of this weakness was yet to emerge and in any case Hitler was largely preoccupied with strengthening his position in Germany. The point is not that *Mein Kampf* and its prescriptions provided Hitler with a blue-print for policy, but that its basic ideological principles gave a direction to Hitler's policies while permitting him latitude for manoeuvre. The prescriptions in *Mein Kampf* can be taken as illustrations of the directing principles that, when the former were invalidated by changing circumstances, remained constant as a guide to proper practice. It was this combination of rigid and unchanging views about the constitution of politics and expediency in reaching long-term aims derived from them that made Hitler such a dangerous and successful politician. He knew what he wanted but he was prepared to wait until the situation had changed in his favour or had been manipulated by him so that he could realize his ambitions. This was opportunism with a direction. I want to argue that his manoeuvres and his actions and decisions are explicable, not in terms of the programmatic elements of his early writings but in terms of the political principles explicitly stated in them and that I have outlined. Further I want to argue that an imperialist programme, regardless of its direction and content, axiomatically followed from his political beliefs. That its actual implementation fell in Eastern Europe is not so important as the broad objectives that were sought. These last follow directly from a consistently held ideology.

Hitler himself was deeply conscious of the difficulties in converting ideological principles into action, especially in view of his need to create a party with a mass following. He stressed the importance of defining the aim rather than seeking closely to define the means. Given clarity of ends, the means could be as devious and as opportunistic as circumstances directed.[27] Essentially, he argued, a programme of action should not be directed to specific short-term ends with stated conditions and timing, but should consist of a few guiding principles related to aims. He wanted neither controversy over basic doctrine nor commitment to objectives that were influenced in their fulfilment by contingent factors such as the will of the opposition to resist.[28] What he called the 'outward formulation' of a programme should be subordinated to a few essential ideas. Adherence to a faith, particularly a faith based on his leadership, was the prerequisite for a national—socialist party. Given this, its leader was free to adopt his own policies untrammelled either by considerations of ideological orthodoxy or by apparent inconsistencies between his immediate actions and a programme of action that specified specific intentions. Statements of aim were thus couched in terms that begged the question of the means and conditions of their fulfilment.

Before going on to consider the level of action itself, and in particular Hitler's decision to attack the Soviet Union, something should be said about the nature of the problem in relating theory to practice.[29] Let me restate my thesis: essentially I am arguing that Hitler possessed a set of beliefs that, *inter alia,* postulated territorial expansion. Such beliefs constituted part of the reasoning that was the basis for his actions in extending German power and authority beyond the German state. In short, in order to understand and explain the level of action, we need to relate his actions and decisions to this system of reasoning. Only when we have done so are we in a position to know what his actions really were. Until we have done so his actions remain only putative. Thus a knowledge of his intentions derived from an elucidation of his beliefs tells us something of the nature of his actions. It is my thesis that his intentions were derived from his ideological beliefs and that he was consistent in adhering to them.

A distinction must be made between reasoning associated with a specific action in its situational context and what I have called the belief system, to which the former is related. Any political decision is related to the perceived constraints and opportunities of the situation in which it is made. Calculations of this kind are clearly related to an appreciation of circumstances. Alternative courses of action, the possibility of inimical or favourable consequences, the reactions of friends and opponents, considerations of capacity, and so on, are all relevant considerations for the political practitioner and, clearly, a reconstruction of this reasoning is a necessary part of the historian's task. But a full explanation of the action, that is, a complete statement of its nature, depends upon the reference of this situational rationality to a context of beliefs that transcend it. We need to know about aims and purposes related to ends rather than means if we wish to explain fully. It is this reference that makes the action itself intelligible. In some cases, it is true, what is desirable is subordinated to what is expedient. Many actions are in a sense 'forced' upon the agent. But few politicians, least of all Hitler, are so caught up in the immediate demands of a situation that they do not have the possibility of choice between alternative courses of action. And in my view it is this element of choice that makes ideological beliefs relevant. We can regard this type of reasoning as directly linked to aims and purposes and these have no necessary connection to circumstances and contingent factors. The conditions for their fulfilment are in a sense 'open'. It is when they are, as in Hitler's case, consistently held and have a prospect of fulfilment, or when a situation has been engineered rendering them so capable, that they become directly relevant in directing choice. For, as I have argued, no belief entails action, but choices are based upon beliefs and, in the case of ideological beliefs, are directed by them, even if only in the negative sense of dictating what is illicit.

I have stressed above that a reconstruction of reasoning is done in terms of the perceptions of the agent. A reading of Hitler's expression of thoughts in their various sources and forms cannot simply be correlated with the record of his actions in order to 'prove' a consistent programme of imperialism. Quite apart from its ambiguities and the perils of exegesis, what would be missing in such an account would be evidence of Hitler's actual reasoning at times of decision and action. Evidence is necessary, but there are considerable problems in providing it. This is not simply a matter of the survival of documents or the accounts of eye-witnesses and participants, but one of determining 'real' reasons from *ex post facto* justificatory 'explanations' designed to persuade or placate or from any other form of rationalization. The *actual* reasons of an agent are inaccessible to the historian and an element of interpretation based on inference of necessity creeps into the argument. The only criterion of adequacy that seems appropriate here is consistency between the various pieces of evidence and the removal of inconsistencies and anomalies. The account should thus be coherent in terms of the available evidence.

The question of intention is not treated as it was at the Nuremberg Trials, that is, as the basis of a conspiracy designed to promote 'ideological war and race conquest', conceived well before Hitler's accession to power. *Mein Kampf* was not a blue-print for policy. The thesis considered here is that consistency of aim can be established but that this does not *entail* consistency of action. Hitler was in many respects an opportunist but an opportunist with a sense of direction. The opportunities that presented themselves to him were *his* opportunities and the range of possibilities that gradually unfolded permitted a degree of choice that, in the issue, reflected *his* long-term aims. The choices he made, in a sense, were directed by his beliefs. But of course complete freedom of action was never open to him. He was restrained, in his own view, from accomplishing his desires by a number of opponents, internal as well as external. Only in one respect was he free, and that was in his treatment of the Jews and other 'racial' minorities, and that only after the war had become 'total'. Even the elimination of the mentally ill and chronically sick was done with utmost secrecy under the awareness that public knowledge of this would be politically dangerous. The churches could never be directly eliminated and Hitler was always conscious of the existence of opposition to his policies within Germany. With the war he was freed from many inhibitions but not totally so.

So a desire for *living-space* can be considered an aim where ideological justification is provided without specifying the conditions necessary for its fulfilment or the form and direction that it would take. For example, were Hitler's actions in Eastern Europe after March 1939 the consequence of design, or were they purely opportunistic? Even if Hitler simply seized an opportunity to increase the area under direct German rule, the fact that he saw it as an opportunity at all implies some preconceptions about what is desirable. It is an unreal dichotomy in practice to separate actions as either planned or as opportunistic. The question of choice, where several possibilities are perceived to exist, often turns on what is deemed desirable, and this in turn depends on an associated reasoning that is ideological in character. The question here is not the compatibility of Hitler's actions with his ideological preferences, but whether he held these preferences as clear intentions preceding his decisions and actions. Both Ribbentrop and Goering, admittedly on trial for their lives and the latter, for what it is worth, not under oath, stated that Hitler's colonial policies only emerged once the war had proved so successful with the defeat of France.[30] But Hitler himself recognized that a break with his policy of creating a united Germany came with his assumption of a protectorate over Bohemia and Moravia in March 1939.

> For in March 1939, for the first time, we put ourselves in the wrong in the eyes of world opinion. No longer were we restricting ourselves to reuniting Germans to the Reich, but were establishing a protectorate over a non-German population.[31]

There is some evidence in his policy towards Czechoslovakia after this date and in Poland from September 1939 about what his long-term aims were. But the general point I wish to make is that it is not the direction that his imperialism took but its necessity that is at the root of his decisions and actions. Before turning to the question of his reasons for attacking the Soviet Union, I want to examine Hitler's statements of aims to see what consistency they had over his political career.

The distinction between aims and action is central to this thesis. Aims are related to aspiration; that is, they specify no conditions for their fulfilment. Intentions specify such conditions, and are formulated within their terms. Action is related to intention, which in turn is related to aims. An act is to be understood not solely through a knowledge of intentions but through a knowledge of aims. An explanation of Hitler's actions in terms of a desire for living-space must distinguish therefore between aims that make subsequent intentions and actions intelligible and the intentions themselves, which are intimately bound up in the perceived conditions for action. Neither evidence of aim nor of intention is sufficient to provide an explanation of Hitler's actions. It is the relation between the two, especially in this case where a well-articulated ideology forms part of the reasoning of the agent, that provides us with this. Much of the evidence concerning intentions deals with problems of circumstances, contingencies, timing, the intentions of other agents, and so on, and it is difficult to evaluate this or estimate the significance of particular factors in the absence of evidence about aims, or the context of the agent's beliefs about the situation in which he conceives himself to act. Moreover, any attempt to separate special pleading or *ex post facto* justification from 'real' reasons for an action is supported by reference to a context of stated aims that permits us to see a direction or consistency in practice, overriding particular circumstances and arguments. This should not, of course, be imposed upon the agent, and the problem of the relation between aims and intentions is not easy to resolve.

Evidence of aims largely consists of statements made by Hitler when he lacked the requisite power to implement them. Thus *Mein Kampf*, his early speeches made before he came to power, his Party Rally speeches, speeches in the Reichstag and conferences with his generals, together with recorded conversations including those of the last impotent year of imminent defeat, provide us with some evidence of his aspirations unrelated to the context of practice. These correspond to four major preoccupations: firstly, with the need to provide an ideological basis for his party and to win support; secondly, with the need to create a pliant instrument to carry out his will through rearmament, control over the army and the consolidation of his personal authority over the German people; thirdly, to establish priorities in future policy, tempered by the need to achieve military victories; and finally, his last musing over his political career in the hour of defeat. Throughout these phases there is, as I hope to show, a sustained and consistent concern for the creation of an empire in Europe overriding his immediate concerns and activities. Only in the third of these preoccupations were aims and intentions closely related in practice, and even here only briefly.

In *Mein Kampf* Hitler makes a distinction between the acquisition of colonies that were not contiguous to the racial state, and the creation of an empire.[32] An empire for him was a homogenous racial state that expanded territorially through a process of conquest and racial assimilation, and its corollary, the elimination of racially inimical elements. The process of assimilation of new territory took time, and was achieved through settlement in 'racial colonies' by Germans and a programme of germanization. The impetus to the achievement of this empire was seen as stemming partly from the birth right of a superior race and partly as the consequence of an expanding population. The choice of policies was seen as between 'territorial policy or a colonial and commercial policy'.[33] The former meant the acquisition of new soil, and the latter an attempt to achieve a balance between resources and population through investment and trade abroad, together with control over markets and raw materials through colonies. This last he rejected on ideological grounds as favouring the Jewish international conspiracy and weakening the race, but he also urged the pragmatic ground that pursuing it would bring about the opposition of that quasi-European imperial power, England. No conflict of interests could occur, he argued, if Germany pursued a 'territorial' policy in Europe whilst abstaining from challenging British interests abroad. The restoration of the ex-German colonies, whilst desirable, was not central to this 'territorial' policy.[34]

But which direction should this 'healthy European land policy' take? Hitler answered this by saying, 'If we speak of soil in Europe today, we can primarily have in mind only Russia and her vassal states'.[35] True, France was a major opponent of Germany, but, as he argued,

> Much as all of us today recognise the necessity of a reckoning with France, it would remain ineffectual in the long run if it represented the whole of our aim in foreign policy. It can and will achieve meaning only if it offers the rear cover for an enlargement of our people's living space in Europe. For it is not in colonial acquisitions that we must see the solution of this problem but exclusively in the acquisition of a territory for settlement which will enhance the area of the mother country and hence will not only keep the new settlers in the most intimate community with the land of their origin, but secure for the total area those advantages which lie in its unified magnitude.[36]

The racial purity of this newly acquired area was to be secured by 'specially constituted racial commissions' that would issue settlement permits to intending colonists.

So the primary aim for Germany was to secure living-space at the expense of Russia and the neighbouring Eastern states. Although a war with France was postulated, the purpose of such a war was to secure Germany's rear while achieving her objectives in the East. Britain was to be an ally or at the least neutralized through a studious avoidance of any clash of interests. The new empire was to be gradually assimilated within the racial state. Whatever the other aims — the reversal of the Versailles Treaty, the restoration of the 'lost territories', an *anschluss,* rearmament, and all short-term objectives — these were but pre-conditions for the realization of the destiny of the German racial state in the creation of a European empire. And as Hitler explicitly argued, this could only be achieved through force.

> Our task, the mission of the National—Socialist movement, is to bring our own people to such political insight that they will not see their goal for the future in the breath-taking sensation of a new Alexander's conquest but in the industrious work of the German plough *to which the sword need only give soil* [my italics].[37]

Diplomacy was useful in providing the greatest chance of success in war when it became necessary. But diplomacy could not replace war, for this was of eugenic necessity for the race. This argument was stressed throughout the two volumes of *Mein Kampf* published in 1925 and 1926, and emerges clearly out of the rambling and convoluted rhetoric. In this phase of Hitler's reasoning, as he himself pointed out, 'It is not the task of a theoretician to determine the varying degrees in which a cause can be realised, but to establish the cause as such: that is to say: he must concern himself less with the road than with the goal.'[38]

When Hitler came to power in 1933 he was primarily concerned with the problem of keeping it. This preoccupation, together with the fulfilment of a programme of rearmament and the destruction of the Versailles Treaty, precluded an expansionist policy. Nor could he indulge himself in urging its importance without alarming neighbouring countries. The complexity of the diplomatic scene is beyond this study, but one element in it — the attempt at wooing England — did reflect one argument at least in *Mein Kampf.*[39] But Hitler's public image was certainly not one of a latter-day Genghis Khan bent on conquering Europe. He was at pains to suit his arguments to his audience and he had ample material arising out of the treatment of Germany by the victor powers to arouse his people, while at the same time pricking the consciences of the European states. Much of his case was based on the acknowledged injustices of the Versailles Treaty and on the blatant self-seeking of the victors.[40] What would not be conceded by his repentant opponents might perhaps be taken by force, but this possibility was always tempered by appeals to reason.

In his early speeches and press interviews Hitler based his case largely on the alleged iniquities of the post-war settlements. In spite of the injustice of the lost colonies, he argued that Germany would never go to war to recover them. 'We are', he said in May 1935 'by conviction and basic tenet, not only non-Imperialistic but anti-Imperialistic. Just as we wish not to be assimilated so we do not wish to assimilate others.'[41] As late as March 1936 he asserted in an interview that 'In Europe we have no territorial claims to put forward'.[42] Justice required that the lost colonies be returned and that the German people had adequate living-space, but this could only be achieved through some indefinite process of negotiation.

But the moderate tone of this argument changed by 1937. In November of that year Hitler said in a speech,

> Today we are faced with new tasks, for the living space of our people is too narrow. The world seeks to evade the examination of these problems and the answering of these questions. But that it will not be able to do. One day the world will have to pay attention to our demands. I do not for one second doubt that just as we have been able to raise up the nation at home, so too, abroad we shall secure the same vital rights as other peoples.[43]

From this point on his tone became increasingly strident. The period of domestic consolidation was over. Yet he was at pains to insist in his public utterances that he wanted nothing that had not been German. In the middle of the Czech crisis in September 1938 he insisted that Germany had no 'further territorial problem in Europe'.[44] 'We want no Czechs', he said. All he wanted was the right to self-determination on the part of the Sudeten Germans and the return of Germany's lost colonies. Nevertheless, the colonial question had become central to his foreign policy and it was justified in terms of the necessity of living-space for the German people. Its limits were not defined and there was no indication, other than his insistence that Germany would make no more territorial demands in Europe, about exactly what constituted a *German* living-space. And this promise was broken in March 1939 with the occupation of Prague. It became clear that Hitler sought a fundamental revision of the political and territorial status quo in Europe and that he was prepared to resort to force if he could not achieve this through negotiation. His object in seeking this change was not the revision of the unjust treaties, or the creation of a Germany that united all the Germans, but the acquisition of an empire. His colonies were to be in Europe.

To that element whose cooperation was crucial to the realization of his aims — the army — Hitler was less diplomatic. His programme of rearmament was popular with the military and his abandonment of revolution or what the generals took to be revolution, with the purging of the SA, assuaged their fears. Between 1934 and 1938 Hitler had achieved an almost universal popularity in Germany. But having created a strong army, to what end? The difficulty for Hitler was that while he had no intention of allowing any element, political or military, to be involved in his policy-making, he needed not merely the cooperation of the army but its direct involvement in the execution of his plans. Hence the generals had to be persuaded, or at least given some hint of the direction his policy was taking, if they were to be obedient. A loose indication of the 'goal' was insufficient for them. But neither could they be closely informed as to his diplomacy for fear that they would either seek to check it or inform his opponents. Hitler's ambivalent relation to his generals was never so clear as in his treatment of them over this period. He needed them but could not trust them. Again it is beyond this study to go more deeply into this question, but this point is important in interpreting the conferences with them in which Hitler stated his aims.

Again it is important to stress that we are dealing with aims and not intentions. Hitler's immediate concerns in the four conferences that will be considered here[45] were related to his diplomacy. He wanted agreement from his generals but not participation in decision-making. So in a sense they were exercises in persuasion. But at the same time they provide evidence of his aims in so far as they are consistent with his earlier statements. He was in effect saying what he wanted, not necessarily what was realizable at the time. Perhaps the clearest statement of his long-term aim was made in the earliest of these conferences in November 1937. As reported, Hitler said: 'We live in a period of economic empires in which the tendency to colonize again approaches the condition which originally motivated colonization. In Japan and Italy economic motives are the basis of their will to expand, the economic need will also drive Germany to it.'[46] But the direction of expansion was not to be outside Europe; it was in 'the raw material producing territory in Europe directly adjoining the Reich . . .'.[47] The central argument used by Hitler was economic necessity, especially the need for food. Germany could not become self-sufficient in food, 'Consequently, autarchy becomes impossible'.[48] A thoroughgoing policy of autarky within the boundaries of Germany's existing resources was not possible given the demands being made on the German economy by rearmament. Hence, for the generals, expansion was dictated by economic necessity. The racialist argument was underplayed. Similarly, the principal target — the Soviet Union — was ignored. It was Czechslovakia and Austria that were to be the immediate targets. But living-space was the objective. 'The German future is therefore dependent exclusively on the solution of the need for living space.'[49] This particular conference took place before the series of crises that preceded the outbreak of war. Hitler concerned himself in his speech with speculations about the possible attitudes of Britain, France and Poland in the event of a German attack on Austria and Czechoslovakia. But the significant part of this speech was a reference to the objective of securing a common frontier with Hungary through the conquest of Czechoslovakia.[50] This entailed rather more than the recovery of 'lost territories'. How it was to be achieved was problematic. Hitler argued that his chief opponents, Britain and France, would not intervene, the former because this move would not challenge any major British interest, and the latter because of her consequent isolation. Hence any conflict over these targets would be limited. The generals were sceptical, but it was reassurance on this point that Hitler was hoping to achieve. No one questioned the objective itself, which unlike the *anschluss*, entailed the absorption of non-German territory and non-German people; it was not merely the Sudetenland that Hitler wanted. In the event, the Munich settlement ceded Hitler's apparent demands, but the occupation of Prague and the establishment of a protectorate over Bohemia and Moravia in March 1939 showed that Hitler's real objective was what he had stated at this conference. And he achieved it in stages and through diplomacy and not by war. At the time of the conference, however, the conditions for the realization of this aim could not be foreseen or stated fully. Only the aim itself was clear. But the army was necessary, for only the threat of war could achieve diplomatic success.

In the Obersalzburg speech of 22 August 1939, Hitler took the opportunity of stating his aims concerning Poland. This time he had the gains of the *anschluss* and of Czechoslovakia behind him. Again, contrary to his public pronouncements and the limited nature of his demands on Poland, Hitler revealed that his objective was not simply the removal of the anomaly of Danzig and the Corridor, but the conquest of Poland.[51] Again he was at pains to reassure the generals that 'Now Poland is in the position in which I wanted her'.[52] He was master of the political situation and he had succeeded in nullifying any attempt to support Poland. The master-stroke of the Molotov—Ribbentrop Pact not only prevented any military assistance from reaching Poland but also provided Germany with food and raw materials and so removed the blockade weapon from Britain. There might be war this time but it would be a war that Germany could win. He did not think, with the odds against them, that Britain and France would carry out their threat to the extent of fighting a major war in the West once Poland had been eliminated. It should also be noted that the pact with Russia provided for the partition of Poland and the acquisition by Germany of non-German territory and non-German people.

After his victory Hitler summed up at a conference on 23 November 1939.[53] He had defeated Poland and the allies had been proved impotent to prevent this. However, there remained the problem of an undefeated and hostile France, to say nothing of Britain. He had long said that France was a constant threat to Germany and had to be dealt with if Germany was to succeed in her objectives. His diplomacy had enabled him to strike at Poland successfully but he still had to tackle the West. He gave his generals a recital of his programme; after rearmament and the building of fortifications in the West he succeeded in achieving the *anschluss* with Austria.

> . . . the next step was Bohemia, Moravia and Poland. This step was also not possible to accomplish in one campaign. First of all the western fortifications had to be finished . . . It was clear to me that from the first moment that I could not be satisfied with the Sudetenland German territory. That was only a partial solution. The decision to march into Bohemia was made. Then followed the erection of the Protectorate and with that the basis for the action against Poland was laid, but I wasn't clear at that time whether I should start first against the east and then in the west or vice versa . . . Under pressure the decision came to fight with Poland first.[54]

And the purpose of all this? 'My goal was to create a logical relation between the number of people and the space for them to live in.'[55]

In turning to the pact with the Soviet Union, Hitler argued

> Pacts are however, only held as long as they serve the purpose. Russia will hold herself to it only so long as Russia considers it to be to her benefit. Now Russia has far reaching goals, above all the strengthening of her position in the Baltic. We can oppose Russia only when we are free in the West.[56]

He went on to assure his generals of the military superiority of the German forces: 'Now there is a relationship of forces which can never be more propitious, but which can only deteriorate for us.'[57] His opponents were themselves rapidly rearming and the French forces in particular were formidable. He therefore decided, he told his generals,[58] to attack France and England 'at the most favourable and quickest moment' and this entailed the invasion of Belgium and Holland. He wanted neither a negotiated peace nor a defensive war, for his objectives were not only the defeat of the enemy forces but the seizure of territory that had to be won by force of arms.

After the defeat of France and the withdrawal of British forces from Europe, Hitler was in a position to take decisions that most directly reflected his aims. Before coming to the question of his reasons for invading the Soviet Union, I want to look at his statements of aims expressed during the phase of military success and in the time of defeat. In the former case, Hitler initially was able to implement a programme of action in the conquered territories that directly reflected his aims. The deterioration of the military situation, however, meant that the demands of the war were paramount. As he said himself in 1942, 'The essential thing for the moment is to conquer. After that everything will simply be a matter of organisation'.[59] And so increasingly Hitler confined himself to making statements of aim rather than directing a colonial and imperial policy.

Running through Hitler's conversations with his staff over the years 1941-2 was the constant theme of empire. The space between the Reich and the Urals was to be a German India, exploited and ruled over by Germans.[60] Germans were to settle this area much as the pioneer fringe of the West was settled by Americans. Indeed, Hitler compared the non-Aryan population of this vast area to 'Redskins',[61] drawing perhaps on his readings of Karl May. The German empire proper was to consist of the Baltic states, the South Ukraine, including the Crimea, the Cracow and Lublin districts of Poland as well as the Wartheburg.[62] Within ten years he envisaged ten million Germans settled in the East. Moscow and Leningrad were to be erased.[63] The non-Aryan inhabitants were to be treated as slaves working for their German masters. No industrial production was to be permitted.[64] Only agriculture and extractive industries were to be exploited for the benefit of the German economy. Occupied states such as Norway, Denmark, Holland and Belgium were to be incorporated within this empire and their peoples encouraged to settle in the Baltic states and the East.[65] Their Aryan blood entitled them to this privilege and the hard conditions of pioneer settlement would refine its qualities. Allies such as Romania and Finland were to be incorporated into the New Order[66] but to confine themselves to the production of food and raw materials. The neutrals, Sweden and Switzerland, were to lose their autonomy as states.[67] France, the principal defeated enemy, was to lose Alsace, Lorraine and Burgundy,[68] as well as other territory on the Mediterranean littoral to Spain and Italy.[69] Her North Atlantic coast was to be permanently occupied by German forces.[70] Britain was to enjoy her imperial possessions unimpeded, although the former German colonies were to be returned.

The end in view was the winning of 'a continent to rule'. As he put it, 'Europe is not a geographical entity; it is a racial entity.'[71] Conquering it would provide a genuine independence for the new German state. 'There is no country that can be to a larger extent autarchic than Europe will be. That's our most urgent task for the post-war period to build up the autarchic economy.'[72] Hitler gloated over the prospects before him:

> We have the richest and best colonies in the world; in the first place they are next door to us, in the second they are inhabited by healthy peoples, and in the third they produce an abundance in everything we require except coffee . . . Our gains in the West may add a measure of charm to

our possessions and constitute a contribution to our general security but our Eastern conquests are infinitely more precious for they are the foundations of our very existence.[73]

What was the justification for this programme of imperialism? It was the argument that 'According to the laws of nature the soil belongs to him who conquers it. The fact of having children who want to live, the fact that our people is bursting out of its cramped frontiers. These justify all our claims to the Eastern spaces.'[74] Here is the same emphasis on the pressures of population growth, the need for expansion, the appeal to social Darwinism, the same notion of world anarchy, and the same direction for living-space as he expressed in *Mein Kampf.* After the years of political impotence, followed by the years of manoeuvring, Hitler at last found himself on the point of fulfilling his ideas of German destiny. Germany was not to be satisfied with relatively minor revisions of the territorial settlements made after the last great war. The conquests of Europe were not enough, for his ultimate aim was the creation of a huge empire at the expense of Russia.

Even in this moment of exultation Hitler realized that the lightning victory he had hoped for in his invasion of the Soviet Union had eluded him. The war was to be one of prolonged struggle. Although he expressed no doubts as to its result, his extrication of his forces from near disaster in 1942 and a reversion to defensive warfare designed to hold ground and to maintain control over resources compelled him to concentrate on short-term aims. The empire in the East had to be postponed until the final victory was achieved. War needs dominated his policies.

In the hour of defeat, when only a miracle could save Germany,[75] Hitler summed up his aims. The *raison d'être* of national-socialism was the destruction of Bolshevism and this entailed the 'conquest of wide spaces in the East'.

It is eastwards only and always eastwards that the veins of our race must expand. It is the direction which Nature herself has decreed for the expansion of the German peoples. The rigorous climate with which the East confronts them allows them to retain their qualities as hardy and virile men; and the vivid contrasts they find there help to keep fresh their love and longing for their own country.[76]

Although he would not survive the defeat, nevertheless he wanted to leave this advice behind for a future leader. In his view the only proper empire was one contiguous to the territory of the conqueror. Not for him the drive to expand in the world at large following the examples set by the great European empires in Latin America, Africa and the Far East. Such a drive, he argued, enfeebled those states that had achieved vast colonial possessions. They had the resources only to loot and not to develop and this contributed to the eventual weakening of their hold.[77]

He was equally consistent in his belief that the world was inherently anarchic. Only the fittest survived, and the major conditions of being fit were an economic independence won through domination of sources of food, raw materials and markets, and racial purity. In his view his greatest and lasting contribution to Europe was ridding it of its Jews.[78] Although he had failed in all else he had not failed in this, and it was his legacy to Germany and to Europe. In this thought lay hope even in defeat, for here lay the seeds of a future German regeneration. It was a basic condition for the realization of national destiny. All else depended on this. His failure he considered to be due to lack of time in that he attempted too many objectives and had to divert resources from one task to another. Time was against him.[79]

In terms of what evidence we have of Hitler's thought, from its first expressions when he was winning power to his final eclipse, there is a remarkable consistency in his aims. He is clear as to what he wants to do.[80] The conditions under which this might be realized had to be treated pragmatically. It was not easy to create them. And so there is this tension between opportunism and planning in Hitler's policies. Nothing could be done without a viable army. But this again depended upon his opponents and their rearmament programmes. If he was to use force in order to obtain his objectives it had to be timed accordingly. And this consideration was paramount in 1941 when he realized that the Soviet Union was rearming rapidly while he had not succeeded in either defeating Britain or bringing her to the conference table.

I want to turn now to Hitler's decision to invade the Soviet Union and to try to place this within the context of his declaration that 'all our aspirations were *in reality* [my italics] orientated eastwards'.[81] I want to follow this by a study of practice, that is of evidence of Hitler's intentions in situations where action replaced general statements of aim. In what sense was he putting his aims into practice? My thesis is that, whatever the ostensible reasons given for this particular decision, the fundamental one was to acquire an Eastern empire for the Reich. In essence the argument makes a distinction between the context of reasoning that is ideological in character, concerned with aims and aspirations rather than with conditions and circumstances deemed necessary for their fulfilment, and reasoning directly connected to the object in view and with conditions for success in achieving it. An explanation of action is in my view inadequate if it does not include both forms of reasoning.

The point was made earlier that aims in general do not stipulate any precise link between their satisfaction and the necessary conditions. They are simply desirable states of affairs. Hence any link between theory and practice in terms of the realization of aims depends upon a clear relationship between intentions and action, which in turn relates the intentions to the larger aim and the actions to the creation or appreciation of the conditions for fulfilment. For Hitler it was pointed out that this possibility arose only after the elimination of those obstacles to his larger ambitions posed by internal conditions in Germany and by the opposition of other states. After the defeat of France and the isolation of Britain, Hitler was free to consider his next step without the immediate constraints of opposition. We need not consider all that had happened since 1938 — that is, from the *anschluss* or even earlier — as a progressive and inevitable fulfilment of a grand design. All that is being said here is that where choices between alternative courses of action are perceived by an agent, the actual choice will reflect what is deemed the most desirable of possible ends. And in this case ideological considerations enter intimately into choice. There is, I argue, a consistency in Hitler's choices that reflects a continuity of belief. The apparent shifts and vacillations in policy and in policy statements are reflections not of infirmity of purpose but of the difficulty of estimating probable reactions on the part of his opponents. More immediate factors were paramount in this sort of calculation.

It is perhaps true that appetite grows with feeding, and new possibilities had certainly been created with German success in diplomacy and war. Hitler had staked a good deal on success. The weapon of *blitzkrieg* was chosen for a variety of reasons, including domestic politics and their uncertainty as well as the dangers inherent in a total war of resources. If he won, his victory was complete; but if he lost, so was his defeat. And Germany lacked the resources for a prolonged war. The point here is that Hitler's calculations and his military strategy indicate that he was fighting *political* wars designed to achieve political ends. They were intended to be wars in the Clausewitzian sense of policy by other means. In short, war was a means to an end and the end was the creation of an empire. It could not have been achieved otherwise.

> War becomes inevitable if for no other reason that in order to avoid it we should have been compelled to betray the fundamental interests of the German people. As far as our people are concerned we could not and would not be content with the mere semblance of independence.[82]

In establishing the connection between ideology and action what is necessary is to show that the possibilities considered to be both viable and worthy of fulfilment were consistent with the ideological aims expressed earlier. Were Hitler's decisions in his moment of triumph consistent with an ideological commitment? The period between June 1940 and June 1941 marked a time of relative freedom of choice. There were a number of things he could do, and indeed he contemplated a number of courses of action. The immediate problem was that of an undefeated Britain. Britain was impotent to take action against Germany, but this would not of course hold for the future.

After the defeat of France, Hitler made a peace overture as he had done after the defeat of Poland.[83] It was summarily rejected. His forbearance at Dunkirk was taken to be either a mistake or a miracle and not a deliberate act of restraint in seeking to prepare grounds for negotiation.[84] Hitler certainly expressed his desire to make peace with Britain but it is clear that he did not think that he had to pay too high a price for this. He did not believe that his contemplated course of action directly challenged British interests. But what *was* his projected course of action? In this period Hitler ordered a plan of invasion and embarked on the series of air attacks known as the Battle of Britain.[85] Was his purpose one of invasion?

Hitler's proposed peace terms included an offer to 'guarantee' the British empire. By this it would appear that he voluntarily renounced any designs on it. The return of Germany's former colonies and the acceptance of Italian aspirations in the Mediterranean were the only major concessions demanded of Britain.[86] This was to accept the paramountcy of Germany in Europe but at the same time provided for a recognition of the equivalent for Britain overseas. With it went the implication that Britain, Italy, and perhaps Japan, could satisfy their imperial aspirations at the expense of France. If this is taken seriously then it indicates that Hitler saw no challenge to Britain in what he wanted. He could not make this explicit however, if his ultimate target was to be the Soviet Union. To do this would not only reveal his hand but it might provide an opportunity for Britain to escape from her isolation and ally with the USSR. Given the negative response of the British government, this is academic. However, if we assume that Hitler wished merely to neutralize Britain in order not to be constrained in pursuing his objectives elsewhere, we can view operation Sea-Lion and the Battle of Britain in a different light. Their purpose was two-fold: they were designed to persuade Britain to negotiate, preferably by toppling the Churchill government, and to eliminate the only threat that Britain could make — the use of her airforce. Hitler did not intend to invade Britain. He had something else in mind.[87]

What of other constraining factors in this period? It is equally true that the United States remained a potential belligerent and was actively engaged in supplying Britain in order to keep her in the war.

Here Hitler reasoned that the threat posed by Japan's imperial ambitions and policies kept the USA in check. No active involvement in a European war was likely while Japan threatened the Pacific. It was part of Hitler's policy to direct Japan away from mainland Asia into blue water.[88] He was also well aware of the anti-war feeling in the United States and of Roosevelt's difficulties during the electoral campaign of 1940. Roosevelt sought to appease fears of an American intervention. The visit of Sumner Welles in early March 1940, whatever its object, was not a success, but it persuaded Hitler that the United States had no interest in intervening in Europe. Like Britain, the United States was isolated. In any case, the state of American rearmament and the logistical problems involved in waging war in Europe precluded any immediate challenge. And the *blitzkrieg* was designed to preclude any future challenge; by the time the United States, or Britain, were in a position to intervene it would be too late.

What of the Soviet Union? The Molotov-Ribbentrop Pact of 1939 stipulated Soviet neutrality in the event of German hostilities with other countries, changes in the frontiers of Eastern Europe, including the partition of Poland, and economic exchanges between the two signatories in which raw materials and food from the Soviet Union were bartered for manufactured goods from Germany.[89] Hitler's subsequent victory over Poland and his expansion into Scandinavia together with Stalin's defeat of Finland and his occupation of his share of Poland brought them directly into contact. Whatever Stalin's expectations of German involvement in a prolonged struggle paralleling the First World War, Hitler's *blitzkrieg* against France presaged a new settlement. Negotiations began after the defeat of France over territorial divisions in the Baltic, Eastern Europe and the Balkans and culminated in Molotov's visit to Berlin in November 1940.[90] The price for Soviet neutrality had risen to include not merely the Baltic states and the demands on Finland and Polish territory that had been agreed, but also the annexation of Bessarabia and North Bukovina from Romania, bases in Bulgaria and Turkey and a sphere of influence in the Middle East. Hitler was not the only one with imperial ambitions. At the same time the USSR was preparing for the possibility of war and was rearming rapidly. As the only major power left undefeated on the continent, any lasting agreement would have to be based on some measure of acceptance of Soviet demands for territory and influence. The alternative was to remove the necessity to compromise by defeating her.

Yet Germany was dependent upon the Soviet Union. The pact and the subsequent economic agreement of February 1940[91] provided for an exchange of food supplies and raw materials for manufactured goods and coal from Germany. These deliveries from the Soviet

Union were 'a very substantial support of the German war economy'.[92] The Four Year Plan had failed to create autarkic conditions; the cost of substitutes and the enhanced demand on domestic resources created by rearmament had underlined German dependence on external supply. This was particularly the case in food, for by September 1940 the national food reserve had been used up leaving no grain reserve for the following year. A guaranteed supply of food was essential.[93] Continued dependence on the Soviet Union, however, meant accepting the political concomitant of Stalin's territorial aspirations. And this meant that the necessary conditions for the survival of the Reich through autarky and expansionism either had to be abandoned or sought through expansion to the West or outside Europe. The former course was contrary to Hitler's ideological beliefs, while the latter would bring him into direct conflict with the major maritime powers, Britain, the United States, Japan and, at that time, Italy. He would have to build and maintain a large navy designed for quite another purpose from the existing navy. It would also mean sharing power in Europe with the Soviet Union and accepting a permanent inhibition on his policies imposed by the uncertainty of an alliance with a growing military power with territorial ambitions and contiguous with Germany. He could never be certain that the USSR would not intervene while he was preoccupied abroad.

At the same time, the fact that Britain had not sued for peace in spite of the defeat of her continental ally and the eclipse of her forces, meant that Hitler had not succeeded in getting a political endorsement of his military victories. So long as the prospect of a prolonged war existed, then the problem of supply remained acute and his dependency increased. The Reich was not prepared for such a war. The notion that Churchill would play the part of a latter-day Pitt was certainly in Hitler's mind and the solution to the problem was seen as removing the one hope that Britain entertained − a Soviet intervention against Germany. Such an intervention was not immediately likely, but there were disturbing signs that Hitler noted − increased demands for territory and bases, and rapid rearmament − that made this a possibility for the future. At the very least the Soviet bargaining position would be strengthened by a war capacity and by continued British hostility. Time was running out.

So Hitler's decision to invade the Soviet Union can be seen as a decision to fight a preventive war, but a preventive war in the sense that the Soviet Union was an obstacle to his ambitions. Hitler could not sustain a major war capacity without Soviet supplies, but a dependence on them reduced the political value of such a capacity, since it could not be used either as a threat or as an enforcement of his political aims. Defeat of the Soviet Union would not only remove the obligation to maintain a major war footing but also provide the necessary resources to match anything his remaining opponents could put up. Britain would have to come to terms. Continuing the agreements with the Soviet Union meant in the short term reducing the scale of weapons production in order to meet Soviet orders. He had no wish to strengthen the Soviet Union while at the same time weakening his own war effort. By September 1940 Germany was delivering only half of her quotas to the Soviet Union, which was threatening to suspend deliveries — a threat that both Germany's dependence and her weakness in the event of future threats. The solution was to cut the Gordian knot and remove the Soviet Union as a potential opponent. Such a decision also permitted the realization of his long-term objectives — autarky, living-space and the racial purification of the Reich. The question of timing and of political contingencies, which had so perplexed him after the fall of France, and the fulfilment of his ideological programme came together in the autumn of 1940.

Let us look more closely at what evidence we have of Hitler's reasoning. Hitler himself said that he took the decision to invade the USSR in August[94] 1940. Operation Sea-Lion was postponed indefinitely on 17 September and it had been accepted that with the failure to destroy the Royal Air Force, Britain, while incapable of any offensive, was nevertheless capable of defending herself against an invasion. Directive No. 1 for Operation Barbarossa was issued on 18 December 1940 and the date set for the invasion was in May 1941. Between August and December detailed planning for Barbarossa was undertaken and Soviet complaints in September at the German failure to deliver her appointed quotas produced a memorandum that referred to the directive made by Goering banning the delivery of materials 'which directly or indirectly would strengthen the Russian war potential'.[95] Confirmation of the timing of the decision to invade is found in testimony made in interrogations of German generals. Von Brauschitz said the first hints of this came in a conversation with Hitler in August,[96] while a specific directive to prepare for this contingency came in the following month. Koestring, the military attaché in Moscow, who had an important role to play in assessing Russian military capacity and monitoring reactions to German policy, testified that early in August he was instructed by Halder to prepare for operations against Russia.[97] Clearly only a few were so involved in the early stages of preparation and it was not until early 1941 that the possibility of a war with the USSR was more generally released. According to Goering in his unsworn testimony it was in November that the final decision was taken.[98] This he argued was the consequence of Molotov's demands made in the negotiations of that month for Finland, Bessarabia, North Bukovina and for spheres of influence in the Balkans and bases at the exit of the Baltic. Rosenberg, too, confirmed this in his testimony:[99] it was the Soviet occupation of these two Romanian provinces that brought Hitler to conceive of the USSR as an expansionist state. The notion of preventive war was put forward as a reason for the invasion by the generals. Brauschitz, Manstein, Keitel, as well as Goering,[100] all argued that the growing strength of the Soviet Union and the increasing scale of its demands, together with the problem of an undefeated and hostile Britain, meant that war with the USSR was necessary in order to safeguard German security. Goering referred to Soviet attempts to exert economic pressure on Germany in the February and September negotiations over the economic provisions of the Molotov—Ribbentrop Pact. Hitler seemed to confirm this when he argued in the autumn of 1941 that 'I had to foresee that Stalin might pass over to the attack in the course of 1941. It was therefore necessary to get started without delay in order not to be forestalled and that wasn't possible before June'.[101] He expressed his feelings of alarm at the rapid pace of Soviet rearmament.

So from this we have a picture of a situation in which Hitler was faced with an obstinate, if impotent, opponent in the form of Britain, and a neutral neighbour that seemed to be not only increasing its territorial demands, but was developing a capacity to enforce them if need be. In his so-called last testament in the hour of defeat Hitler went over his reasons for going to war with Russia.[102] He confirmed Goering's later testimony that Molotov's visit in November clinched matters. He cites as reasons those given by his associates and generals — the refusal of Britain to treat with him, the failure of the air offensive to achieve its objectives, the dangerous dependence on the Soviet Union for raw materials and food necessary to the war effort, the rapid rearmament of the Soviet Union, and so on. A prolonged defensive war was not possible for Germany, given her relatively scarce resources, and such a war was inevitable if he accepted the position as it stood after his failure to reach an agreement with Britain. As he said, in that event, 'Time, and it is always Time you notice, would have been increasingly against us'.[103] So he decided, he said, to take the initiative and to 'settle accounts with Russia as soon as fair weather permitted'.[104]

On the face of it we have in this reasoning nothing that is peculiarly ideological. Hitler decided on war with Russia for reasons that appear pre-eminently practical. Such reasoning, if we can show it to be based on adequate evidence — and in this case this is problematic: Hitler in giving his reasons was either persuading his generals, concealing his actions, justifying his failures or giving *ex post facto* a gloss on his performance as Führer of the German people for posterity; and his generals or associates were seeking to avoid complicity in order to save their necks — appears to explain why Hitler invaded the Soviet Union. But it begs the larger question of why Hitler believed it impossible to come to an accommodation with the Soviet Union. Why was the Soviet Union the principal target? The reasons given above are reasons of expediency and unconcerned with questions of a larger purpose. Timing and those problems concerned with means are of the essence and not the ends themselves. The 'logic of the situation' was a limited logic.

The war that Hitler planned was to be of short duration but its end was to leave the Soviet Union as prostrate in defeat as France in the previous year. What he intended to do in that event was largely concealed. As he put it after his invasion,

> Now it was essential that we did not publicize our aims before the world: also there was no need for that, but the main thing was that we ourselves knew what we wanted. By no means should we render our task more difficult by making superfluous declarations. Such declarations were superfluous because we could do everything wherever we had the power and what was beyond our power we would not be able to do anyway.[105]

As in the case of the Czechs and the Poles, the inhabitants of the conquered territories were to be left in ignorance as to their ultimate fate. But there is evidence that allows us to offer a more complete explanation of the reasons for the invasion of the Soviet Union. It falls into two categories: the evidence discussed earlier in the form of Hitler's statements of aims expressed within his ideological framework and the evidence in the form of decisions and actions. That the war was not simply designed to eliminate a rival in European power politics is shown by Hitler's concern for achieving certain ideological ends in the event of success. The war itself, of course, was a reflection of Hitler's beliefs in the primary of force and the anarchic nature of inter-state relations. In the struggle of all against all, diplomacy was merely a cloak for the creation and the deployment of the means of violence in order to obtain national supremacy. War was a fact of life and, through preparing for war and actually fighting, the nation achieved strength. So in a sense his wars were ideological in their very nature. This of course does not explain any particular use of violence but it explains his readiness to go to war. Although intended to achieve political, and so limited, ends, his wars were in reality total, for he presupposed permanent struggle. No victory could be final given that view. Even the condition of world hegemony that Hitler glimpsed as within his grasp was conceived as unhealthy for the future of the Aryan race. Wars were necessary in order to maintain the conditions for racial purity and, from this, racial supremacy.

We couldn't require a better activity on nature's part than that which consists in deciding the supremacy of one creature over another by means of a constant struggle.

As a general principle I think that a peace which lasts more than twenty-five years is harmful to a nation. Peoples, like individuals, sometimes need regenerating by a little blood-letting.[106]

What then was the purpose of his war with the Soviet Union, if we seek to qualify the contingent reasons given by Hitler and his associates? Hess stated in his interview with the Duke of Hamilton on 11 May 1941 that 'Germany had certain demands to make of Russia which would have to be satisfied either by negotiation or as the result of a war'.[107] He knew at the time that it was the latter that was in train. Here we have a direct hint that Hitler was not concerned with fighting a preventive war but had objectives over and above this. As in the case of France, the elimination of an enemy's capacity to resist also allowed the satisfaction of aspirations other than the removal of a rival. The Vichy government was never told what Germany sought from France once the war was over.[108] Hess had on his own account made three attempts to get to England, the first being in December, the month in which Barbarossa was made operational, and we can assume that plans for the treatment of Russia were formulated at the same time as the military programme. In April, Rosenberg was made Reichskommissar for the Central Control of Questions associated with the East European Region, and in the same month Goering, in his capacity as director of the Four Year Plan, was placed in charge of the integration into the German economy of the areas about to be conquered.

This programme of conquest and integration closely follows that adopted in Czechoslovakia and earlier in Poland. Hitler's first seizure of non-German territory came with the creation of the protectorate of Bohemia and Moravia in March 1939.[109] Although it was 'incorporated in the territory of the Greater German Reich' it was decreed both 'autonomous and self governing'. With the advent of war, the pretence of autonomy was dropped and after the fall of France it was decided to colonize the protectorate, eliminating half of the population and 'germanizing' the rest.[110] Poland's case was rather different in that not even the pretence of autonomy was made. Hitler annexed the four western provinces directly into the Reich. The remainder was placed under a German civil administration and was known as the Gouvernement-General. This latter area was designed to be the dumping ground for the Jews and for those Poles considered to be incapable of being 'germanized'. It was also to receive German colonization with a double transfer of one million Germans to be settled while four million Poles were to be transferred to the Reich.[111]

Thus before the invasion of the USSR we have in the treatment of these two countries what a Nuremberg prosecutor termed the 'testing ground' for the expansionist policy.[112] Part of the conquered territory was to be assimilated into a Greater German Reich. The justification for this, apart from the rights of conquest, was that much of the area was 'historically' German. And this argument was also made for the assimilation of the Baltic and Eastern territories. But this 'historical' right was itself based on the social-Darwinian view of the state that was part of Hitler's vision of history. The boundaries of the state were effectively the boundaries of its conquests. The racial element of the ideology appeared in the treatment of the indigenous inhabitants. Those people who for racial reasons were unable to be 'germanized' were to be transferred beyond the frontiers of the racial state. Those in the limbo of the non-racial hinterland who were deemed to be suitable material for 'germanization' were to be transferred into a totally Germanic environment and subjected to an indoctrination and eugenic programme designed to turn them or their offspring into Aryans. The territory beyond the racial state was to be systematically exploited and colonized. The colonies had a three-fold purpose: they were to be a proving ground for the race, toughening the stock by subjecting it to pioneer conditions; they were to be a means of controlling the 'natives', much as, Hitler argued, was the case in India where a small number of expatriates dominated a very much larger number of indigenous peoples;[113] and they were to be a means of extending the boundaries of the racial state itself, pushing the pioneer fringe further and further East as the colonies enlarged and expanded. There was a clear precedent here too in the settlement of the Americas.

This was the broad programme and it was deemed appropriate only to the Eastern territories. The thrust of colonization was to be in the East, which was wholly consistent with aims stated long before at a time when the conditions for their realization were unknown. But the chief condition *was* known and stated. Whatever the nature of the opposition, both domestic and international, any territorial expansion to the East entailed the elimination of the Soviet Union. Nowhere else could this programme of racial hegemony and imperial expansion be realized.

Anomalies, as, for example, in his differential treatment of the Czechs and the Poles, can be explained by the belief that the former were more capable of germanization than the latter,[114] and by the existence of an industrial base in Czechoslovakia necessary for the German war effort. The Czechs were racially different from the Slavs in Hitler's view, and so the necessity for island colonies did not exist. Similarly, Southern Europe was seen more as an area of assimilation or of association than of colonization. The geo-politics of this area, containing as it did a number of states useful as allies or with racially acceptable inhabitants, and with the existence of Italian aspirations and involvement, made for a more complex situation than was the case for Eastern Europe. Here again, Hitler wove both questions of expedience and ideological predeliction together into a practical programme.

This was also the case in his demands for the return of the former German colonies. This can be seen as an attempt to get Britain to agree to his other demands and to urge the 'legitimacy' of German colonial aspirations. His interest in colonies outside Europe was largely as bargaining counters or as bait for his allies. His chief European ally Italy, for example, was to be rewarded by French colonial territory and by taking Britain's place in the Mediterranean as the dominant power. This would take Italy out of direct competition with Germany and also place her in permanent competition with his enemies. He sought the same object with Spain, but France was more wary.

So in the realm of practice we have evidence of a clear programme of annexation, colonization and exploitation deemed necessary to the survival of a German racial state. In conjunction with this was a policy of racial purity that entailed the murder of millions of people deemed to be racially impure or in some way dangerous to the racial state. Only part of this programme was carried out. The exigencies of war dominated Hitler's policies and actions after his invasion of the Soviet Union failed to achieve the lightning victory he sought. And this abortive programme, successful only in the slaughter of defenceless people, was ideological in nature. If we ask the question what the series of wars conducted by Hitler was for, it was for this.

I have been concerned in this study with the role an ideology has in providing an explanation of political practice. In particular I have tried to relate an imperialist ideology to imperialism. An imperialist ideology — that of national—socialism — it was argued, provides the key to an understanding of Hitler's foreign policy. Adherents of the belief system were constrained by their beliefs to conceive of the external world as creating both an opportunity, and a necessity, for imperialist expansion. True there were other perceived constraints of a contingent and practical nature. But a study of the ideology allows us to make sense of or, as I would prefer to put it, *explain* the actual choices they made. They explain actions that on the face of it could be *described* or interpreted in a variety of ways.

The three principal elements of the ideology — race, social

Darwinism and autarky — together produced a programme of action designed to acquire living-space for the German people. Expansion was the only logical conclusion of the fusion of these elements into a coherent argument and this made it an imperialist ideology. Fundamentally the key concept was that of race, for the whole point of expansion was, as Hitler himself continually stressed, the survival not of the state or of the nation, but of the species. And it is this racial element that is the chief distinguishing mark of Hitler's ideology. His intention was to create a new type of political entity — a racial state with an empire. A genuine racial state once purged of its impurities was in a position to fulfil its destiny in the world and to assert its superiority over its racial inferiors, and over those states that had degenerated through miscegenation and impurity. It was this aspect of the ideology that made it unique as a political philosophy and that presented such a challenge to those other imperial powers bent on preserving the status quo. Nothing could alter a racial identity. No compromise could be sought as a permanent basis for inter-state relations, for any compromise challenged the very essence of the premise of racial superiority. Acting on it enabled its adherents to justify their crimes against humanity, for they could claim that they were more than merely human instruments, and deny the force of that judgement. Only nature was responsible for the racial types and racial divisions in the world. It was after all a *natural* hierarchy they were asserting.

> Peace can result only from a natural order. The condition of this order is that there is a hierarchy amongst nations. The most capable nations must necessarily take the lead. In this order the subordinate nations get the greater profit, being protected by the more capable nations.[115]

They only wanted their birthright. The imperialism they pursued was merely the reassertion of a natural order that had been corrupted by a conspiracy of the Jews. The other elements stemmed from this.

The struggle of all against all simply reflected nature. The world of politics was a eugenic testing ground in which, once free of the handicap of racial impurity, the superior race could assert itself. War was a natural state of affairs and indeed necessary if the race was to maintain its superiority. To ignore this reality and to subscribe to ideals of world peace and cooperation was to acquiesce in racial suicide. Naturally the Jews were promoters of this sort of internationalism. And so a racial state was a state armed, not merely for self-protection but for expansion.

The pursuit of autarky also followed from this, for no state could survive if it was enmeshed in a web of economic interdependence with other states. Again such a web was spun by Jews. But more important, a racial state had not only to be able to live off its own, it had also to have a military capacity sufficient to overcome opposition from other states. Its domestic resources thus had to cater both for a scale of living commensurate with its racial status, and for a war capacity superior to other states, alone or in combination. If they were not equal to this, then an extension of its living-space was a necessity. And so, given Germany's position *vis-à-vis* other states in the 1930s, a policy of imperial expansion was dictated.

War was inevitable. It was to be both a political instrument and a condition necessary for the purity of the race. Hitler believed that permanent struggle was the common lot of mankind and he approved of this as providing testing conditions for racial survival. Too much ease led to racial degeneracy. But he also believed in political wars, that is, wars fought with lesser rational objectives in mind, and within limits recognized by his opponents. Not for nothing was he a disciple of Clausewitz.[116] Given an initial superiority in armaments and speed of execution, Hitler believed that he could obtain political success through military victories. In this sense he prepared and fought for limited objectives that required recognition by his defeated enemies. He intended to change the European map by force and to create a European empire for Germany.

So, although Hitler believed that war was endemic in inter-state relations, he regarded his wars as imperialist wars in the tradition of the eighteenth and nineteenth centuries. They were designed to obtain concrete advantages for Germany — natural resources and territory. Few wars were wars of life and death for the states that fought them. Total war was only a theoretical possibility. The defeat of Germany in 1918 and the consequent loss of the gains of the Treaty of Brest-Litovsk was a political and not a military defeat. Even so, Germany was left intact as a state and was able to rise again. In creating a racial state Hitler believed that he had eliminated the chief cause of that defeat. No future stab in the back could occur.

But his naive assumption that *realpolitik* governed the reasoning of all statesmen, and his failure to understand the implications of weapons technology and the organization of the modern state for total war, blinded him to the nature of the opposition his policies aroused. To his chagrin the logical implications of his pact with the Soviet Union in 1939 were lost on the British and the French.[117] They persisted, contrary to all military and political logic, in challenging him over Poland. His demonstration that they were impotent brought no peace overtures. The defeat of France did not persuade Britain to withdraw from the war. His peace overtures, concessionary though they were, brought about no political solution. He was forced to invade the Soviet Union without resolving the issue with Britain. His hope that a lightning victory over Russia would bring about a political settlement was dashed in his failure to achieve that victory. Even then he was puzzled about why Britain persisted in continuing the struggle allied to a power whose interests were in direct conflict. The defeat of Germany could only mean the aggrandizement of the Soviet Union in Europe. His conclusion was that Churchill was not only an alcoholic and senile, but was governed by the Jews. But the reality was that the war had become total because it was German war capacity and not German intentions that was seen as the direct threat.

Like Clausewitz himself, Hitler was unable to prescribe the limits to violence between states, which alone made war rational. His opponents either did not understand, or refused to accept, his use of violence in the pursuit of his ends. For them it was the German capacity to take this course that alarmed them and led them to total war. And so Hitler found himself fighting for his very existence, rather than for the empire he sought to gain. He had not helped himself by his Machiavellian diplomacy. No undefeated opponent could accept the legitimacy of his conquests given a continued capacity to make them, for their turn might be next.

So in a sense it was the war that Hitler did not fight that was the touch-stone of his imperialism. He wanted to change the map of Europe, creating a unity directed and controlled by a German racial state possessing a vast colonial area in the East. The national identities of the small states, opponents, allies and neutrals alike, would disappear. Only Italy, France, Britain and Spain would remain of the old Europe and of these Britain was deemed to be a non-European power, France was to be severely reduced in territory, while Italy and Spain were to be very junior fascist partners and encouraged to seek their fortunes outside Europe. Such an empire, Hitler argued, was no different from those his European rivals had acquired for themselves at the expense of the coloured races.[118] It was at least commensurate with the French and the British empires. The smaller states, in any case, had no title to their imperial possessions.

The illusion that this was *politically* acceptable to his opponents, albeit that he had to convince them by military victories, persisted even in the hour of defeat. Their refusal to enter into his world was inexplicable to him. For his enemies the struggle was apocalyptic. This was true not only of the small states he conquered but of his principal European opponents, Britain and the Soviet Union. France, perhaps, was an exception, with its popular neo-fascist government; although, had this government known what Hitler planned for France, it too might have rebelled. But Hitler kept his plans to himself and was well aware of the dangers their disclosure would bring should he reveal them before his final victory. The war that Hitler actually fought, as opposed to the one he intended, was a war of national survival. This was implicit in his policies. The rationale of his imperialism could only be accomplished through a total victory. The implications of this were realized by his opponents. The Clausewitzian paradox that war was 'policy by other means' and that war 'tended to the extreme' was never resolved. For the former to be true there had to be both limits set to the use of violence and an acceptance of their rationality by contending states. Since they did not share Hitler's ideological framework, it is not surprising that the war ceased to be political and became total.

I argued at the beginning of this study that beliefs do not entail actions. What then is the relevance of ideology to practice? The central argument is that the adequacy of an explanation of human action depends on its relation to the reasoning of the agent. In order to explain Hitler's actions in Eastern Europe, and indeed the whole basis of his policy, it is necessary to transcend the 'logic of the situation' — the *immediate* context of reasoning — and refer to the overall context of beliefs — a basic rationale. The question at issue is the relevance of the rationale to an explanation of particular actions. Answering this question does not entail a *theory* of action, but constitutes a historical exercise that seeks to establish a relation between evidence of belief and evidence of action, in which the former explains the latter by establishing its precise nature.

Putting it simply we do not *know,* other than in a nominal fashion, what the action really was until we have discovered an associated reasoning. But this associated reasoning, in cases where an explicit belief system is professed or adopted, includes not merely that surrounding the immediate action or decision, but that of the belief system too. Otherwise we do not know the significance for the agent of his actual or contemplated action or decision, and it is this that constitutes its character. It was argued in this study that we can explain Hitler's actions and decisions in terms of an adherence to an ideology that prescribed imperialism. He was possessed of a rationale that was inherently imperialistic. If we are to place his actions within the rubric of imperialism it is because of the nature of the ideology and its relation to practice and not because we superimpose a theory of imperialism.

The characterization of imperialism as ideological is based upon the connection of ideas with action in the sense that the latter is rendered explicable by reference to the former. For Hitler his wars were imperialist wars. Instead of focusing our attention on *events* as if they had a quality and an existence independent of our thinking about them, or, alternatively, describing or characterizing them in terms of some overriding conceptual framework, we are concerned with referring *actions* to the intentions of the agent, that is, to *his* conceptual framework. This entails reconstructing the latter on the basis of the available evidence if we wish to explain his actions. The focus thus shifts from the interplay of factors, forces, circumstances and events, which we might label 'imperialism', to the reasoning of the agent.

We can thus define *imperialism* in phenomenal terms in two ways: Firstly, we can ourselves adopt an ideological stance, or a conceptual framework, and so characterize 'phenomena' *qua* events as imperialist and detach them from the perceptions of the agents who enacted them. Or, secondly, we can derive this characterization from the reasoning of the agents themselves: it is *their* rationale for action that matters. Now I am not designating the former approach as illegitimate or as inferior to the second. I shall say more about this question later in this study. But I am asserting this distinction as important, for the two approaches have very different references in terms of their status as empirical explanations. The distinction is clear if we consider the economic imperialist argument discussed earlier. There is no doubt in the mind of a neo-Marxist that Hitler's actions were imperialist; it followed as night follows day from his nature as a *capitalist* agent. But this is a very different form of imperialism from that conceived of by Hitler. If we accept it, we are then constrained to apply an ideological view to the world of practice. And this would be equally true if we adopted national—socialist beliefs. For the adherent there would be problems of relating theory to practice, but regardless of the content of the theory they would be intrinsically the *same* problems.

What has been done in this study is to relate actions to the perceptions of the agent, and this entails relating theory to practice. Given that national—socialism is an imperialist ideology, at least in Hitler's version of it, does this necessarily mean that Hitler practised imperialism? Can we designate his actions as imperialist? Now it is the practical aspect of this ideology that is important if we are to distinguish between *ex post facto* justification and ideological reasoning that directed choice. A belief, for example, in the survival of the fittest as the central characteristic of human behaviour in general and in international politics in particular, does not constrain the believer to undertake any action. And all actions, whatever their motivation or associated reasoning, can be justified by that belief. The tautological element in it begs the question as to what constitutes the necessary and sufficient conditions for survival. *But,* when it is wedded to the notions of race and racial purity, then a programme for action is immediately entailed, for specific conditions are laid down for success in the struggle for survival.

In short, there is a programmatic element in Hitler's ideology that prescribes certain conditions and certain courses of action as necessary for the achievement of survival in the struggle of all against all. Among these conditions were the elimination of inimical and alien elements from the race, the creation of autarky and the acquisition of living-space. It is true that such prescriptive elements constituted long-term aims that did not include in their statement any precise definition of the means deemed necessary for their fulfilment, but, on my argument, almost all of Hitler's actions can be explained as an attempt to create those conditions that would allow him to realize them. He held to a consistent purpose. His political and diplomatic manoeuvrings were attempts to gain freedom of action. And when at last he was in a position to pursue these ends directly, he did so. The successive steps he took from the beginning of his power were not predestined steps in an inexorable programme of action dictated by his beliefs. He was no sleepwalker. And no one could be clairvoyant enough to know which political situations would arise out of the complexities of European politics. But they were steps in the sense that they were consistent with his ideology. His decisions and actions, constrained as they often were by the immediate circumstances he found himself in or had contrived, had a direction that is explicable only in terms of his beliefs. Alone of all the politicians, he knew what he was doing; he sought to put his ideas into practice. What evidence there is of his reasoning reveals a distinction he continually made between the immediate situation and its problems, and the conditions necessary for the realization of his long-term aim: the creation of a European empire for Germany.

NOTES AND REFERENCES

1 This needs qualifying, since those neo-Marxist theories of imperialism that focus on the problem of underdevelopment tend to reduce the nation-state to a passive rather than an active role in the workings of the capitalist system.
2 This argument was the basis of Julius Streicher's defence at Nuremberg. Although he propagated anti-Semitism in violent terms, he was not in any way involved in the Final Solution. Nor did he hold high rank in the Nazi Party or participate in policy-making. It cannot be shown, his defence argued, that *action* against the Jews was a necessary consequence of the propagation of his ideas. There is some force in this argument.
3 'The staggering blow for us was that the situation was entirely unexpected, and the fact that our men were not equipped for the temperatures they had to face' (Hugh Trevor-Roper *Hitler's Table Talk* London, Weidenfeld & Nicolson, 1953) p. 220. This was part of his explanation for the failure to obtain a decisive victory over the Russians in 1941.
4 Another reason he offered was the delay in starting the invasion as a result of

Mussolini's invasion of Greece. See *The Testament of Adolf Hitler. Hitler-Bormann Documents. February-April 1945* (ed. François Genoud, trans. R. H. Stevens, intro. H. Trevor-Roper, London, Cassells, 1960) p. 65.

5 Adolf Hitler *Mein Kampf* (trans. Ralph Mannheim, London, Radius Books/Hutchinson, 1969) pp. 191, 268, 416.

6 *ibid.,* pp. 360, 361.

7 *ibid.,* p. 132.

8 See intro to *Mein Kampf* by D. C. Watt, pp. xxvii-xi.

9 *Table Talk, op. cit.,* p. 422.

10 There are, of course, others: for example, the organization of the state; the principle of leadership; education and propaganda; the role of the party; and so on, which are not directly relevant here.

11 *Mein Kampf, op. cit.,* pp. 277-96.

12 *Testament, op. cit.,* pp. 55-6.

13 *Main Kampf, op. cit.,* pp. 356-9.

14 *ibid.,* p. 137.

15 *ibid.,* p. 347.

16 *Mein Kampf, op. cit.,* pp. 124-6, 368, 596.

17 *ibid.,* pp. 249, 362.

18 *ibid.,* pp. 128, 603.

19 *ibid.,* pp. 559-60.

20 *The Speeches of Adolf Hitler 1922-1939* (hereafter *Hitler's Speeches*) Vol. II (trans. and selected by Norman H. Baynes, London, Oxford University Press, Royal Institute of International Affairs, 1942). Speech made to the Reichstag on 30 January 1939, p. 1623.

21 *Mein Kampf, op. cit.,* p. 121.

22 *ibid.,* p. 121.

23 *ibid.,* pp. 126-7.

24 *ibid.,* p. 128.

25 *ibid.,* p. 155.

26 *Mein Kampf, op. cit.,* p. 193.

27 *ibid.,* pp. 314, 326.

28 Hitler compared the role of national—socialist doctrine to Catholic dogma. They were both sets of general fundamental principles immune from critical review. 'The task of the present and future members of our movement must not consist in a critical revision of these theses, but rather in being bound by them' (*ibid.,* p. 418).

29 See *ibid.,* pp. 191, 192, 314, 326, 343, 414. Hitler recognized the considerable problems in relating theories to programmes of action: 'Even more seldom, however, is a great theoretician a great leader ... And conversely of what avail would be all the genius and energy of a leader if the brilliant theoretician did not set up aims for the human struggle? However, the combination of theoretician, organiser, and leader in one person is the rarest thing that can be found on this earth; this combination makes the great man' (p. 528). Clearly he had cast himself for this role.

30 Ribbentrop said in his interrogation on 10 September 1945, 'The Fuehrer, to my mind, had absolutely no sketched-out definite program of any sort of forming what later on was called the Gross Germanic Reich or the Gross Germanic State ... He never had that idea. It all came during the war. He never had that before' (*Nazi Conspiracy and Aggression* (eight vols, Washington, US Government Printing Office, 1946-48, Vol. 2, p. 1202). Goering in his evidence at Nuremberg denied categorically that Hitler's main purpose in going to war with the Soviet

Union was the acquisition of living-space (*The Trial of German Major War Criminals* (hereafter IMT) London, HMSO 19 , Vol. IX, p. 317).

31 *Testament, op. cit.*, p. 85.

32 Hitler made a distinction, not always clear, between a policy of colonization, by which he meant the acquisition of colonies overseas following the example of the major European empires, and *lebensraum* (living-space), which meant the acquisition of land around the national heartland. He always insisted that he wanted soil and not people; indeed, people embarrassed him unless they were capable of being germanized. He considered a policy of colonial expansion overseas was a mistake for Germany, since this form of empire was a source of degeneracy for the metropolitan state; it brought Germany into conflict with the other empires; and Germans lacked the inclination to colonize abroad. He also conceived of this form of colonization as a loss to Germany through the emigration of her best people. See *Testament, ibid.*, pp. 43-6.

33 *Mein Kampf, op. cit.*, pp. 126-19.

34 *ibid.*, p. 580.

35 *ibid.*, p. 598.

36 *ibid.*, p. 597.

37 *ibid.*, p. 599.

38 *ibid.*, p. 191.

39 The Anglo-German Naval Treaty of 1935, which gave Germany a lower ration of capital ships to Britain, may be regarded as one of Hitler's attempts at allaying British fears of German rearmament and of his revisionist policies. Germany's submarine programme was kept to a minimum for the same reason.

40 'I considered these two lectures on "The True Causes of the World War" and on "The Peace Treaties of Brest-Litovsk and Versailles", the most important of all, and so I repeated and repeated them dozens of times' (*Mein Kampf, op. cit.*, p. 426).

41 In an interview with E. Price Bell in May 1935. See *Hitler's Speeches, op. cit.*, Vol. II, p. 1216.

42 In a speech to the Reichstag, 7 March 1936 (*ibid.* p. 1300).

43 In a speech to the Old Guard of the Party at Augsburg, 21 November 1937, he said, apropos his expansionist policy, 'I am convinced that the most difficult part of the preparatory work has already been achieved' (*ibid.*, p. 1370).

44 Sportpalast Speech in Berlin, 26 September 1938 (*ibid.*, p. 1526).

45 These four conferences — of 5 November 1937 (the 'Hossbach Memo'), 23 May 1939 (the 'Schmundt Memo'), 22 August 1939 (the 'Oversalzburg Speech', and 23 November 1939 (the 'Boehm Memo') — have all been cited as evidence of Hitler's *intentions*. It was argued by the defence at Nuremberg (especially that of Raeder) that no actual text, verbatim or otherwise, existed for any of the speeches alleged to have been made by Hitler at these conferences. It was also argued that those attending did not receive copies and so their records, which form the basis of the evidence for what Hitler said, cannot not be checked at source. And finally, it was argued that these speeches were merely pieces of rhetoric designed to convince the generals as to the wisdom of *Hitler*, and not necessarily of his intended actions, which he kept largely to himself. While accepting these points, the reliability of those who kept a record seems indisputable since they were not themselves arraigned, nor can they be shown to have any particular axe to grind since they held no senior position or were responsible for military operations. But more important, what was recorded as having been said seems entirely consistent with what Hitler said and did in other contexts. Their failings as legal evidence can be counterbalanced by reference to historical evidence, such as that relating to the negotiations between the Soviet

Union and Germany after the Molotov—Ribbentrop Pact, which the Nuremberg lawyers could not use since one of the parties was also a judge. The point in any case is not the one the Nuremberg prosecutors were trying to establish, namely the culpability of the Nazi leaders in a *conspiracy*, but the continuity of Hitler's thoughts on the subject of living-space.

46 Hossbach Memo, Doc. 386-PS in IMT, *op. cit.*, Vol. III, p. 297.
47 *ibid.*, p. 298.
48 *ibid.*, p. 297.
49 *ibid.*, p. 296.
50 *ibid.*, p. 301.
51 Obersalzburg Speech, Doc. 798-PS, *ibid.*, p. 585.
52 *ibid.*, p. 585.
53 Boehm Memo, Doc. 789-PS, *ibid.*, p. 572.
54 *ibid.*, p. 573.
55 *ibid.*, p. 574.
56 *ibid.*, p. 575.
57 *ibid.*, p. 577.
58 *ibid.*, p. 579.
59 *Table Talk, op. cit.*, p. 33.
60 *ibid.*, pp. 15, 24, 33, 92, 395.
61 *ibid.*, pp. 69, 469.
62 *ibid.*, pp. 16, 34, 53, 68, 405.
63 *ibid.*, p. 5.
64 *ibid.*, p. 128.
65 *ibid.*, pp. 16, 25, 34, 128.
66 *ibid.*, p. 14.
67 *ibid.*, pp. 25, 660.
68 *ibid.*, pp. 19, 460, 471.
69 *ibid.*, pp. 477, 661.
70 *ibid.*, pp. 477, 471.
71 *ibid.*, p. 19.
72 *ibid.*, pp. 53, 73.
73 *ibid.*, pp. 625, 697
74 *ibid.*, p. 261.
75 Hitler believed the death of Roosevelt in April 1945 would prove to be the same solution to his predicament as the death of the Tsarina had been to that of Frederick the Great.
76 *Testament, op. cit.*, p. 46.
77 *ibid.*, pp. 43, 45.
78 *ibid.*, pp. 50-7, 105, and Hitler's 'political testament' in W. Maser *Hitler's Letters and Notes* (London, Heinemann, 1974) p. 349.
79 '. . . where all others have all eternity at their disposal I have but a few short miserable years' (*Testament, op. cit.*, p. 94).
80 'I have restricted myself to making promises that I knew I could keep and that I had every intention of keeping' (*ibid.*, p. 83).
81 *ibid.*, p. 86.
82 *ibid.*, pp. 35-6.
83 On 6 October 1939 Hitler made a speech in the Reichstag in which he proposed a peace on the following terms: (1) Western recognition of the German conquest of Poland (and by implication its partition); (2) satisfaction given to German colonial claims overseas; in return for (3) no German demands on France including Alsace and Lorraine. On 19 July 1940 he made another speech in the Reichstag after the defeat of France. His terms of this time: (1) the removal of

Churchill from the British government; (2) British recognition of German hegemony in Europe; and (3) the restoration of the former German colonies. These he considered to be mild terms and in return he was prepared to 'guarantee' the British empire.

84 There is some evidence that Hitler, in the words of Sun Tsu, created a 'golden bridge' for the British forces. Warlimont cites Rundstedt, who explained the order to halt the German advance on Dunkirk by saying that 'Hitler stated that he had hoped to come to some rapid agreement with England if he let the British expeditionary force escape' (W. Warlimont *Inside Hitler's Headquarters 1939-45*, trans. R. H. Barry, London, Weidenfeld and Nicolson, 1964, p. 99). This is supported by B. H. Liddell Hart in his account of his interview with Rundstedt. Rundstedt told him that Hitler gave as his reason for halting the advance, that he did not want to risk losing tanks, that Britain was out of the war anyway, and that 'his aim was to make peace with Britain on a basis that she would regard as compatible with her honour to accept' (B. H. Liddell Hart *The Other Side of the Hill* London, Cassell, 1948, pp. 139-43). Hitler himself said: 'Churchill was quite unable to appreciate the sporting spirit of which I had given proof by refraining from creating an irreparable breach between the British and ourselves. We did, indeed, refrain from annihilating them at Dunkirk' (*Testament, op. cit.,* p. 96). Hitler's views on the character of the English make this entirely credible. D. Irving's view that the halt order did not emanate from Hitler in the first instance but was Rundstedt's own decision (see note to p. 121 on p. 826 of *Hitler's War* London, Hodder and Stoughton, 1977) does not alter the fact that Hitler endorsed it.

85 Operation Sea-Lion was ordered on 16 July 1940. It received none of the attention that Hitler gave to his other operations and was postponed indefinitely on 17 September 1940. The Battle of Britain lasted over the period 13 August — 17 September 1940.

86 *Testament, op. cit.,* pp. 30-5.

87 Hitler had hoped that the success of the British in the Battle of Britain would have been seen as a basis for opening negotiations without humiliation. But this very success also confirmed his inability to invade Britain (*Testament, op. cit.,* pp. 33, 63).

88 For example, Hitler undertook to mediate between the Soviet Union and Japan in 1939 (Telegram from Ribbentrop to Schulenberg *Nazi-Soviet Relations 1939-1941,* ed. R. J. Sontag and J. S. Beddie, Washington, US Dept. of State, 1948, p. 58). And on 26 March 1941 he urged Matsuoka to attack Singapore (*Hitler's Interpreter* (Dr Paul Schmidt) ed. R. H. C. Steed, London, Heinemann, 1951, p. 228).

89 For the text see German—Soviet Boundary and Friendship Treaty in *Nazi-Soviet Relations 1939-41, op. cit.,* pp. 105-7.

90 For example, Soviet demands for North and South Bukovina, which were not included in the original Pact. See *Nazi-Soviet Relations 1939-41, op. cit.,* pp. 157-8, 163, 237.

91 This originated in the German-Soviet Trade Agreement of 19 August 1939, which provided for the provision of 200 million Reichsmarks for the purchase of machinery, industrial installations and armaments, in exchange for Soviet raw materials.

92 See Foreign Office Memorandum dated 28 September 1940 in *Nazi-Soviet Relations 1939-41, op. cit.,* p. 201.

93 In the event of a Soviet suspension of grain deliveries Germany would have been in a serious situation. 'Russia is the only country that has a good grain harvest and therefore might be in a position to continue with large shipments. The Reich

Food Ministry points out that the national grain reserve will be used up in the current crop year so that we would enter the next crop year without such a reserve' (*ibid.*, p. 200). The problem of food supply was important to Hitler because he did not want to jeopardize his political position by introducing rationing or reducing the standard of living in any way. He meant to pay for his wars by the spoils of conquest.

94 '[I] arrived at my decision on the very anniversary of the signing of the Moscow Pact' (*Testament, op. cit.,* pp. 96-9).

95 *Nazi-Soviet Relations 1939-41, op. cit.,* p. 200.

96 IMT, *op. cit.,* Part 21, p. 29.

97 *Nazi Conspiracy and Aggression, op. cit.,* Vol. 5, p. 724.

98 IMT, *op. cit.,* Series B, Interrogations, p. 1110.

99 *ibid.,* Vol. XII, p. 12.

100 *ibid.,* Vol. IV, p. 594, Part 21, pp. 29, 50, 90.

101 *Table Talk, op. cit.,* p. 31.

102 *ibid.,* pp. 63-6.

103 *ibid.,* p. 65.

104 *ibid.,* p. 66. See also Hitler's letter to Mussolini dated 21 June 1941 in *Nazi-Soviet Relations 1939-41, op. cit.,* pp. 349-53.

105 See the memorandum of the Conference of 16 July 1941 cited in IMT, *op. cit.,* Vol. VIII, p. 1046.

106 *Table Talk, op. cit.,* pp. 396 and 661.

107 *Nazi Conspiracy and Aggression, op. cit.,* Vol. 8, Report on Interview with Herr Hess by Wing Commander the Duke of Hamilton, Sunday 11 May 1941, pp. 37-40.

108 See *Table Talk, op. cit.,* pp. 476-8 and p. 661, and also Goebbels' remark 'If the French knew what the Fuehrer is one day going to demand of them their eyes would probably fill with tears' (*The Goebbels Diaries,* trans. and ed. Louis P. Lochner, London, Hamish Hamilton, 1948, p. 146).

109 For the text of the decree see *Nazi Conspiracy and Aggression* Vol. 4, pp. 751-2.

101 *ibid.,* Vol. 6, pp. 1038-9.

111 *ibid.,* Vol. 1, pp. 1025-35.

112 *ibid.,* Vol. 1, p. 1023.

113 'The Russian space is our India. Like the English we shall rule this Empire with a handful of men' (*Table Talk, op. cit.,* p. 33).

114 *ibid.,* p. 263.

115 *ibid.,* p. 314.

116 In his 'political testament' of 19 April 1945, Hitler urged his people to fight on 'faithful to the ideals of the great Clausewitz' (Maser, *op. cit.,* p. 354). Carl von Clausewitz was one of the few writers Hitler cited in *Mein Kampf* as having influenced him.

117 'Churchill by refusing to come to terms with me has condemned his country to suicide' (*Testament, op. cit.,* p. 30).

118 Hitler always maintained that, although colonies were sometimes desirable in that they were sources of raw materials that could not be obtained in Europe, nevertheless the ideal imperial policy was to achieve 'complete economic independence inside a territory compatible with her population' (*ibid.,* p. 88).

5

Sociobiology and Imperialism

The fact that man is an animal, whatever his other attributes, has led many commentators to insist that this aspect of his nature deserves some consideration in explaining his behaviour. In this chapter I am concerned with a sociobiological account of imperialism. The focus is the alleged phenomenon of aggression in man, with its associated territoriality — the acquisition and preservation of biological living-space. In concentrating on this aspect of human nature and ignoring other features such as mating, reproduction, family relations and organization, and socially cooperative forms of behaviour, I am not subscribing to the view that aggression is the dominant characteristic of the human species, although this is a view put forward by some biologists.[1] Rather I am interested in the notion that wars, violence between human groups and the seizure by force of territory and empires can be explained by reference to the biological constitution of the human species, in particular its seemingly ineradicable propensity to engage in intra-specific aggression.

For the first time we shall be considering a model that claims to provide an explanation of human behaviour within the terms of natural science. While there are cross-disciplinary links in ethology — the study of animal behaviour — notably with psychology, anthropology and sociology, the basis of the argument is rooted in biology, in the theory of evolution and in genetic theory. So it is necessary for us to look at this basic theoretical context before going on to examine those extensions into the realm of animal behaviour that concern themselves with the phenomena of aggression, conflict and imperialism.

If follows from this that since we are concerned with human nature in terms of fundamental causes of behaviour, the type of reason-giving explanation discussed in the previous chapters is irrelevant. Imperialism, conceived of as the product of aggressive drives emanating from innate characteristics of the human species, is an inherently irrational phenomenon. Man acts as an instrument rather

172

than as a conscious reasoning being. To put it another way, his ostensible reasons for his actions are really manifestations of underlying causes. Whatever his conscious will, his actions are to be explained in terms of unconscious forces that are part of his nature. The implications of this argument will be considered later. The point here is that unlike the other models of imperialism considered earlier the sociobiological argument is unambiguous in that it excludes the possibility of an explanation based upon intention, motive, purpose and reasoning. Hence we are confined to the general theoretical form of explanation in our assessment of the explanatory adequacy of the argument.

There are other possibilities within this form that we shall have to consider as potential explanations. They are peculiar to biology or rather to evolutionary theory. These are, firstly, that the argument is teleological in character and, secondly, that it postulates a functional 'explanation'. By teleological is meant an account that posits a purpose in the occurrence and development of phenomena, so that some form of ordered continuum exists. In this case evolutionary theory is said to be teleological in that it asserts a retrodictive (as opposed to predictive) form of argument in which a phenomenon occurring in the past makes a contribution to an undetermined future phenomenon. We can only determine the contribution made by the former through an inference based on the latter. Thus a present organism survived *because* of the prior existence of some characteristic of its former being. It is this that is defined in terms of the survival of the fittest.

Given that we have a surviving organism in the first place (one that is accessible to observation and enquiry), we can then assess what are taken to be those factors conducive to its survival. In a sense this is a projection into the past biological history of the organism. These factors, genetic and environmental in nature, have a special significance in terms of the future and continued existence of the species: they fulfil a goal or have a purpose. Such a notion of purpose is of course natural and not human. The former constitutes the survival of the species, while the latter is referrable to an individual rationale of choice. In short, the explanation of biological characteristics is directly linked to the idea of a super-riding purpose, that of the continued existence of species. The past history of a species and changes in its biological and environmental constituents are interpreted accordingly. In this sense the notion of evolution is a colligatory concept and is used to organize a wide variety of 'facts' in the construction of a 'history' and an explanation of present species.

When we come to functional explanation there is some difficulty in distinguishing it from teleology, for the notion of function is sometimes used as synonymous with purpose. A functional argument is one that asserts a contribution made by one element to the maintenance or existence of another. In the context of systems theory in the social sciences, or more specifically of structural—functional theory in anthropology, the parts of the system or of the social group contribute to the continued existence of the whole. For example, social practices such as religion or economic exchanges, whatever their nominal character, have the function of acting as a means of social cohesion. They help to maintain the character of that society. An explanation of such practices therefore takes the form of establishing this connection. In biology, however, a functional account can be extended from relating the component parts of an organism to an assertion of the relationship between these and the survival of the species. In other words, a functional relationship may be said to have a goal other than the simple constitution and maintenance of the life and processes of an organism. It is directed to the further goal of the survival of the species of which it is a member. This is particularly important, as we shall see, where genetic changes occur. The concepts of adaptation, natural selection and fitness are part of a functionalist argument. There is rather more to this argument than simply showing what contribution an element in a physiological system plays in maintaining it, as, for example, in explaining the function of the liver in terms of the circulation and purification of the blood. We may say of a diseased liver that it is malfunctioning, that is, that it is not doing its job properly. But in the case of a species, as apart from an individual organism, dominant genetic mutations that are maladaptive in terms of survival are said to be dysfunctional. Given radical environmental changes, the genotype of the species may be dysfunctional in the same way. And so the species may dwindle and become extinct.

When we come to the behavioural aspects of this argument and to the notion of cultural evolution, the functionalist argument assumes another dimension. Although there is a biological basis stemming from the genetic composition of the species, the emphasis is placed on social practices that regulate (i.e. are functional to) sexual selection, breeding, nutrition and living-space, and that optimalize the survival of a population and of a species. Such practices are thus explicable in terms of the purpose they serve, as well as in turn explained as responses to stimuli that are part of the biological composition of the organism and of the species. As we shall see, aggression has a special function of its own.

Now the question whether these arguments are explanatory is debatable. Some commentators think that teleology is ineradicable from biology. And whether anything is explained in terms of its alleged 'function' is open to criticism. The postulated relationship between physical or cultural characteristics, in which one is said to maintain or contribute to the other, may be causal. That is, we can conceive of such a relation as that of cause and effect within the terms of a general law on the lines of the theoretical mode of explanation discussed earlier. Similarly, each of these characteristics may itself in turn be explicable in terms of causality either through genetic theory or through some other theoretical construct. In which case, teleological and functional arguments may be subsumed within such a theory. Alternatively, it may be claimed that evolutionary theory is not concerned with causality or with eliciting a predictive mode of explanation. It stands as an explanatory mode in its own right. At this stage I leave these possibiilties open and turn to the specific arguments posited by the theory of evolution.

Before doing so, some preliminary comments on the choice of the empirical example used as a test-case should be made. Given the irrelevance of human reasoning and volition for this type of theorizing, it may seem odd that Japanese imperialism in the 1930s is considered an appropriate area of reference for sociobiological argument. On the face of it, it seems something of a quantum jump to move from the generalities of evolutionary theory to a complex set of human decisions and actions within a very limited historical context, whose interpretation seems to be totally bound up with an analysis of reasoning. Indeed, if a formal historical analysis of Japanese foreign policy and diplomacy during this period were presented as an appropriate 'case' for an empirical application of sociobiological theories of human behaviour, this would be a serious category mistake. For two completely incompatible conceptual frameworks and associated explanatory modes would thus be conflated. History cannot be interpreted in terms of science nor science in terms of history.

The sociobiological argument with all its variations can hardly be described as a complete theory with a clearly defined set of empirical references. It is concerned with *general* propositions about categories of behaviour rather than with specifics. Where it turns to the empirical its enquiry is directed to highly specialized studies of animal behaviour.[2] And even here it stands more as a framework for investigation than as a finished mode of explanation. Its conclusions are tentative. How then can it be tested in any meaningful way by reference to such a specific case as Japanese imperialism? Is such a phenomenon of its nature susceptible to sociobiological explanation?

According to some biologists, 'politics is about genetics'.[3] And, although the conclusions of this genre are more tentative than conclusive, its explanatory claims are far-reaching. In principle, all cases of imperialism are explicable as a generalized phenomenon that is characteristic of human behaviour. Without anticipating the substance of the argument to be discussed shortly, the sociobiological argument does contain a fundamental explanation of human conduct in terms of innate propensities to perform certain actions under appropriate stimuli. Aggression is only one such behavioural trait, but it is central to imperialism. We should therefore find evidence in the course of Japanese imperialism to substantiate this thesis. While much of the detailed actions and events are extraneous and may be dismissed as irrelevant or mere epiphenomena, there should be a central core that is explicable through this argument and that constitutes its test. Clearly, the roots of Japanese imperialism, and indeed of all cases of imperialism, lie in the nature of man and his social relations. So in using this as an example I am not begging any questions as to its nature by juxtaposing a historical interpretation against a biological thesis. Such an exercise would be futile. Rather I am treating Japanese expansion into mainland Asia and into the Pacific as a phenomenon that in principle might be explicable in sociobiological terms. And indeed, given the nature of the socio-biological argument, it *should* be explicable within its terms.

Although much of the argument concerning human aggression and territorial expansion emphasizes behavioural and cultural aspects of human development, it is derived from evolutionary theory. So before looking at these aspects I want to consider the basic ideas of evolution — natural selection, adaptation and genetic inheritance — that either directly, or indirectly, permeate the discussion on man's biological composition and his allegedly aggressive tendencies. I should stress that these ideas are largely concerned with the acquisition and transmission of *physical* characteristics common to a species and their relation to survival, and further that they are largely the product of enquiry into non-human species, either through the palaeon-tological record or through experiments on species capable of reproducing through many generations in a comparatively short period of time. Man's existence as a species is brief in evolutionary terms.

What then is evolutionary theory? What is its relationship to an explanation of human behaviour? I am concerned at this stage with giving an account of the main ideas in what is termed the synthetic theory of evolution and indicating their relevance to ethology, or the study of animal behaviour, and not with their explanatory value or the status of the theory. This last will come later following the attempt to apply the derived ethological argument to the example of Japanese imperialism. The basis of modern or synthetic evolutionary theory is a theory of genetics. This concerns the transmission from one generation to another of genes that act as a kind of programme for the development of the organism's physical characteristics. Although genetic theory is still unclear on a number of problems, the basic process explains how the transmission of heritable characteristics occurs. The gene is carried in the nuclei of cells on strips called chromosomes, which in animals occur in pairs. A set of genes is termed an allele; in each pair of chromosomes there are two alleles. It is believed that the gene consists of a segment of DNA (deoxyribonucleic acid).[4] In large organisms, including man, the gene performs two functions. It replicates cells and, using RNA (ribonucleic acid), it forms proteins. The units of heredity, the cells, which form the main physical characteristics of an organism and which are also the sources of variation, are 'caused' by the DNA molecules, which in a sense are 'coded' for each organism and for each species. The composite genetic characteristics of an organism are termed a genotype. It is important to note that this theory concerns processes within cell structures that explain heredity, that is, the transmission of physical characteristics from one generation to another. Nothing else is explained. The genes concerned are those related to reproduction. A Mendelian gene, that is the notion of a gene as a unit of function that transmits heritable characteristics, is here merged with the molecular biological view of a gene as performing this function but composed of a section of DNA. The process of transmission is given a theoretical explanation.

This genetic theory thus provides us with an explanation of how the main physical characteristics of an organism and of a species are transmitted through reproduction. The explanation of change in these characteristics is through the existence of mutations. Variations occur in the actual process of coding and transmission that impart new characteristics to succeeding generations. They are transmitted in the same way as those belonging to the 'normal' genotype, but they introduce change into the genetic pool of a species. As we shall see, genetic variations are extremely important in evolutionary theory. Mutations are one of the major causes of a change in the physical characteristics of a species. Their cause is as yet unknown and they are generally considered to be random. The point to be stressed at this stage is that the genotype and the mutational changes that alter it are independent of any environmental influences in the sense that they are not acquired characteristics. The so-called Lamarckian thesis of the heritability of acquired characteristics is generally rejected by biologists.[5] Genetic inheritance occurs as a result of molecular processes within the organisms of a species, regardless of its environmental consequences.

The phenotype constitutes the characteristic behavioural or physical traits of a species. While the phenotype may be the product of the genotype as well as environmental conditions, the reverse is not the case. The genotype is determined neither by the phenotype nor by changes in the environment of the organism. The behavioural and physical characteristics of an organism (and of a species) are thus partly the product of its genetic structure — its genotype — and partly the product of a relationship with its environmental conditions — its habitat, which includes other members of the species and other species. There are thus two influences upon the behaviour of the organism: its genetic inheritance and its environment. Its range of capacities — the possibilities of behaviour — are determined by the genotype as well as by the habitat. But it is the genotype that is transmitted, with or without mutation, to succeeding generations, while learned behaviour is not. It is, however, argued that a *capacity* for learning is heritable and this will be considered later on.

The relation of this argument to the Darwinian concept of evolution lies in what is termed natural selection. The 'gene-pool' of a population is altered by the circumstances in which that generation finds itself. A differential mortality or fertility will, in principle, change the genetic characteristics of a population. And clearly, environmental conditions that affect mortality or reproduction will in turn affect the gene-pool. Similarly, individuals possessing a mutation that confers a special advantage in terms of their environmental relationship will tend to dominate the gene-pool by virtue of their superior capacity to survive and breed. Through reproduction they pass on their mutated form and, assuming that the favourable environment does not change, the mutant form will come to dominate the genotype of the species. The point about natural selection is that there is a genetic basis to the survival of a species and this capacity for survival confers advantages on the species relative to others. In effect, each species has a genetic potential for adaptation to its environment. It is realized when an appropriate set of stimuli occurs in the external environment. Changes in this potential occur with random mutations, which may or may not be conducive to adaptation. Evolutionary theory is basically an attempt to explain the success or persistence of a species in maintaining its existence over a long period of time.

Fitness is defined as the existence of a postulated relationship between the genotype, its phenotype and the environment, for a given species or a population within a species. Adaptation is in effect a synonym for this relationship, although it also implies a response to environmental change. As we have seen, the existence of mutations provides a means of responding to changing environmental conditions, although this is a matter of chance since the mutation occurs without any reference to such conditions. It may thus be adaptive or maladaptive. Given that, fitness becomes a function of reproductive success in that the survival of a species is linked to the domination of the gene-pool by the adaptive mutant.

Anticipating later argument, many of the behavioural characteristics of a species are linked to the successful breeding of individuals within a population. This success depends upon the existence of innate (genetic) mechanisms designed to regulate this breeding and ensure the dominance of those genes most conducive to the continued survival of the species. Aggression is said to be one of these mechanisms. Clearly, the transmission of genes through reproduction, and their efficacy in promoting the survival of a species, are dependent upon a number of non-genetic factors. And it is the relationship between the genotype and these factors constituting an 'environment' that is at the core of sociobiological theories of human behaviour. Such factors as population distribution, food resources, inter-specific predation, intra-specific competition, and so on, are obviously relevant. The problems arise, as we shall see, when 'culture' is conceived of as an environment for the human species. Aggression is both inter- and intra-specific and it is the latter that primarily concerns us in considering a biological explanation of imperialism. Whether 'culture' is an effect of human genetic composition, or is an environment that acts as a stimulus to innate genetic determinants of behaviour, are questions that will concern us.

However, the point here is that a theory of population genetics is the centre of the synthetic theory of evolution. Whatever arguments are derived from it in terms of animal behaviour or the general notion of natural selection depend ultimately upon the theory of the transmission of phenotypic characteristics through genetic inheritance. The *history* of a species may or may not be explicable in terms of contingent factors, but the *nature* of a species, its central characteristics as a population of organisms, depends upon an atemporal genetic theory. Evolution thus does two things: it offers a description of the past of a species in terms of its biological development, and it offers an explanation in terms of the genetic basis for adaptation and survival.

Before looking at arguments more closely associated with animal behaviour and human aggression, let us look at an example of adaptation in a non-human species in order to see more clearly the nature of evolutionary theory. In recent times the peppered moth (*biston betularia*)[6] changed its 'normal' speckled colouring to an abnormal black. While both the original and the new forms coexist, the latter has become dominant in the species. The explanation for this change is found in the need of the moth to camouflage itself more successfully. Its habitat on the bark of trees in urban surroundings became blackened through industrial pollution and so placed the original peppered form in jeopardy from predators. Consequently those strains or mutants with melanistic characteristics became dominant. In the language of evolutionary theory, there was a strong selection pressure induced by the change in the peppered moth's environment, which placed a high premium on adaptation if the species was to survive.

Now the question arises, what was the process of interaction between the habitat and the genetic structure of the peppered moth? It could be argued that the melanistic form existed independently of its habitat as a genetically transmitted mutant. It had a superior chance of survival since the gene-pool of the species was influenced by predation affecting mostly the originally dominant peppered form. Before the change in environment the reverse could be argued. But the change in habitat was merely contingent and, given the random nature of mutation, the dominance of the melanistic form was an accident, merely a matter of chance. As it turned out, it proved adaptive but its existence is not explained by any reference to environmental factors. On the other hand, it could be argued that the change in habitat triggered off a change in the genetic structure of the peppered moth. It is true that this hypothesis finds no favour amongst biologists. It implies a form of Lamarckism in that the actual genetic processes are treated not as random or autonomous but as induced or affected by extraneous factors other than the contingent factors that affect reproductive success. Such factors are environmental and would have a causal relation. The point is that the former 'orthodox' explanation simply states that the melanistic mutation was better at surviving than the 'normal' form, and so became dominant. The reason why it was better at survival was because its colouring protected it from predators given the change in its environment. That this was actually the case is a matter of observation. Although the mutation and the way in which it is transmitted as a heritable characteristic is explained by genetic theory, the process of natural selection is not explained in any *theoretical* sense. There is no causal relation between the random mutation and the changing environment. In the case of the 'heterodox' explanation there is. And so, if we claim the status of a theoretical explanation for evolutionary theory, a full statement of necessary and sufficient conditions, the laws governing their relationship and the ensuing process of survival has to be made. As we shall see, this becomes particularly important when we examine the postulates of arguments that seek to establish a link between human behaviour and its environmental context. On the basis of this example we can see that, as it stands, orthodox evolutionary theory

simply postulates an *ex post facto* link between physical characteristics and an environment conducive to the survival of a species.
The 'proof' of the link lies in survival itself. It is not testable in any
other way. The implications of this argument will be considered later
on.

We can see from this necessarily brief exposition of the main points
of evolutionary theory that its central theoretical basis is that of
genetics. The inheritance of certain characteristics is through genetic
transmission. Now, while physical or morphological characteristics
such as colouring can be shown to be of genetic origin, that is, they
are explicable in terms of genetic theory, is this the case for behaviour?
If we can show that physical characteristics are 'caused' by genetic
transmission, can it also be shown that the phenotype of a species is
caused in the same way? This is the crucial question for the application
of biological concepts to human action. In the case of aggression, can
we treat it as a behavioural phenomenon that is susceptible to a
biological explanation?

Before seeking an answer to this question, let us look at various
attempts to explain social behaviour in the human species in terms of
biology. It should be clear from what has been said in preceding
chapters that the problem is not one of subsuming 'observed'
behaviour within the rubric of a general conceptual framework.
Rather it is one of relating such phenomena to a testable causal
theory that states necessary and sufficient conditions governed by a
law-like principle and enables the occurrence of the phenomenon in
question to be predicted. It is a necessary consequence of the
fulfilment of these conditions, and as such it is open to empirical test.

There are two main aspects that need consideration here. One is
the argument that evolutionary forces and genetic programming
have produced innate tendencies in the human species that take the
form of drives, instincts, motor patterns, etc., and that produce under
certain conditions a specific behavioural response. The other has a
broader social basis and incorporates this argument into a wider
framework of cultural evolution. In both cases they are asserted as
part of the synthetic theory of evolution and so provide a biological
explanation of some aspects at least of human behaviour.

Ethologists argue that in terms of his basic biological nature
contemporary man is a palimpsest. His present sociobiological
character is derived from previous adaptations to environmental
conditions.[7] The human species in this sense is a product of a
relationship between a genetic structure and a phenotypic adaptation
to an environment that no longer exists. The point here is not whether
this relationship is any longer valid in that what was formerly adaptive
is now maladaptive, although this is part of the ethological thesis, but

that it is impossible to prove or disprove the asserted relationship between genetic programming and environmental adaptation — the selection pressures and the evolutionary process — by referring to the past. The palaeontological record only provides evidence of a very basic physical structure. Environmental features can only be inferred from very scant evidence of coeval species and hence are extremely conjectural. Similarly the genetic structure of early man is not open to scrutiny. In short, only evidence that such a relationship and the innate propensities stimulated by it actually existed is found in modern man himself. Cultural evolution in terms of the development of social forms through an interaction between the human genetic structure and the environment over a long period of time, and the existence of genetic programming, would seem to be linked to historical evidence that is far from conclusive and that is related to the present.

However, this is not a major problem if the ethological argument is taken to be not historical but theoretical in nature. Evidence that, for example, aggression in man facilitated his survival in a hostile environment is not proof of the central thesis. If it were treated as such, then not only is the evidence inconclusive it also contains a circularity. Survival is survival. The point here is that the postulated link between genetic structure and environmental conditions can in principle be treated in the same way as any scientific hypothesis, that is, it is susceptible to testing through experiment and observation. Such a test would confirm or disconfirm a theory of genetic change. This brings us back to the explanation of mutations and genetic change central to evolutionary theory. But it takes us away from the alleged behavioural consequences and 'observable' social forms accessible to us only through unique 'historical' reconstructions. If this argument is accepted then the focus shifts from the sociological to the strictly biological. An explanation of the genetic changes in the composition of a species over a long period of time is strictly atemporal. A description of the changes themselves does not amount to an explanation. Nor can the effects of such changes be treated in terms of their effects, as axiomatically following from an interaction between them and an unstated or undefined environment. One side of the equation, that of genetic change, may be explained. But the other side, that of natural selection, adaptation and survival in cultural terms, cannot. Yet the latter is dependent upon the former since the root cause is seen as a favourable mutation or genotype. Evolutionary development in short is *caused* by genetics.

The problem is how can a relationship between genetics and alleged behavioural consequences — the genotype and the phenotype — be established where the environmental conditions cannot be stated with any precision? Natural selection, as we have seen, postulates such a relationship. The case of *cultural* evolution, as opposed to the development of morphological or physiological characteristics, poses great problems in that behaviour constitutes the environment and environment the behaviour. An adaptation in terms of a physiological adjustment to changing conditions of food supply, for example, in comparing man as an unspecialized omnivore to creatures such as dinosaurs with their relatively specialized diet (so far as we have any knowledge of this), makes the survival of one species as opposed to the other intelligible, but does not explain it. Leaving aside the problems of evolution in physical terms, what of the notion of cultural adaptation? What is the genetic basis for this? How can we distinguish between the notion of culture as behaviour (phenotypic) and culture as environment for the human species? There are two problems with the idea of cultural evolution. One is establishing the genetic basis of allegedly cultural or innate behavioural traits in man, and the other is distinguishing between such traits and the environmental conditions that stimulate them.

Few biologists are prepared to assert that cultural traits in human behaviour are the product of human genetic composition. Culture is taken by ethologists to mean an identifiable set of practices, customs, traditions and habits that is independent of the individual and that, together with environmental conditions, determines his behaviour.[8] It is taken to be universal. Regardless of the apparent diversity of human customs there is a basic conformity to biological norms. A fundamental culture specific to the human race is asserted. But the link between biology — the genetic element — and anthropology — the cultural manifestation — is imprecise. While the biologist is dubious about the genetic heritability of cultural traits, the sociobiologist postulates a link between genetics and such aspects of human behaviour as language, intelligence and capacity to reason.[9] These are inherent capacities that are heritable and are the product of the human genetic composition.

The basic argument is one of genetic assimilation.[10] Behavioural traits that have a particularly adaptive function under certain environmental conditions exist in certain individuals in a population. Such traits are phenotypically 'caused' by the environment and not by the genotype. However, natural selection results in those individuals possessing such behavioural traits dominating that population and, it is argued, the gene-pool. The trait that permitted this success becomes fixed in the population through breeding and so becomes part of the genetic endowment of that population, and possibly of the species. As we shall see, this argument is of particular relevance in the explanation of aggression in man. But the point here is that it is an argument that asserts the formation of a genotype through acquired characteristics becoming genetically fixed and thus heritable. This is, of course, a reversal of the argument that 'the relationship between genotype and phenotype is unidirectional'.[11] Learning, for example, is conceived of as based upon a genetic coding that transmits the capacity to learn from one generation to another. The capacity to learn is part of the basic genetic programming of the human species.[12] It proved extremely adaptive since it gave the species an advantage in terms of survival in that information could be rapidly assimilated, stored and transmitted from one generation to the next. Those individuals who showed particular aptitude in this faculty possessed an advantage over their less gifted fellows and so dominated the gene-pool. Selection and adaptation gave the human species an advantage in a varied and changing physical environment.

But, some ethologists argue, rather more than this is entailed in the notion of cultural evolution. Culture itself constituted a selection pressure favouring species with these genetic attributes.[13] *Behavioural* characteristics that include aggression, a drive to power and dominance, and the assertion of rank and hierarchy, all favoured particular members of a species and gave their genes an adaptive advantage. They dominated the gene-pool through a quasi-monopoly of successful breeding. The 'lesser' members were excluded. Social mechanisms such as aggression that secured to the species an adaptive advantage became genetically based. They also extended the range of behaviour from dominance within sub-groups of the species to extend across whole populations. Imperialism is a direct product of this innate aggressive drive. As two proponents of this argument have it, 'it must be understood that the process which gives rise to empire is the very same process that primates engage in simply in order to exist and persist. The hierarchical encounter and the rank order are the cells out of which whole and larger systems are built'.[14]

While the early antecedents of human behaviour are not known, our present cultural forms are asserted as being the product of evolution. It is a cultural or more precisely a behavioural, evolution that has emerged from a genetic base that favoured those species capable of learning and translating the things learnt into purposive action, which could be delayed or planned and was not necessarily an immediate response to the environment. The earlier *raison d'être* of human adaptation — the advantages conferred on the species by the reproductive dominance of its better equipped members — became a cultural adaptation in which cultural fitness evolved in response to the physical environment changing into a virtually man-made one. As Tiger and Fox put it, 'the leaders could not ensure that they controlled the future merely by peopling it with their own offspring, they had to ensure that their offspring controlled the future by having the monopoly on wealth and power'.[15] On this argument the most perfect example of successful cultural evolution would be the Saudi Arabian royal family! The point is that social forms are the product of a genetic composition, itself the consequence of selection pressures emanating from a physical and social environment. As MacBride argues,

> Man is unique in his acquisition of a superb system of cultural genetics which has almost replaced the genetic system as the mechanism of coding and transmission of behaviour. The mechanism here is the use of human speech and language for the coding of all behaviour which makes culture and its transmission from generation to generation by societal teaching or socialization.[16]

It is the capacity to do this that is heritable and part of the genetic composition of the human species.

So far this argument is general and refers only to a capacity to learn that allegedly stems from a genetic origin mediated by selection pressures. What is actually learnt, and actual behavioural phenomena such as aggression, are explained as having a genetic basis in that there is an inherited capacity in the human species to perform certain actions. The actions themselves are not prescribed by this argument. So the ultimate explanation for any regularity of behaviour in the human species lies in its genetic endowment. But such behaviour is not determined. It is one of a range of possibilities open to man. The realization of a particular possibility depends upon contingent factors such as the nature of the environment and factors affecting reproductive success. An explanation of any particular behavioural aspect thus has two dimensions. Firstly, it provides an account of the specific relevant circumstances in a temporal context for a population. Such an account 'explains' in terms of biological needs and interactions between the species and its environment. Such needs are related to fundamental biological concepts such as natural selection, adaptation and fitness. Secondly, an explanation of this nexus is provided in the basic genetic theory that underlies it. The former is not a logical or empirical necessity of the latter. The implications of this argument will be considered later on.

However, when we move away from the general to specific aspects of human conduct such as aggression, the argument asserts a link between genetic endowment and a propensity to act in a specific way. The link is causal. We are thus concerned with a theory of behaviour that asserts a behavioural necessity based upon a form of biological determinism. Given appropriate environmental conditions, a specific form of action will be undertaken as a consequence of a 'motor mechanism' itself the result or the product of the genetic endowment of the species. We are not concerned here with the more general view that 'educability' is an inherited characteristic without any prescription about what is learned. Such a view does not entail any specific form of action at all. Aggression could be learnt or part of a tradition. In a sense it is voluntary.

The argument we shall be discussing stresses the involuntary nature of much of human action. Before turning more directly to the aspect that chiefly concerns imperialism, that of human aggression, I want to look briefly at two other 'biological' views of human nature, the psychological and the ecological. Both of these are related to ethology and their arguments are not incompatible with the basic ethological thesis of a genetic basis to specific human behaviour. They take as their respective points of departure, however, the human neurological structure and relationships between social and physical environments.

The notions of instincts and drives innate to the human species are susceptible to a number of interpretations. There is a psychological theory of instinct, which should not be confused with ethological usage. Freud, for example, asserted that aggression was 'an innate independent instinctual disposition in man'. Others have argued that aggression stems from anxiety neuroses and frustration.[17] But these notions of instinct are distinct from that used, for example, by Lorenz who asserts a *genetic* basis for the 'instinct' of aggression while agreeing that the phenomenon of aggression corresponds to its description in psychoanalytic terms as a drive towards violence manifesting itself in situations of conflict and frustration.[18] Lorenz accepts that the form that aggression takes in social behaviour is of a reflex-like compulsion. Fundamentally, however, ethologists accept the notion of aggression as an instinct created through genetic programming as a product of, and response to, selection pressures. It is not therefore dependent upon psychoanalytic theory. It is a mechanism of survival belonging to the evolutionary pattern of human development. The point about this notion of instinct or drive is that it is an inherited disposition to act in a particular way when confronted with an appropriate stimulus. The action itself is the main evidence for the alleged existence of the 'instinct'. Violent or aggressive acts are caused by the prior existence of a disposition to act in this way. So while the phenomenon of aggression is in a sense held in common by both psychological and ethological theorists in terms of its description as a performance, there is a difference in the way in which it is explained. Both depend upon the notion of innate tendencies in the human species, but the former stops with the human psyche, while the latter goes further and subsumes that within a more fundamental genetic theory.

Similarly, explanations of aggression based on the notion of 'ancestral' memory and on the structure of the brain have a biological basis in that the neurological system is part of human genetic endowment. Such arguments assert the existence of a fossil brain inherited from man's reptilian past.[19] Together with this coexist a paleo-mammalian limbic system and a neo-mammalian cortex. The reptilian portion of the brain consists of the matrix of the brain stem, the reticular system, the mid-brain and the basal ganglia. It is alleged to be responsible for basic functions such as mating, breeding, establishing territory and 'forming group hierarchies'. The limbic system 'elaborates emotions and guides adaptive behaviour in a changing environment'.[20] The neo-cortex is responsible for the linguistic development of the human species and contains its reasoning faculty. What are termed 'agonistic interactions', which include aggression, are thus the product of the original brain structure of the species. Setting aside the speculative aspects of this theory and the difficulty of testing its adequacy as an explanation, the point here is that such an argument can be subsumed within the ethological thesis. Behaviour is explained through the genetic structure of the human species. It is thus possible for one prominent sociobiologist, E. O. Wilson,[21] to assert 'If aggressive behaviour under stress has a genetic basis it is likely to be due less to Pleistocene genetic inertia than to the fact that such behaviour has continued to be adaptive into modern times'. This is to accept the origins of innate tendencies while at the same time to argue that their original adaptive function remains. And of course such an argument places the emphasis upon the other side of evolutionary theory, that of social or environmental interactions that are adaptive.

This brings me to the other variant argument — that of the notion of ecological fitness. Behaviour here is seen as a response to selection pressures emanating from the environment. In the case of aggression and imperialism these manifestations arise as a consequence of an 'unstable ecological community'.[22] On this argument it is the selection pressures generated by this instability that produce evolutionary fitness. The consequence is a modifed genotype that is passed on to the next generation. Instead of an instinctive basis to the phenomenon of aggression, it is population pressure on territory that is the basic cause. Aggression and warfare are the consequences of a population explosion and competition for scarce resources. Where there is a balance between population and living conditions, there is stability, and aggression is conventionalized or ritualized into non-destructive channels. A change in the conditions for survival results in territorial behaviour and a struggle for existence that eventually restores the balance.[23]

However, as we shall see later on, this view confuses what is fitness for the species with what is fitness for the individual organism. An emphasis on environmental conditions and related behaviour, and the attribution of the latter to the former, is a strictly temporal argument based on contingent factors. Genetic fitness cannot be attributed to notions of ecological balance or instability in prospective terms. The reverse may be argued, that is, behavioural responses are a function of genetic endowment and the environment, but, as was argued earlier, an account of the former in historical terms gives us no clue as to what is adaptive for the future. There may be, as is alleged, a change in the genotype due to acute selection pressures, but this can only be assessed, if it can be established, retrospectively. Therefore, an emphasis on contemporary human ecology, however this is understood, will tell us nothing about the survival of the species in genetic or evolutionary terms. In short, a behavioural response to environmental conditions, such as aggression, can in principle be explained through reference to genetic endowment as its pre-condition but not the other way around. We cannot know in advance what is adaptive given our lack of knowledge either of genotypic change or of future environments.

I do not want to dwell on these two views of human conduct except to say that in their extreme form one shades off into psychological theory and the other into sociology. Those aspects they have in common with ethology are best discussed in the context of specific propensities to act under given conditions, such as aggression. Whether the 'motor mechanism' is instinctual and psychologically derived, or whether a given social or environmental situation induces particular forms of action and creates or modifies a disposition to do so, are subordinate to the theoretical question of their origins. If the roots of human conduct lie in the neurological system or in social interactions stimulating appropriate responses to specified situations from a genetically endowed organism, then our attention should be focused on the processes involved and not on the alleged behaviour that stems from them.

I come at last to the concept of aggression central to the biological notion of imperialism. The way in which this is defined constitutes a problem as with all concepts about human behaviour. We can make nominal distinctions such as, for example, distinguishing it from predation or from warfare. Similarly we can distinguish it from any anthropomorphic or ethical connotation as a form of unjustified violence. So far as ethology is concerned, it is a form of violence of a particular kind, intra-specific in nature performing adaptive functions, and with a genetic basis.[24] Clearly the identification of aggression as a behavioural phenomenon must be separable from any preconception as to its nature or cause if we are to explain it. Otherwise the 'observation' of aggression will be prejudiced by the postulates of a supporting hypothesis, and will lead to circularity. This is not so much of a problem as would appear since a distinction can be maintained between the hypothetical element — as a conjecture or set of conjectures — and what is observed, providing due caution as to the status of the hypothesis as a conjecture is observed. No observation can be neutral in the sense that the conceptual framework and its language through which the phenomenon is observed and expressed can be eliminated. But so long as the associated explanation and the phenomenon to be explained are logically independent of one another, and the putative explanation is susceptible to empirical testing, then circularity can be avoided. If these conditions are observed, then conjecture ceases to be mere conjecture and questions may be formulated capable of being adequately answered.

This is particularly important in the case of any investigation into aggression as a phenomenon found in the behaviour of a number of species including the human. There is a danger of adopting a view derived from the language in which we commonly describe human behaviour, transposing it into an examination of animal behaviour and then referring conclusions from that study back to man. As one commentator has it, 'First we anthropomorphise the animals and then we discover that we are just like them'.[25] Although ethology is largely concerned with animal behaviour in its actual investigations, it considers the human species as sharing the same biological characteristics. There is a 'biological continuum linking man with other forms of life'.[26]

Having said this I want to examine the argument chiefly associated with Konrad Lorenz although generally adopted by a number of ethologists.[27] Aggression is conceived of as a behavioural phenomenon within a species consisting of a competition for a resource in scarce supply. So far as imperialism is concerned, aggression consists of a competition for territory and material resources between organized sub-groups of the human species. As such it is not purely an individual trait, although some individuals and populations may be more inclined to aggression than others. It is a trait of the species. War is seen as its main social manifestation, although aggression may take other forms of violence. It is manifest at all levels of social activity. More specifically, aggression is an innate trait related to sexual selection, social bonding, the distribution of food, population distributions, and other activities necessary for social existence. Competition between individuals and sub-groups in a population is directed to the fulfilment of these basic social needs. As such it is characteristic of a wide variety of species, including the human, and constitutes a form of adaptive selection pressure. Success in this competition is due to the possession of superior mental and physical characteristics, which enable the possessor to dominate the gene-pool. His successful challenge to his rivals places him in a superior position in the hierarchy giving him the widest range of breeding opportunities and a prior claim on resources. In return the sub-group or population receives an undisputed territory commensurate with their needs, and, in normal times, an equitable and stable distribution of its members.

Aggression, in this view, fulfils certain basic requirements of a species. It ensures that the gene-pool is dominated by the strain most capable of ensuring the survival of the species, given a stable and unchanging environment. It regulates a population through the establishment and maintenance of a hierarchy, which restricts competition between its members through dominance. It provides a basis for reproduction and breeding by restricting this to dominant males. It rations food supplies in the same way. It distributes the population more evenly over a protected territory through the ejection of young adults from the nuclear group. And finally it provides security against other groups and other species.

I shall discuss the functional argument implicit in this view later; for the moment I want to concentrate on its biological aspects. Clearly this argument stresses the adaptive nature of aggression — it enhances the survival value of the species. Of course this does not explain its origins. These are found in the genetic structure of a species. Innate to man and to other organisms is a drive or motor mechanism that is heritable. It constitutes an inbuilt set of responses to an appropriate stimulus. Where this stimulus is present, the genetic programming towards aggression takes effect. The explanation for aggression is thus fundamentally an inherited, that is genetically transmitted, drive or instinct that finds its expression in actual aggressive behaviour where the environment, both social and physical, triggers it.

This basic drive is controlled, that is, kept to its fundamental purpose, by the existence of countering drives.[28] In other words, an inbuilt inhibition coexists with the drive to aggression. In behavioural terms such control occurs in what has been called ritualization,[29] which is essentially a displacement activity that, according to Lorenz and other ethologists, forms a basis for a bonding relationship with individuals of the species. Display, greeting, conventions governing contacts and social intercourse, are all manifestations of the displacement of the aggressive drive to other members of the species into a controlled form. Thus in most species, excluding the human, intra-specific fighting is regulated by innate mechanisms of control. These allow aggression to be channelled into its functional or constructive role. Only under exceptional circumstances, for example in cases of very high population densities, does it escape this control, and the result is the disintegration of that population as a stable and harmonious group. Aggression in animals is thus controlled by a kind of biological overdrive that allows it to optimalize its adaptive function. If it did not exist, interbreeding would not take place and the gene-pool available to the species would be limited and impoverished. Similarly, population distribution would not optimalise resources. Excessive intra-specific aggression would become mal-adaptive. Regulated aggression thus consists of a form of selection pressure within the species that is conducive to the survival of that species by producing a high level of reproductive fitness. As two ethologists put it, 'Aggression in the human species is the same as aggression in any other animal species. It springs from the same causes and subserves the same functions. It is a necessary force in the evolutionary processes taking place in any sexually reproducing species. There has to be competition in order for natural selection to occur.'[30]

The origins of aggression in the human species are linked to primitive man and his hostile environment with its severe selection pressures. It was in this environment that aggression was selected as part of the human genetic endowment. As Lorenz argues, aggression is 'the consequence of intra-specific selection which worked on our forefathers for roughly forty thousand years, that is, throughout the early Stone Age'.[31] But in modern times intra-specific aggression in the human species has ceased to perform its adaptive function. It has escaped control.[32] How this can happen, given that controlling mechanisms on this argument are equally innate, is not explained. The reason given is 'the rapid change wrought in human ecology and sociology by cultural development',[33] but aggression and its controlling conventions are equally 'cultural' in nature.

War and imperialism are explained as the direct consequences of this aggressive drive. 'Unreasoning and unreasonable human nature causes two nations to compete, though no economic necessity compels them to do so.'[34] The former balancing function of aggression, which under control created social stability and a harmonious relation between individuals and their respective share of resources, is now lost. And given that one of the major functions of aggression was the acquisition of territory and the balanced distribution of population, the result is an uncontrolled imperialism. Some ethologists argue that what was originally a process of natural selection through breeding governed by aggression has now become a drive for power. Wealth, resources and prestige have taken the place of sexual selection and more basic needs. Consequently, the aggressive drive has become maladaptive because it fulfils functions that are genetically irrelevant or counter-productive to the survival of the species. However, regardless of the question whether aggression is adaptive or maladaptive, the point is that it is alleged to be the result of *cultural* evolution and to have a genetic base. The implications of this argument will be considered later. (Much of this argument is an extension of observations made about animals to human behaviour. There has been little ethological study of man, but this has not inhibited any claims made by ethologists.)

I want to consider now one argument that on the face of it appears to be outside this sociobiological debate. J. A. Schumpeter published his study on imperialism in 1919, well before current concerns with ethology.[35] Yet his thesis is surprisingly 'biological' in tone. Like the ethologists, he believed that aggression is a basic characteristic of human nature and he set out to make an explicit connection between it and the phenomenon of imperialism. His main postulate was that the cause of imperialism is an atavistic impulse in man. He posited the same connection between environment and adaptive response as that made by the ethologists. Schumpeter was at some pains to deny the rationalizing arguments of the economic imperialists discussed in an earlier chapter.[36] In his view men are motivated by irrational impulses that are not recognized in their apparently rational pursuit of interest. To this extent he was seeking to apply a corrective to the insistence placed on economic structure and forces by Marxist and neo-Marxist writers. For Schumpeter, the true causes of war and imperialism lay not in the ostensible reasons offered by the contending states, but in their innate aggressiveness. Aggression is motiveless. The only point in aggression is aggression itself. As he put it, 'And history in truth shows us nations and classes — most nations furnish an example at some time or other — that seek expansion for the sake of expanding, war for the sake of fighting, victory for the sake of winning, dominion for the sake of ruling . . .'.[37] The immediate cause of a war or of imperial expansion is only secondary, and the appeal made by political leaders to their peoples for support in such enterprises arouses the primary instincts: 'the dark power of the unconscious calls into play instincts that carry over from the life habits of the dim past.'[38]

Nationalism and other ideological beliefs such as national–socialism, discussed in chapter 4, are fundamentally appeals to human nature. Imperialism is thus atavistic in character. It emanates from deeply rooted instincts in the human race and leads directly to the 'objectless disposition on the part of a state to unlimited forcible expansion'.[39] Schumpeter argued that the drive to aggression and dominance is the product of a social habit, itself in turn the result of a time in the human past when fighting and territorial expansion were necessary elements in a struggle for survival. Then imperialism had a *raison d'être*: it provided a means of subsistence for the social group. The social habit assumed in this early time of troubles became a psychological disposition that carried, through inheritance, into the present. In effect what is argued here is that an environmental condition, in this case a hostile and uncertain world, placed a premium on those factors in human relationships that made for survival. These were social cohesion and strong leadership, warrior-like qualities and a commitment to permanent struggle in order to guarantee food supply and possessions. A kind of anarchy prevailed between social groups or tribes, in much the same way as is argued was the case for the world of nation-states by the power-security theorists. The stability, both social and economic, necessary for breeding and subsistence could only be achieved through successful violence. The consequence was a psychological disposition to aggression that needed to find an outlet. The modern age in Schumpeter's opinion provides few if any outlets for this entrenched instinct. As he put it, 'Aggressive nationalism . . . the instincts of dominance and war derived from the distant past and alive down to the present — such things do not die overnight. From time to time they seek to come into their own, all the more vigorously when they find dwindling satisfaction within the small community'.[40]

There are some striking similarities between this argument and that of the ethologists. Of course there is no suggestion that the transmission of this clearly heritable characteristic of man is genetic. The references to instincts and dispositions echo more the psychological view referred to earlier, and are directly related to an innate propensity to act in certain situations, including that of frustration. But the notion that a social disposition to act in a particular way both is a product of an environment and is transmissable from one generation to another is very similar to the ethological view of aggression. It is an atavistic impulse derived from a time when it served a social purpose that it no longer fulfils. From being adaptive in a past environment, it has now become maladaptive and purposeless. The point that Schumpeter continually stressed, rather like Lorenz, is that aggression is inherently irrational and dysfunctional in a modern society. It serves no purpose in modern human society, whatever its original function.

The central argument echoes the ethologists in that the roots of human action are found in the human biological constitution. Man is motivated by something that he does not control and of which he is unaware. It is part of his inheritance from an earlier age and an earlier being. In the evolution of human culture, with all its complexities and sophistications, there remains an element of a more primitive and savage past that he cannot eliminate. Given appropriate conditions, a stimulus is provided for the realization of this primitive inheritance. Man becomes aggressive. And it is this aspect of his character that explains large-scale violence and the ceaseless struggle for power that typified ancient societies and is now the central characteristic of the world of states. Wars and imperialism, as Schumpeter says, reflect 'the ancient truth that the dead always rule the living'.[41] And as Lorenz asserts, 'no politician ever could make men really fight if it were not for very archaic instinctive reactions of the crowd on which to play'.[42]

Schumpeter's theory of psychological momentum, or the persistence of traits formed under past conditions into a totally different present, does not tackle the question of the process by which such traits are transmitted. He is primarily concerned with what has been termed a phenotype, that is a set of behaviour characteristic of the species. The ethologists, of course, argue that there is a genetic origin to aggression. Atavism, if it exists, is the consequence of a genetic endowment that under certain conditions triggers off an appropriate behavioural response. It is this endowment with its innate propensity to act in a particular manner that is transmitted, not the behaviour. As we have seen earlier, the process is asserted to be one of genetic assimilation. Aggression is conceived of as a trait that can be acquired partly or wholly by learning. Such a capacity for learning, as we have seen, is asserted as having a genetic basis. The point here is that the phenotype is produced by environmental stimuli as well as by the genotype, and is then fixed by selection of genes. A genetic programme is thus created by selection pressures and establishes a set of innate tendencies that respond to appropriate stimuli. On this argument learned behaviour becomes biological behaviour and is thus heritable. The question of its adaptive function is open, as environments change, but it is presumed that originally it was adaptive or it would not have become genetically fixed in the population or the species. It contributed to the 'fitness' of the species.

Let me restate the theoretical propositions of the argument so that we can have a clear idea of what is at stake in assessing it as an explanation of human aggression and imperialism. The phenomenon of aggression in human society is said to stem from man's biological nature. This in turn is conceived of as a complex of genetic programming and cultural evolution. As Lorenz argues,

Both phylogenetically and culturally evolved norms of behaviour represent motives and are felt to be values by any normal human being. Both are woven into an immensely complicated system of universal interaction to analyse which is all the more difficult as most of the processes take place in the subconscious and are by no means accessible to self-observation.[43]

We have thus a fusion of evolutionary theory, which includes not only genetic change but also cultural development, psychological concepts such as instincts, drives motor patterns, etc., and structural—functional theory using concepts such as system, function and purpose to explain social interaction. Essentially the argument stipulates a relationship between a genetic structure and an environment in which adaptive functions are served by aggression. The tendency to be aggressive serves a variety of functions across most animal species, including man. It establishes a basis for sexual selection, through the dominance of the biologically 'fitter' individual; it serves as a basis for the allocation of food and territory for a population; it disperses young adults over as wide a territory as possible, thus optimalizing resources; and it ensures that competition between individuals is adaptive in that selection pressures are set up that place a value on intelligence, speed of learning and innovation. It also reinforces the solidarity of the group against other competitive groups or species by providing a basis for hierarchical dominance, leadership and discipline in the face of countering aggression. The gene-pool of the species is thus improved through the existence of aggressive tendencies subject to countering or controlling forces that coexist with them. Aggression is an agent of natural selection and an important aspect of human evolution.

Aggression in the human, and other species, is thus an innate trait, heritable and genetically based, which appeared when the appropriate circumstances occurred in the environment. It gave an aggressive species a high survival value and so conferred evolutionary advantages on it. However, since this trait was innate and acted as an involuntary instinct, drive or motor pattern, its functioning and, more important, its control were equally instinctive. A means of control was necessary to prevent innate aggression becoming maladaptive and to realize its adaptive functions. On this argument a radically changed environment could, and in fact did, break the controlling mechanism, and so aggression in man became dangerous to the survival of the species. Wars and imperialism are the consequences of man's inability as a species to produce a control over aggression in environmental conditions that make maladaptive what was formerly a balanced and adaptive form of natural selection. Such controls, as in the case of ritualized conduct in other animal species, are in any case unconscious and, in this sense, beyond reason.

Rather paradoxically, some ethologists assert the possibility of substituting rituals for war, sport for example, in order to nullify the dangerous effects of an uncontrolled aggression.[44] But if this can be done for the rational end of reducing the dangers of aggression, it is hard to see why aggression itself could not be more directly controlled through rational policies of disarmament or arms control. The answer clearly is that aggression in man cannot be *eradicated* because of its innate biological nature, but it can be *contained* by appeasing it with some substitute other than wars and violence. There is in this a curious mixture of biological theorizing and ethical concern. The point here is that the argument insists that man is a prisoner of his biological nature and driven by forces that he cannot consciously or rationally control. The equilibrium between his genetic programming and his environment is fortuitious. Contingent factors in the latter can radically change it.

The third element in this conceptual framework is that of the functional relations between these evolutionary and psychological aspects and social interaction. The central question asked in this kind of approach is not what *causes* a particular behavioural phenomenon but what is its purpose. For example, aggression *inter alia* has the function of inducing dispersal of a population over as wide an area of territory as possible. Dispersal is both a product of aggression and a means of controlling aggression through 'distancing' individuals and sub-groups of a population and minimizing contact. The purpose of this is to optimize resources and to prevent the aggressive drive from having destructive or dysfunctional effects on the population and on the species. Overcrowding is dangerous not only because of the possibility of aggression escaping control, but because of the strain on resources and the debilitation of standards of living. Disease and malnutrition become adverse environmental conditions. Furthermore, the selection pressure of aggression is nullified given the breakdown of its functioning under extreme conditions of overcrowding. It is pointed out that the aggressive drive is at its minimum or non-existent in species that herd.[45]

The overall purpose of aggression is to maintain a population in some form of stability. If the population is conceived of as a system of behavioural practices, each component making a contribution to the maintenance of the whole, and each kept in check by counteracting or feedback relations, then this constitutes a model of a functional argument. The reason why a particular phenomenon or phenotypic behaviour exists is explained by the assertion of a prior logic which relates it to the maintenance of society. It is not so much a 'cause' of society, nor is the practice itself explained in causal terms, as subsumed in this notion of purpose. Aggression exists in order to perform a social function, not because of specific necessary and sufficient pre-conditions that are independent of any application to function and purpose. The point here is that, although, as we have seen, some biologists conceive of a causal basis to social behaviour in the form of genetically transmitted behavioural traits, others either blur this distinction or abandon it by using functional argument. As we shall see, this is of significance when we come to assess the explanatory adequacy of these arguments.

Finally, not only is functional argument the basis of some ethological enquiries, evolutionary theory itself has a teleological aspect. The distinction was made earlier between evolution as a form of historical description and as an explanation of the series of changes in organisms and species over time. The concepts of natural selection, fitness and adaptation are linked to the former and not to the latter. By this is meant that while the synthetic theory depends upon Mendelian and molecular genetics for an explanation of change and the transmission of the genotype, the relationship of the phenotype to the actual environment is contingent. Adaptation is a matter of chance, because while the physical characteristics of the organism are transmitted through reproduction, the question of the 'fitness' of the organism and of the species can only be 'explained' retrospectively. Survival itself is not explained in terms of fitness unless the conditions for survival, which would presumably include the genotype and mutational forms, can be specified in the context of environmental conditions relevant to them. Such a specification would be theoretical and not historical, and survival could then be a predictable outcome if the theory was proved adequate through testing.

In short, any consideration of adaptation in the absence of such a theory is historical in the sense that natural selection itself is a non-theoretical concept, just as society in the functional argument cannot be treated as a theoretical entity independent of the practices that constitute it. Society is behaviour and behaviour is society. In terms of evolution, the process alleged to be at work that selects those species that survive and those that do not, is not given a theoretical specification nor is it explained.

In the case with which we are primarily concerned, that of aggression in human behaviour, the argument asserts the existence of a behaviour mechanism, the product of genetic programming, that is created by a form of selection arising out of the interaction of environmental and genetic factors. For this argument to be other than circular it is necessary to isolate those conditions that, create firstly, the genetic element and, secondly, the appropriate responsive behaviour. It is also necessary, if we are to have a genuine explanation of aggressive and competitive behaviour in the human species, to establish the relationship between causes — the mechanism — and the effects — the actual behaviour. And this must be done not merely rigorously but so as to produce a *testable* hypothesis.

At the core of the ethological thesis and of the synthetic theory of evolution is a hypothesis about the acquisition and transmission through inheritance of behavioural characteristics. In the former case general features of human life such as the existence of aggression, war and imperialism are said to be explicable in terms of man's biological nature. And by this is meant that as an animal species, human behaviour can be explained by reduction to a thesis of the heritability of characteristics. No account of behaviour can prove this theory true or false. Only a vindication of the genetic theory central to the hypothesis can do that. If we take cultural evolution to be literally, a development of behavioural traits in the human species, consisting of a phenotypic response to genetic composition and environmental change, the latter being both social and 'physical', then, unless we can isolate the genetic basis as causes and the phenotypic responses as effects, we are not engaged in a biological explanation. This is because, as was pointed out earlier, while the phenotype is derived from the genotype, the reverse cannot be the case. The genotype is the product of a process within DNA that is completely independent of the physical environment of the organism and of the species. Its consequence in terms of adaptation and survival is, as we have seen, fortuitous. Cultural evolution is a derivative of biological evolution and is simply the record of phenotypic responses, allegedly explicable in terms of the genetic composition of the human species and of the various environments that it encounters.

If, alternatively, it is claimed that cultural evolution consists of responses to environments *per se,* then it is non-biological, for the genotype of the species is not responsive in this way. It is neutral in terms of its processes and, while it may have a favourable outcome in terms of adaptation, this cannot be induced through environmental conditions. At best it permits the realization of a wide variety of possibilities. In short, the phenotype is either the product of the genotype, in which case we can explain behaviour in genetic terms, or it is independent of the genotype in the sense that it is the product of the environment, in which case we must seek a non-biological explanation of human conduct. The transmission of cultural traits from one generation to the next is the consequence of non-genetic factors. They are not heritable in the genetic sense of heredity. Traditions are accessible to reasoning and are part of human consciousness in a way denied by the ethological theory. An explanation of this kind of transmission would depend upon relating human thought to action, and would constitute a radically different kind of explanation to that postulated by sociobiological theory. It would take the form of the type of reason-giving explanation discussed in earlier chapters.

Having these possibilities in mind, we can now turn to the example of Japanese imperialism in the 1930s to see if sociobiological theory can help us towards an explanation. After discussion of this case I will turn back to the problem of explanation and trace out some of the implications of the arguments I have just considered. How then can we apply a sociobiological theory of aggression to an explanation of contemporary human behaviour? The case for an ethological explanation of aggression rests largely on analogies with animal behaviour. But it is difficult to place humans in laboratory or experimental conditions in the same way as animals, and even more difficult to study them in their native 'habitat', given the problems of defining 'culture' and distinguishing behaviour from environment. I have chosen the example of Japanese imperialism in order to see whether the sociobiological approach can lead to an explanation of this phenomenon rather than as a rigorous test of a finished theory. I have chosen it largely because, superficially at least, it seems to have some resemblance to the ethological case of behavioural characteristics, aggressive in nature but strictly controlled, transmitted through generations, entering into a new phase with a radically changed environment. The consequence is an unbridled imperialism. The dramatic changes that occurred with Japanese exposure to the West in the middle of the last century produced a new environment. They were imposed on a society that was isolated from cross-cultural contact, that was hierarchical and homegeneous in nature, and that had a large and elaborate set of rituals for controlling social relations. Aggression seemed to be an important element in Japanese society, embodied in military virtues, the samurai and the cult of *bushido*. After Western penetration the Japanese transformed their economy from a self-sufficient and highly organized agricultural base into an industrial economy heavily dependent upon the import of raw materials and on trade. It was also linked to a programme of armaments manufacture designed to turn Japan into a major power in the Far East and the Pacific.

Parallel with this radical change in the economy was the dominance of the military in Japanese politics and society. Increasingly, government became influenced by the demands of the armed forces and massive armament production became the basis of an imperialist policy. From an inward-directed society, Japan turned to the outside world with a civilizing mission designed to create an empire and a set of dependencies paying tribute to the metropolitan power. Such a transformation was accompanied by social changes that were based upon existing institutions and practices, and were not so much revolutionary as modifications. Instead of a balance between the component elements of Japanese society — the aristocracy, the military, the merchants and the peasants — the military came in the end to dominate and to govern. And their declared end was the creation of an overseas empire for Japan.

Now 'orthodox' reasons for this surge of militarism and imperialist expansion, such as have been discussed in earlier chapters, do not seem to fit this case of Japanese imperialism. It seems anomalous. The nature of Japanese society seems to be relevant in a way not apparent in the cases of European imperial expansion. The drive to empire appears to be not a consequence of rational planning designed to achieve objectives, such as the provision of national security or material advantages, although, as we shall see, elements of these exist in the form of rationalizing arguments designed to eliminate opposition and to justify measures already taken or in train, but the consequence of a drive in the ethological sense.

Economic motivation has been alleged to be the mainspring of Japanese imperialism. The Greater East Asia Co-Prosperity Sphere, which was the ostensible goal of the Japanese, has been likened to the major capitalist empires created by the Europeans. But Japanese society in this period bore very little resemblance to Western capitalist societies, regardless of the weaknesses of the economic imperialist argument discussed in chapter 3. This is not to say that economic motivation was irrelevant to an explanation of the decisions to expand, but that it was not paramount or self-sufficient as an explanation. The conduct of the Japanese army cannot be explained in economic terms, nor can the attitude of the Japanese cabinet or of the Genro.

It is also argued that the 'overpopulation' of the Japanese islands, and the consequent strain on resources occasioned by this, and the radical changes in the Japanese economic structure provide basic reasons for imperial expansion. But of course the ethological view of territorial expansion and of aggression 'explains' these phenomena not in terms of any rationalization, economic or political in character, but as a drive designed to secure the survival of the population and of the species. The need to secure access to resources and to respond to severe selection pressures occasioned by environmental changes such as population growth and territorial limitation constitutes a biological trigger releasing aggressive impulses to expand. Rationalizations based on security or economic needs are subsumed within this argument.

Similarly the ideological aspect of Japanese militarism, the cult of bushido, the hierarchical and highly organized nature of Japanese society, Emperor worship, Shintoism and the dominant position of the armed forces, and the sentiments and beliefs that reinforced them, are simply expressions of basic biological drives. These features were to be expected of a society that was experiencing acute selection pressures. Extreme nationalism and the constantly expressed fear of confinement by the powerful Western powers to the cramped islands of the Japanese homeland were the manifestations of a population under pressure. Debate on this predicament was constantly emphasizing the need for 'space' and the importance of the use of force in attaining it. Diplomacy and negotiation were seen only as adjuncts to that end.

I hasten to add that this recital of 'factors' in Japanese imperialism during this period is not intended to beg the question of its nature or of those features that would constitute an 'ethological' explanation. As we shall see, the descriptive language we use to identify the phenomenon that is the subject of an explanation should not result in the tautology that Japanese imperialism was both an aggression and evidence of an innate tendency to aggress. There are serious problems with the use of concepts such as survival, adaptation, drive and selection that involve circularity. The language used to describe Japanese imperialism — indeed the very use of the term imperialism — is in a sense tentative, and the suggestions made about it at this stage at least are mere conjectures. We need to make a clear logical distinction between the phenomenon to be explained and the explanation. This means that the concepts used both in the delineation of the phenomenon and in the explanatory framework must not be merely descriptive or circularity will result.

Hence the real point is not that the manifestations of Japanese national consciousness referred to above are relevant to an explanation, but that consciousness itself is the product of underlying causes. The form it actually takes is not important although one would expect some consistency with the actions undertaken. But expansion beyond the nation state is, as we have seen, justified in a wide variety of ways from an admission of national self-interest, to the civilizing mission and the preservation of world peace. So where these features of Japanese society appear to reflect the ethological thesis of a population under pressure embarking on aggressive imperialism, this coincidence is not causal. It is the aggression itself that matters; and this is explained by an innate drive released under certain conditions, which are latent in all societies. In the case of Japan they occurred in a particularly acute form. Existing social practices became instrumental rather than were causal.

On the ethological argument, aggression is an individual response to an environmental situation originally directed and controlled so as to perform certain social functions such as sexual selection, distribution of resources, social protection and cohesion, and the spatial distribution of population, all of which were conducive to the survival of that population and of the species. While aggression is a product of individual behaviour — and individuals have differential degrees of response in this respect — the result is an aggregate *social* behaviour. Hierarchy, leadership, dominance and submission are all features of a population in which aggression is a central characteristic.

Instability in the form of acute selection pressures in the environment places a premium on aggression, and the gene-pool for that population is dominated by the genes of the most successful aggressors through their control over breeding. Thus, given a population with a net reproduction rate commensurate with resources and territory, a balance exists between aggression and the fulfilment of these basic social functions. If, however, instability is introduced through radical changes in the environment, either in the physical terms of existence, or through competition from other populations, then the aggressive drive is directed towards containing such changes. If it succeeds in doing this and restoring the balance, then it is adaptive. During the period of adjustment however, we may expect a rise in the incidence of aggression as the individuals in the destabilized population respond to change.

If we translate this to Japanese society in the later part of the last century we can see on the face of it a society exposed to radical environmental changes. Prior to Commodore Perry's expedition, Japan had a balanced economy, a hierarchical political system and a religion and a set of beliefs that emphasized family affiliations. The vision of Japanese society it perpetuated was that of an extended family with the Emperor at its head. Social divisions were in a sense functional with everyone occupying his appropriate place. Interchange between these social classes was not encouraged; each had its own order and degree. It was a stable society and one insulated from the outside world. Such changes as were occurring were assimilated or accommodated within an existing structure of rules and beliefs. With the intrusion of the outside world all was changed. The important point to be considered here is the impossibility of explaining the drive to expansion without relating it to Japanese society and its attempt to adjust a rigid, if stable, social structure to radically changed conditions. Whether this relationship follows the ethological model outlined above is another matter. But clearly the kind of explanation for Western imperialism based on a rationale for action taken for granted in Western social mores does not have the same force in explaining Japanese policy and actions. Without begging the question of the relationship between socially derived beliefs and political action, the former appear to be relevant in a way not so apparent in 'Western' accounts of international politics and diplomacy. Whether this entails a qualitative difference I leave open at this stage. But if social mores are relevant, this brings the Japanese case within the scope of the sociobiological argument.

What then can be said of Japanese society during this period and what bearing does it have on a sociobiological explanation of Japanese imperialism? One of the major features of Japanese nationalist sentiment that radically departs from that of the West is Emperor worship. This itself was based on a modification of existing institutions and practices. The Meiji Restoration replaced the shogunate with a ruling monarch. Although prior to 1868 the Emperor played an important role in Japanese society, that role had become increasingly symbolic. The crisis initiated by Perry resulted in a progressive shift towards the dominance of the Emperor in the political system. As well as representing the element of continuity through an unbroken line of succession and through a divine origin, the Emperor came also to represent a new nationalism. He became in this sense an instrument of change. He was a transcendental monarch in the sense that he represented the Japanese people. He was the embodiment of the state. All virtue emanated from him. In almost a literal sense he was considered to be the father of the Japanese family. The idea of the family constituted the basis of Japanese views of their society. Filial piety, the acceptance of parental authority, the performance of family duties and the coherence of the family unit all contributed to the idea of the state as a corporate entity with the imperial family as its symbolic form. Loyalty to the state meant loyalty to the Emperor. As in filial relations within the family, with its established order and degree, so the individual related in the same way to the Emperor.

The only acceptable motive or grounds for action in moral terms was *chukun,* or sincerity in heart towards the Emperor.[46] Thus a justification of an action could, and as we shall see did, ignore any reference either to expediency or to the authority of rank or of institutions within which the individual had his place, by identification with the Emperor. This notion of personal honour cut across personal position or social identity and allowed an individual to act on his own initiative provided he did so with *chukun.* His superiors had to take this as a valid and sufficient reason. Each such act was in effect *de novo* and an individual need be consistent only in terms of this 'sincerity of heart towards the Emperor'. Apparently irrational behaviour, paradoxical and contradictory, is thus explicable in terms of this overriding moral dictate. The balance of calculation for any decision in moral terms depended on its relation to the Emperor.

Thus, in considering the level of action and decision in Japanese imperialism, this factor is clearly relevant. As we shall see, what to Western eyes is indiscipline or lawlessness in the form of assassinations, suicides, factionalism, decisions taken without authority and the curious ambiguities of the Japanese political system, is consonant with this principle. It explains both the independence of the individual and the delays and inconsistencies in policy-making. While in his observation of the duties and obligations incumbent on his social and official position the individual was following the divinely inspired example of his Emperor, he could eschew these ties and follow his own conscience given *chukun*.

This is particularly important in the case of one section of Japanese society — the army. The army came to represent the epitome of Emperor worship as well as of ultranationalism. As with the Emperor himself, the army changed its role from that of a constituent, if not particularly respected, component of the Japanese 'family' to become the predominant element. It was associated very closely with imperialism and with an extreme form of nationalism. An imperial destiny was urged for Japan, whose aim was the extension of the Japanese 'way' to the outside world, so that all nations accepted the divine role of the Emperor and took their appropriate place in an international hierarchy with Japan at its head. Such sentiments were peculiarly the expression of the junior officers of the armed forces, although they found wide support among the 'common people' and sympathy from their superiors. Drawn from the land-owning and peasant sections of Japanese society, these officers represented an intense and radical conservatism. The agrarian economy had been disrupted not only by the effects of the world economic crisis but by the Japanese government's efforts to industrialize. The urban areas had gained at the expense of the country. These officers played a role in Japanese politics and in the important decisions taken on imperial expansion incommensurate with their rank. Both as individuals and as members of ultra-nationalist factions they exercised an influence in a society that respected *chukun*. Senior officers and politicians were either sympathizers or dared not confront them with strong disciplinary action, at least in the early stages of imperial expansion in the 1930s. Such independence and influence would be unthinkable in contemporary Western societies.

The junior officers were not the only source of independence and decision in the context of Japanese imperialism; their superiors also considered themselves independent of the government. The Chiefs of Staff and the service ministries held an autonomous position in the

Japanese political structure. They represented a major locus for decisions affecting imperial expansion on mainland Asia. With the eclipse of the embryonic party system, and closely associated with the *zaibatsu,* the major industrialists in Japan, in major rearmament, they were able to exert an influence on Japanese politics far beyond that of any contemporary 'military—industrial complex'. It was only in major war, however, that they were able in effect to undertake the functions of government. In this period, while they could take initiatives, they could not direct or control all the institutions involved in decision-making in the Japanese system.

The Japanese cabinet and ministries were somewhat amorphous in political terms. Few prime ministers were directly associated with political parties in this period. They governed within a framework of constraints imposed by the necessity to secure the agreement of the armed services, the Genro (Council of Elder Statesmen) and the Emperor himself, and to comply with popular sentiment, which increasingly became zenophobic in tone. Imperial and Liaison Conferences in any case became substitutes for the Cabinet and Diet and important decisions were made at these meetings outside the nominal political framework. The major parties or party coalitions — the Seiyukai and the Minseito — ceased to have any political significance and indeed by 1940 all parties were suppressed and replaced by the Imperial Rule Assistance Association.

The Genro was another source of influence in Japanese politics. Its main function was to proffer advice to the Emperor on the choice of prime minister. It was composed of court officials and former prime ministers. Later in the thirties it became the Jushin, or Council of Senior Retainers. While it cannot be said to have had much political influence in this period, for the army tended to have the last say in choosing a prime minister,[47] it acted as a source of indecision and weakened the role of the Emperor as well as that of the government. Issues tended to be debated exhaustively so that events often overtook decision. This allowed scope for independent initiative that forced the issue.

The Emperor himself, the key figure in Japanese society, was not so much a ruler as a spiritual leader. His involvement in politics was that of an endorser, rather than an initiator of action. In a sense he was at the end of the political process. By the time decisions came to him for approval circumstances had moved, or been contrived, to force his judgement in one direction. All was done in his name, yet he could at best only intervene and not direct. It was what he represented and not what he was as an individual that mattered. Followers of *kodo,* or the 'imperial way', while professing eternal allegiance to the Emperor, could and did treat the actual Emperor as subordinate to their policies. He could be used to endorse what they believed to be the right course for the fulfilment of Japan's destiny. Yet this endorsement was all-important, for without it Japanese unity would collapse. He was central to it.

We have in this necessarily brief summary of Japan's political institutions a picture of a society peculiarly homogeneous in mores and social attitudes, yet in political terms extraordinarily diffuse.[48] There were many loci of decision. There was no clear chain of command or of authority other than that of the Emperor, who neither governed nor presided over the political process but symbolized it. He was the state. Order and degree prevailed to the extent that everyone knew his place. But while this led to the acceptance of a hierarchical form of authority, it was more a case of obeying one's superiors. At the top and at the bottom of Japanese society there was no clear direction. Nationalist sentiment took the place of political ideology governing a political programme. The only common ground for action was an imperialism that united the Japanese and excluded dissent and debate. All could agree on that. Any alternative programme carried with it the seeds of revolution and opposition. The peasants and the *zaibatsu* could unite with the army in carrying out a programme of imperial expansion to the greater glory of the Emperor. On almost any other issue there were deep divisions between these groups and, worse, no clear political direction or means of providing one.

Commentators on Japanese society at the time stress the importance of frustration and fear as elements in the Japanese psyche.[49] A traditional society was experiencing profound changes imposed by the intervention of the outside world. There appeared to be two alternatives and both were to be feared. The first was revolution and a radical change in the structure of Japanese society on the lines of the Russian revolution. And the second was the possibility of Japan becoming an imperial possession of the Western powers, or at best an object of contention, following the example of China. Any internal political development that changed the basic institutions of Japan was a potential danger, since it might provide an opportunity for intervention. Civil war or political weakness through the lack of a central government capable of withstanding foreign powers were to be avoided. Yet fundamental changes had to be made in order to strengthen Japan against her external dangers. The economy had to be transformed giving Japan an industrial base for her military power. This in itself had its dangers, on the one hand from the social dislocations necessary for its achievement and, on the other, from the creation of a dependency on trade and raw materials that could be manipulated by foreign powers.

By 1930 both of these prospects seemed imminent. The world economic crisis and changes in Japan's economic structure produced considerable discontent amongst the agrarian population. The growth of the cities and of industries similarly produced an urban class susceptible to revolutionary programmes and ideologies alien to traditionalism. Socialist and communist parties had begun to appear. Democracy itself seemed dangerous since it gave dissent and opposition an opportunity. A cleavage in Japanese society appeared. At the same time the basis of Japanese economic development, the creation of exchange relations with a world market economy, was arrested with the world depression. The rise of tariff barriers and the vulnerability of sources of raw materials and markets encouraged notions of economic nationalism.[50] And the enhanced competition for market opportunities together with imperial preference systems meant that Japan was isolated. China was at once an awful example and an opportunity.

The rigidities of the Japanese social system and these forces of change produced what one commentator calls a 'pressure transfer principle'.[51] Masao Maruyama argues that the corporate nature of Japanese politics and society with its hierarchical structure produced social tensions that could not find any outlet in dissent. On the principle of the ship's cat or perhaps the ship's rats, frustrations were relieved by passing them down the hierarchy. The common people having no such outlet could only relieve their own frustration by finding an outlet in nationalism. As he puts it, 'at the bottom no such transfer is possible . . . People in an undemocratic society are consequently liable to become the slaves of fanatic zenophobia, the frustrations of their daily lives being effectively sublimated into jingoism.'[52] It was, of course, this class that provided the recruits for the expanding army and from which sprang many of the junior officers who formed extreme nationalist groups; while at the top the absence of any 'autonomy of decision' and the fear of revolution and social anarchy led to the encouragement and use of such sentiment. While reserving judgement on this argument for the moment, it is interesting to note that it is compatible with the sociobiological explanation of imperialism. Certainly Japan experienced a rise in violence in the form of political assassinations and coups that had no clear object other than the removal of politicians and military leaders who failed to represent the 'imperial way'.

It was not only the fear of revolution or the collapse of Japan's social and political institutions that inspired the political leadership, but fear of the outside world, which has been suggested by some commentators as a motive for Japanese imperialism.[53] Japan's relations with the West indicate two conflicting tendencies: the first an admiration and a desire to emulate the technological drive seen as the basis of Western superiority and strength, and the second a fear of Western dominance, which as combined with a resentment at the way in which the Japanese were treated as racially inferior. The interference on the part of the West in Japan's economic management and the imposition of unequal treaties implied a quasicolonial status. At the same time, the acquisition of empire by the European states and the United States in the Pacific, South East Asia and the Far East, and their treatment of China, not only threatened Japanese sovereignty but also isolated and excluded her. The sense of inferiority that this engendered was important. It reinforced the move to modernize and to increase Japanese technical and industrial capacity. And it also encouraged the initial policy of seeking to revise the symbols of Japanese tutelage to the West in the form of the unequal treaties and the Western assumption of paramountcy in the East. Fear of the West, on this argument, was a major factor in inducing a programme of industrial development that was a basis for a genuine political independence and an aggressive expansionist foreign policy. If these had not been undertaken, then Japan was in danger of becoming another China, an area of exploitation by contending foreign powers.

Fortunately for Japan, circumstances favoured her. She had, as we have seen, a stable political system capable of changing without disruption. Unlike China, there were no political opportunities for foreign intervention. Her potential exploiters were themselves divided and indeed their quarrels, culminating in the First World War, gave Japan herself an opportunity for expansion. A shrewd policy of alliance and diplomatic manoeuvring exploited this advantage. At the same time, Japan built up her armaments and created a major navy. By the time opposition to Japanese expansion hardened in the inter-war period, Japan was in a strong position. Nevertheless the fear remained. Any retreat or internal weakness would provide an opportunity for foreign intervention. The Japanese saw themselves as essentially on the defensive challenged by an expansionist West whose technological capabilities were to be feared and respected. Until Japan by her own efforts could insulate herself from foreign influence and competition, she remained fundamentally insecure. With the collapse of the world market economy in the early 1930s economic nationalism became wedded to political nationalism, and pointed to the necessity of empire as a means of guaranteeing markets and raw materials for Japanese economic development.

If these arguments are accepted, then the role of the army in Japanese politics and society in this period and the drive to imperialism become explicable in terms of fear and frustration engendered through a traditional and homogeneous society encountering radical changes in its environment. Support for *kodo* and the extreme nationalist feelings that developed in the population at large can be seen as a means of protecting Japanese society in the face of internal and external dangers. All sections of society could unite on this common basis of the imperial way. Divisive issues and dissent could be avoided by means of this common denominator. Whatever the putative gains advocated for expansion abroad, the prevailing imperialist sentiment united the Japanese as nothing else could under the circumstances of the time. And this was clearly understood by the political leadership. It was a solution that while begging all the questions that faced them, nevertheless provided a means of guaranteeing the integrity of their society.

It is interesting to note that during the China Incident of 1937 one of the propaganda posters prominently displayed in public places all over Japan carried the slogan 'A Hundred Million Hearts Beating Like One'[54] over the drawing of a distended ant. The analogy of the ants nest is an apt one for the sociobiological view, for it too is hierarchical, intensively cooperative, functionally controlled and directed, and chauvinistic to the extent that all other groups of ants are enemies.

Let us now look at Japanese imperialism and see what course it took. This is not to suggest that *ex post facto* it constituted a coherent programme or that the narrative that follows is based on any preconception of its nature. The intention is to relate incident with action and decision from 1930 onwards in order to isolate the major questions that have to be answered if the sociobiological argument is to have any force as an explanation. What form such an explanation might have, and the grounds for its adequacy, are central to this analysis and will be examined at the end of this account.

Japan already had an empire in 1930. Her involvement in Korea began in 1894 and the resultant war with China gave Japan Port Arthur and the Liaotung Peninsula in South Manchuria. Formosa and the Pescadores were confirmed as Japanese possessions in the peace negotiations of 1895. But significantly the Japanese position in South Manchuria was challenged by the Triple Intervention of Russia, France and Germany, and Japan was forced to withdraw. The subsequent war of 1904 between Russia and Japan resulted in Japan regaining these territories. Russia also accepted Japanese paramountcy in Korea and her annexation of South Sakhalin. In 1910 Japan formally annexed Korea. The First World War saw the Japanese seizure of the German-held Pacific island groups of the Carolines and the Marshalls, later confirmed as Japanese mandates by the Peace Treaties. Similarly, Japan took over the former German concessions in China at Shantung. The immediate post-war period saw not only Japanese intervention in Siberia during the Russian civil war but a growing involvement in Chinese politics. In 1928 for example some 15,000 Japanese troops occupied Tsingtao and Tsinan and were engaged in heavy fighting with Chinese nationalist forces.

But it was the Manchurian Crisis of 1931 that seemed to indicate a conscious policy of imperial expansion on a grander scale than the piecemeal opportunism of the past. The major moves in Japanese imperial expansion in the later thirties were the invasion of China in 1938/9, the border war with the USSR in the same years, the invasion of Indo-China in 1940, and the major series of invasions beginning with the attack on Pearl Harbor in December 1941.

Japanese policy towards Manchuria had a number of features that qualify the idea of Japanese imperialism as a rational and controlled policy of expansion. The Mukden Incident was an attempt on the part of relatively junior army officers to force their government into a major offensive in Manchuria designed to secure an imperial possession in mainland Asia. It was linked to a plot in Japan itself to replace the existing pluralist political system with a military dictatorship under the nominal authority of the Emperor. Although the plot itself failed, attempts by the Foreign Ministry, the cabinet and the Emperor himself to restrain army actions in Manchuria were unsuccessful. The Kwantung Army was virtually autonomous. It cared little for the international implications of its actions or for the hesitant but threatening moves made against Japan by the League of Nations. On 1 March 1932 Manchukuo was established as a nominally independent state, independent of China but under Japanese tutelage and effectively governed by the Kwantung Army. The pattern of the conquest of Manchuria and of Jehol was one of direct initiatives taken by junior army commanders, followed by weak protest from the Tokyo government and a final recognition of the *fait accompli.*

Was the central government in effect using the Kwantung Army as the indirect instrument of a prearranged plan of imperial expansion? On the face of it, its disavowal of responsibility and inability to control its own armed forces seemed a specious cover for a coherent scheme of conquest. But a closer examination of the situation reveals most of the features of Japanese society and its constraints and inhibitions. Imperial aspirations and their fulfilment in Manchuria met with approval at all levels of society. The army was popular and the actions of the young officers, including their plotting, were deemed to be within the code of honour central to the Japanese nation. Although the government and senior army commanders were perturbed about the loss of control and, in the case of the former, over international repercussions, there was general sympathy with their aspirations. Any move against the Kwantung Army on the part of the Tokyo government in an attempt to assert control would be construed as being counter to the manifest destiny of Japan. It was easier to acquiesce in the actions of the army.

The army, for its part, undertook a wide variety of actions in Manchukuo completely unrelated to its military role. Economic development, investment, the building of railways, as well as policing and administering the conquered territory, were all taken to be its prerogative. It sought to involve the government as much as possible in extending Japanese activity and influence in the area. It saw Manchukuo as a valuable economic asset to Japan and as a solution to the problem of overpopulation. Not only Manchuria but Mongolia, Siberia and North China were potential areas of conquest. China itself, purged of its foreign concessionaries, was to be held tributary to Japan. In effect the Kwantung Army had its own economic and foreign policies.

The government at home, in its endorsement of these actions and in its inability either to control the army or to make an effective opposition, reflected the collective spirit in Japan. The inability of the several loci in Japanese politics — from the Emperor himself, the Genro, the prime minister and cabinet, and the Chiefs of Staff and the Foreign Ministry — to come to a collective solution to the problem in practical terms, did not prevent their approval of the initiatives taken. In this they represented the central features of Japanese society. It was hierarchical but also depended upon a loose coherence of attitudes. 'Social' approval within the spirit of the prevalent code of honour was important. And this combined with the 'order and degree' of social position militated against a formal and institutional responsibility for decisions and actions. Decisions were the result of 'spontaneous' initiatives forcing the issue, or of a kind of political osmosis. Leadership was absent in a society in which legitimacy and authority emanated from an Emperor who was not a secular ruler but had an interventionist role in Japanese politics. The concept of the family bound all, whatever their nominal position, to a collective spirit that robbed individuals of any opportunity to lead and direct the course of Japanese politics. Instead of seeking to impose order on events in the rationalist Western tradition, the political leaders of Japan responded to them. What mattered was the nature of the response for this alone was in the control of the individual. He had the choice to behave with or without honour. And in making this choice he could act not in purely personal terms but in the face of tradition, precedent and the approval or disapproval of his family and society.

The army had a unique role in Japanese politics. The Mukden Incident symbolizes this as well as the general features of the society of which the army was a part. A situation was created in which Chinese forces had the choice of making an unequivocally hostile move towards the Japanese or of tamely submitting to oppressive occupation. This in turn gave the Japanese forces a choice. There was more to this than simply fabricating an excuse for invasion, as Hitler did in the case of the Gleiwitz radio station. It was to create the circumstances in which an honourable decision could be made. Such circumstances were not fabricated so much as induced. The Mukden Incident was not a rational move in the Western sense, but an attempt to choose an 'honourable' course of action. The actions of the Kwantung Army could not be either controlled or condemned by the Tokyo government, because the spirit in which they were made conformed to that accepted by the Japanese hierarchy as legitimizing. In such a situation, faced by a humiliating challenge from the Chinese forces, the army acted with honour. That it had in fact created the situation in the first place, both by being there and by faking the alleged Chinese attack on the railway, was irrelevant. To the Western world it looked like a particularly blatant example of political manoeuvring.

Similarly, the conspiracies and assassinations during the early thirties were considered to be not so much reprehensible as unfortunate. The purity of motive of the conspirators and assassins was recognized by their superiors. When they were brought to trial they received light sentences. Much of this violence was associated with the Kodoha or Imperial Way movement. This consisted largely of junior army officers who were closely involved in the Mukden Incident. They had no clear political programme but wanted army leadership to replace the existing political system and a policy of imperial expansion. In this general aspiration they had the tacit support of some of the political and military leaders. However, their attempt to stage a major coup failed. It is significant that part of the motivation for the coup was the move of the senior army leadership to disperse members of the Kodoha to relatively remote posts and so reduce their influence.

The senior officers themselves had their own faction, the Toseiha or Control Group. The Toseiha was as committed to imperial expansion as the Kodoha. They both believed that the direction of this expansion should be in the North and the USSR was considered to be the major antagonist. Their purge of the Kodoha following the abortive coup resulted in the assertion of control and discipline over the army by the senior officers. Not only did they consolidate their power in this way but they also forged an alliance with the leading industrialists in Japan, the *zaibatsu,* and urged a programme of massive rearmament. Thus, instead of spasmodic and opportunistic efforts to impel Japan into imperial conquest sponsored by fanatical conspiratorial groups, the army became an organized lobby with a coherent policy. From 1936 this coherence became a potent force in Japanese politics. The army not only carried the respect accorded to those following the imperial way, but actually possessed an autonomy and had a continuity of policy and leadership unique in the Japanese political system. In April 1936 the army succeeded in getting the cabinet to accept a policy document — Basic Principles of National Policy — in which rearmament and overseas expansion were major objectives. While it was not a substitute for government and the aim of the junior officers in seeking to achieve a military dictatorship was firmly repudiated, no government could rule effectively without army cooperation. And as Japanese imperialism became central to Japanese policy-making, so the army became more and more influential.

If we return to the course of Japanese expansion, the period between the creation of Manchukuo and the opening moves of the Sino-Japanese War of 1937 was one in which a two-fold policy was adopted of seeking Chinese recognition of Japanese gains and of further encroachment through the creation of local separatist factions under Japanese protection. The Chinese Nationalist government, preoccupied with its struggle against the communist forces and with the existence of other foreign powers on its soil, was forced to accept some of the Japanese demands. Nevertheless, it refused to recognize Manchukuo. It adopted a temporizing policy in the hope that Japanese demands would appear to be so inordinate as to invite opposition from the Western powers and the Soviet Union. Indeed, its only hope seemed tq lie in balancing all the predatory forces directed against Chinese national integrity. In July 1937 the so-called Lukouchiao or Marco Polo Bridge Incident occurred. Again like the Mukden Incident this was instigated by the local Japanese military commanders anxious to force the issue by taking an 'honourable' decision under induced circumstances. The Tokyo government sought to contain the ensuing hostilities, but the War Minister, Sugiyama, asked Konoye to endorse the decision to send reinforcements from Machuria and Korea to the Pekin—Tsientsin area. The Prime Minister reluctantly gave way, and on 27 July the Japanese army occupied Pekin. In the next month fighting broke out in Shanghai and again Japanese troops moved in. Nanking also fell to the Japanese. In October 1937 a Japanese puppet government was created in Inner Mongolia by the Kwantung Army. A similar move was made in North China where General Terauchi, anxious to emulate the Kwantung Army, supported a puppet regime with Pekin as its capital. Tokyo again endorsed these moves.

By 1939 a major colonial war was being waged in China. Fighting had also begun with the Soviet Union in the border areas on a much larger scale than the earlier skirmishes of 1937. The colonial war threatened to become a war with a major power. And this posed a genuine problem of choice for the Japanese government, over and above the piecemeal encroachments in China. The Japanese leadership recognized that the conquest of China was not possible without a major war effort, which would at one and the same time absorb all Japan's resources and leave her vulnerable to intervention from foreign powers. Her dependency upon foreign economic supply was a major weakness. In particular Japan's oil supply was heavily dependent upon foreign sources.

Thus, while the international situation remained both crisis-ridden yet open, in the sense that the major powers had committed themselves neither to formal alliance nor to war, Japanese policy temporized. An attempt to conquer China could not be undertaken without incurring the hostility of the USSR. Yet it was not possible to overcome this opposition without grave risk from uncommitted states. Japan's real opportunity came with the Second World War. It was not a war of Japan's creation but it presented Japan with the circumstances for another 'honourable' decision. It also offered a difficult choice. And this choice was dependent upon the actions and decisions made by other nation-states.

Let us look at the reasoning surrounding the decision to attack the American fleet at Pearl Harbor in order to see whether it was rational in the Western sense of rationality or whether it is explicable in terms of the nature of Japanese society and the mode of thinking peculiar to it. The distinction between the reasoning connected with the immediate circumstances and that concerned with aims, made in the case of Hitler's invasion of the Soviet Union discussed earlier, should be borne in mind. Pearl Harbor and the 'blue water' policy were means to an end. What is important here is whether both the means chosen and the end sought can be explained in 'social' terms.

The defeat of France and the mainland European countries by Germany meant that their imperial possessions in the Far East and in South East Asia were unprotected. Hitler had indicated that Germany had little interest in taking them. Britain, although undefeated, nevertheless was heavily preoccupied with the European war. There remained the United States and the Soviet Union as potential obstacles to Japanese expansion, either in mainland Asia or in the Pacific. If Japan chose one or the other as a zone of imperialist expansion, then a threat existed from the major power that was uncommitted. If Japan adopted a 'northern' policy against the Soviet Union, the maritime powers Britain and the United States could intervene. And similarly a 'blue water' policy left the Soviet Union free in the same way. Japan was not strong enough to fight both a major land war and a sea war. By 1941 the war in Europe had not proved decisive for Germany. The Soviet Union remained intact as a major power and was rearming rapidly. If Japan was to take advantage of her alliance with the Germans and to take the Soviet Union as her principal target, then this meant a land war in the frontier zones of China. The prize would be Siberia and the two Mongolias together with China itself. But if the direction of expansion was to be in this zone then Japan would have to decide before the onset of winter to begin hostilities. Operations could not be undertaken with any prospect of success after the beginning of September. And this was the case even if the German *blitzkrieg* was triumphant. Japan had to decide after June 1941 whether or not to attack the Soviet Union before September.

But a further constraint existed if this was to be the main direction of Japanese imperialism. This was the economic pressure imposed by the United States. Japan had taken advantage of the French collapse and the weakness of occupied Holland to invade Southern Indo-China in 1940. The inspiration for this move appeared to be economic in nature, in order to gain control over materials necessary for any major war effort. Rubber and tin were important. But most important of all was oil. Imports of steel from the United States were also significant. Now the freezing of Japanese assets by the United States in July effectively halted trade. And the oil embargo of 1 August imposed by Britain, Holland and the United States was a decisive move. Japan had oil stocks that gave her two years supply at current levels of consumption.[55] But clearly any disruption of supply would have serious consequences for a policy of imperial expansion supported by a major war effort. Paradoxically this economic pressure forced the attention of the Japanese leaders onto problems of supply — on guaranteeing resources — before undertaking any major operation in the north. As the Chief of Staff, Sugiyama, urged, 'In order to be able to act in the North we have to carry out operations quickly in the South. Even if we start right away [September 1941] operations will take until next Spring. Insofar as we are delayed we will not be able to act in the North. Therefore, it is necessary to move as quickly as possible.'[56] A local supply of oil had to be acquired and this made the initial thrust of expansion into 'blue water'. The principal targets were thus Britain and the United States. If the United States maintained her hostility and continued economic sanctions, then Japan was unable to make a major war effort directed towards imperial expansion in mainland Asia with the Soviet Union as her principal opponent. Success in the Pacific would free Japan for future plans of expansion in the North. And so the United States became the formal enemy of Japan in the pursuit of means to an end. Such success was a necessary pre-condition for the acquisition of empire. Given this reasoning, the American and British move against Japan's oil supply diverted attention from China and the Soviet Union to the Pacific and to the destruction of the American fleet. On 21 November Ribbentrop promised that if Japan should go to war with the United States then Germany would also.[57] No doubt he was relieved that this step would mean that Germany could enjoy her Russian conquests without having to share them.

The war that was planned was a *blitzkrieg* against Britain and the United States, destroying their Pacific fleets and thus eliminating any chance of intervention. In the following spring Japan would then be free to assess the situation *vis-à-vis* Germany and the Soviet Union, and to make a decision about the future direction of Japanese expansion without the uncertainty posed by the presence of the Western maritime powers in the Pacific. In short, Pearl Harbor was not so much a part of a grand design as an expedient action deemed necessary under existing conditions and constraints. American rearmament and her uncommitted position so far as the European war was concerned meant that the Japanese were under threat, a threat that grew stronger as time went on. As the Navy Chief of Staff, Nagano, said:

> A number of vital military supplies, including oil, are dwindling day by day. This will cause a gradual weakening of our national defense and lead to a situation, in which, if we maintain the status quo, the capacity of our Empire to act will be reduced in the days to come. Meanwhile the defenses of American, British and other foreign military facilities and vital points in the Far East, and the military preparedness of these countries, particularly of the United States, are being strengthened with great speed.[58]

This was endorsed by the Army Chief of Staff, who argued:

> We can expect a coalition between the United States and the Soviet Union in the future . . . Therefore if we could take advantage of the winter season and quickly finish our military operations in the South, I believe we would be in a position to deal with any changes in the Northern situation that might take place next spring and thereafter. On the contrary if we should miss this seasonal opportunity, we will not be able to achieve security in the North during our operations in the South.[59]

In this sense the decision to attack the American Pacific fleet at Pearl Harbor was a piece of opportunism that loosely fitted a general scheme of imperial expansion, but that was largely designed to free Japan's hands for a move in *any* direction. It was also the lowest common denominator between those who argued for expansion in the North, largely the army, and those who argued for the South, the navy. It was a compromise. Furthermore, it satisfied the demand for action raised on all sides as the various factions in Japanese politics took heart from the body blow that the Third Reich had dealt, and was dealing, to those states that had long held sway in the East. The only major obstacle to the fulfilment of Japan's destiny was the United States, and circumstances had placed that country in virtual isolation in the Pacific. These circumstances had not been created or willed by Japan. They were the result of others' actions, or perhaps of the Divine will manifest in the Emperor. The Japanese leaders thus found themselves in a situation in which they had to make a choice or forgo the fulfilment of Japan's imperial mission. If they abstained from action then Japan's potential opponents, particularly the United States, could only gain in strength. But to embark on any expansion meant that the prospect of intervention had to be removed. Germany had taken on the Soviet Union and clearly the latter was in no position to abrogate the treaty of neutrality signed with Japan shortly before the German invasion.[60] If Germany proved successful in her struggle with the USSR then Japan might conceivably find herself in the position of Italy and forced to be content with the victor's leavings.

The argument that Japan had a conscious programme of imperial expansion in the form of a Greater East Asian Co-Prosperity Sphere is not borne out by the calculations and decisions of the Japanese leaders. They were all agreed on expansion, but not on the form or direction it should take. These were open questions, not only because of the uncertainties of the international situation, but because to provide concrete answers was to invite discord and contention. Expansion for expansion's sake was the chief motivation. And grasping at opportunities rather than creating them was more consonant with Japanese mores than a rationally conceived policy. Opportunism went with fatalism. Broad agreement on an idealist basis was more important than politics.

The idealism involved in Japanese imperial expansion was peculiar to Japan. The Greater East Asian Co-Prosperity Sphere was an expression of a civilizing mission, and not of a common Pan-Asian nationalist sentiment. The Japanese did not conceive of the other Asian peoples as civilized or as capable of self-government. Their appeal to the colonial peoples of the Far East and of South-East Asia to throw off their oppressors was a reflection of the conviction that the Western nations were alien and barbarous, and that Japan constituted the highest form of oriental civilization. Liberation was not so much a colonial emancipation as the creation of an opportunity to be civilized under Japanese tutelage. While this involved a measure of responsibility for education and progress in the empire, as had been the case in Korea (one of Japan's earlier acquisitions), the liberated areas were to be integrated politically and economically with the Japanese system. In the short term, as the Finance Minister, Kaya, put it, 'it will not be possible for some time for us to give much consideration to the living conditions of the people in those areas and for a while we will have to pursue a so-called policy of exploitation'.[61] In the long term, they were to be part of an economic system that made Japan autarkic.

The calculations that went into the Pearl Harbor decision appear on the face of it to be very similar to those made by Hitler when he decided to invade the Soviet Union. They involved questions of timing, the relative balance of the opposition and its strengths and commitments, economic needs, and security. As with Hitler they even included the season and the weather! But this apparent rationality masked the purpose of this important action against the Pacific fleet. The aim was imperial expansion. While this too could be justified and explained in these rational terms, such argument was curiously lacking in the deliberations of the Japanese leadership. It was taken for granted that this was both desirable and generally acceptable to the Japanese people. And this was generally true, for Japan's imperial adventures were popular. Questions of expediency were thus basically reflections of a unity of purpose that was the imperial aggrandizement of Japan. In what way is this explained by reference to the nature of Japanese society?

In many ways, as we have seen, Japanese society was strikingly different from Western societies. There is a danger of cultural relativity in interpreting the rationale of political action as akin to that of the West. But the point is one of the relevance of social mores to political action whatever the nature of those mores. And this is not a theoretical but a historical question. Actions are made intelligible by reference to the reasoning of those engaged in them. They are not necessary consequences of a social system that acts as a determinant for action. To turn this into a theoretical argument, the point would be that the social system and its mores were the product of specific conditions, and that they acted as *causes* for action. It is of course this argument that is at the core of the sociobiological thesis of human aggression and imperialism.

Thus it could be argued that while individuals *justified* their actions in terms of their beliefs, in their attitudes towards the Emperor and the national 'family', their actions themselves were logically reasoned on grounds other than this. In a sense their beliefs directed not the objectives themselves, or the means of achieving them, but *ex post facto* conferred morality upon them. If this is the case, we seem to have here an explanation akin to that of German imperialism in the Third Reich, that is the assertion of an ideological basis to imperial expansion. Such an explanation is based on the reasoning of those agents chiefly concerned in the actions and decisions surrounding the course of Japanese imperial expansion. If this is indeed the case, the relevance of the sociobiological thesis lies in postulating a link between belief and action while at the same time providing an explanation for those beliefs. The explanation of imperialism is thus removed to a more fundamental level than the level of belief.

Given the traditional element in Japanese society, we should expect some evidence of Schumpeter's atavism having an effect on current practice. Did the traditions of the samurai, the ronin, bushido, etc., produce a kind of behavioural momentum carrying forward into modern times and into an alien environment the values of the past? (Such values being associated with martial virtues and an aggressive expansionist and zenophobic attitude towards the rest of the world.) Apart from the theoretical difficulties of making a connection between cultural atavism and political practice, which will be discussed shortly, there seems little evidence that Japanese society in the inter-war period was traditional in this way. As was pointed out earlier, from the opening of Japan to the Western world by Commodore Perry to the period of aggressive imperialism, Japanese society underwent profound changes. These changes were political as well as social and economic.

The position of the Emperor and the constitutional relations of the major political institutions — the Genro, the Diet, the cabinet and the ministries — were symbolically fixed and politically indeterminate. The Emperor was supreme but the political conditions for the realization of this supremacy were *ad hoc*. Yet this supremacy stifled any independent political development that could provide authority and unity in decision-making. The dominance of the military in the later 1930s cannot be explained in terms of the dominance of cultural values themselves the product of an earlier phase of Japanese history, any more than is the case for the hierarchical structure of Japanese society. Certainly appeals to tradition were made by one faction or another in Japanese politics. The common denominator, that of loyalty to the Emperor, was used quite consciously in order to win support or to justify projected courses of action. But the Emperor was neither sacred nor sacrosant. Factions such as the Kodoha, while justifying their attempts to take over the state and their assassinations in the name of the Emperor, nevertheless believed that the Emperor himself should be forced to follow their dictates. There was an element of opportunism in Japanese politics at this time and an inconsistency of policy that belie the idea of a predetermined disposition to act in a particular manner.

At the same time it is true that while infirmity of will was a feature of decision-making in the highest political circles, there was unanimity over Japan's imperial destiny. Japan was to have an empire in the East and to receive acknowledgment as the undisputed leader of the Asian peoples. Whether the imperial drive should go north or south, and *when* the moment was ripe to do either, were debatable questions; that imperial expansion was Japan's destiny was not. And an explanation of this attitude breaks down when Western rationality is applied to the analysis of the actual decisions and actions taken by the Japanese leadership. It is not simply a problem, as in the case of Hitler and his foreign policy, of identifying a relevant form of reasoning that makes these actions intelligible, but of determining what counted as a reason for those involved. Here social attitudes seem to be particularly important, but they constituted in a sense a justification for acting, or not acting as the case may be, and not a reason for action or inaction.

The drive to imperial expansion appears to be most articulate among the young officers and the civilian population at its lowest level — the peasants. The leadership found these sentiments congenial but were trapped in the complexities of international diplomacy and in their own constitutional and institutional ambiguities. The consolidation of control by the senior army leadership was not so much a conscious policy as a result of a profound breakdown in the embryonic political system in a time of crisis. As we have seen in the deliberations leading up to Pearl Harbor, the general feeling was that time was running out. The spirit of opportunism was a substitute for a clearly defined programme of action with clearly recognizable goals. The other nation-states made the running. This contrasts with Hitler's opportunism, which while pragmatic enough to take advantage of changing circumstances had an objective in mind. Japan wanted an empire but her leaders gave little thought as to its nature or composition. In this sense Japanese imperialism was motiveless. It was defined and justified not in concrete terms, either economic or political, but as a natural and inevitable fulfilment of Japanese destiny.

In the major planning discussions, such aspects as resource procurement, geo-political strategy, logistics, and so on, were certainly considered important, but only in terms of means and not ends. The military leaders, in contrast to Hitler's generals, were foremost in influencing discussion and making their case. The same ambiguities over the absorption of Korea existed over China and South-East Asia. Were the Asian countries to be part of a Japanese empire and the fruits of conquest, or were they to be vassal states sending tribute to Japan? Or were they to be 'associated' with Japan in a loosely integrated and cooperative 'New Order' that excluded Western exploitation and acted as a kind of customs union and free market? Such questions were never answered by the Japanese leadership, which took refuge in the vague and general notion of the 'imperial way' or in the exigencies of the immediate crisis. It can hardly be said that Japanese imperialism was ordered. It can best be understood, not as a conscious rational programme (ideologically inspired perhaps yet committed to a view of the world as governed by *real politik* and to the achievement of specific objectives in it), but as a movement, haphazard in nature and taking its initiatives from a series of actions whose consistency is derived from a general disposition. Such a disposition owed its existence to social attitudes implicit in the Japanese sense of tradition — a sense made all the more acute because of the awareness of the dangers both internal and external that confronted Japan.

We are thus left with the notion of a general drive to imperialism as an attitude or set of attitudes to the external world. Unanimity on this existed at all levels of Japanese society. But can this attitude itself be explained in terms of a psychological or cultural predisposition to perform specific acts of aggression in a given situation?

Let me try to answer this question by drawing all the strands of this enquiry together in a critique of the explanatory adequacy of the sociobiological account of human nature and its consequence for human action. Referring back to the central argument concerning aggression, namely that it is a product of an inherited propensity to act under the stimuli of specific conditions, we can see that the ostensible level of belief, motive, intention, purpose and reason — the level of human consciousness — is irrelevant to such an explanation. Such a level is epiphenomenal, either irrelevant or itself explicable by a thesis that subsumes it. Whatever men think they are doing, the true cause of their actions is hidden from them in the form of a disposition to think and act in this particular way. Aggression is not a rational use of force — as politics by other means — but a fundamental response to competition derived from the human biological constitution.

What can be said of this argument in terms of its explanatory adequacy? If we examine the biological argument — the synthetic theory of evolution — which is at the core of the ethological and sociobiological theories of human behaviour, we find some serious ambiguities. The concepts of fitness, adaptation and natural selection are innately tautological. They are specified in terms of some inherited physical trait or characteristic that produces a response to a set of environmental conditions. Such traits are adaptive where the species possessing them exists or 'survives', and are maladaptive when the species disappears or declines in numbers. Those characteristics conducive to survival become dominant in the species or within a population by virtue of the superior breeding potential of those individuals possessing them. Evolution consists of a successful chain of such adaptations as the species adapts to changing environments, passing on advantages to succeeding generations. Such adaptations are the product of selection pressures acting on a genetic endowment.

But there is no explanation of adaptation as a process in this argument. It is inferred from survival itself. The fact that a species exists is taken as evidence of its fitness. Yet fitness depends upon a relationship between the physical or biological composition of a species and its habitat. What is this relationship? How is it explained? A reason for a specific trait is inferred from the observed behaviour of its individuals and related to the general thesis of adaptive development. For example, present-day giraffes have long necks. The 'reason' for their long necks is to enable them to browse off vegetation peculiar to their present habitat. But this asserted functional relationship between the physiological structure of giraffes and their diet is not explanatory. The 'reason' that giraffes have long necks is *in order to* eat off relatively tall trees. And this characteristic is transmitted from one generation to another, or rather has been so far. The explanation of this genetic transmission — its mechanics as it were — is in terms of genetic theory. We know *how* such traits are inherited. But the question *why* giraffes have long necks is not answered by genetics. A causal relation between genetic endowment and environmental conditions is asserted but not explained. The inferred 'reason', then, for the existence of a trait that allows its possessor and the species of which it is a member to survive, is circular. Given the existence of the species, such a trait provides evidence of fitness, for by definition any handicap is countered by behaviour, or equally any advantage is fostered through propagation. There is sufficient evidence of both 'strengths' and 'weaknesses' in all aspects of animal behaviour to support the general thesis of natural selection. All traits can thus be 'explained' within the rubric of fitness either as successful or unsuccessful cases of adaptation.

The crucial element, that is, a specification of the sufficient and necessary environmental pre-conditions, together with the process of the inheritance of physical characteristics, that interact to ensure the survival of a species, is missing. Selection is thus arbitrary and a descriptive rather than an explanatory concept. Species survive because they survive. The behaviour of a species is taken to mean the causes of behaviour, or rather no distinction is maintained. Selection, if it means anything, implies a reference to specific behavioural characteristics that have a precise role in maintaining the existence of its possessor under stated conditions. Such characteristics are themselves explained in causal terms. Stipulating their functional necessity is a descriptive and not an explanatory exercise.

Thus the conditions necessary and sufficient for successful adaptation, both genetic and environmental, cannot be inferred from actual survival without tautology. If they are not stated in the context of a causal theory, then there is no adequate explanation of evolution. A theory of genetics, that is of the heritability of characteristics, explains how these are transmitted. It does not explain why. Nor can it explain their adaptive of maladaptive function in terms of a given habitat. Genetic change in the form of random mutations is in no way the result of environmental change. It occurs independently of the habitat in which its transmittor and its genetic heirs live. The consequence in evolutionary terms is an argument that can only describe *ex post facto* alleged consequences for the existence of a species.

An argument that asserts fitness as an adaptation between an organism and its environment must state clearly what this relationship is. This entails more than the tautological statement that survival is the test of fitness. It entails at least a description of the environmental 'fit' in terms of those features of the environment and those of the organism that are alleged to be in harmony. The environment is more than a physical habitat. As ecologists have rightly argued, it consists of other members of a species, and other species. 'Social' relations, which include predation, reproduction, breeding, feeding, dominance and hierarchy, and so on, are all relevant to a characterization of an 'environment'. In evolutionary terms there are considerable difficulties in stating these aspects for the past. What lies outside the palaeontological or geological record cannot be known. We cannot readily deduce from a fossil what its eco-system was.

On the genetic side of the argument, we can see that change itself is arbitrary in the sense that no predictive basis for evolutionary theory can be adduced from genetic theory. Whether or not a mutation is conducive to survival, that is, has an adaptive or maladaptive relation to either a static or a changing environment, is impossible to stipulate. As such, the event, that is the fact of survival, is all important. There is no logical or causal necessity involved in the theoretical relationship between genetic change and species adaptation to an environment, even where this 'environment' can be accurately described. An organism that is the agent of genetic change cannot be said to confer a greater or a lesser chance of survival on its genetic heirs in any predictive sense. This can only be established retrospectively, and so constitutes a description and not a theoretical explanation.

The conditions of a covering law explanation are not satisfied by this sort of argument. In order to explain a change from one state or condition to another, in terms not merely of the genetic composition of an organism but of a relationship to a given habitat, an explanation of the process of change is necessary. Such an explanation would take the form of a statement of the necessary and sufficient conditions for the change, together with the covering law governing their relationship, so that the actual change may be predicted. It should be added that while the logical conditions of such an explanatory form must be satisfied, it is also necessary to formulate the derived hypothesis in a testable empirical form. The thesis, if it is to be considered an adequate explanation, needs to be tested under previously stated empirical conditions. Clearly this is not possible for the synthetic theory of evolution. The record of change, in terms of the physiology of organisms for example, is a historical description lacking a supporting explanation. Even if it is correlated with the record of 'environmental' changes, that is with the alleged habitat of a species, this remains merely a correlation and not an explanation. What is missing is a theoretical explanation that connects the two elements of change — genetic and environmental — and explains their interaction in terms of causes and effects. In its absence we have a rationalization that asserts a relationship of utility between a physical trait, such as the long necks of giraffes, and the habitat in which its possessor lives. But the long necks of giraffes are not caused by their environment. The phenotype does not cause the genotype. Nor is the genotype a sufficient and necessary cause of the phenotype. It only at best permits a range of possibilities; the realization in practice of any of these hypothetical possibilities is an imponderable.

So far I have criticized the synthetic theory of evolution as an explanation of the survival of species in terms of the inheritance of adaptative or maladaptive physical traits. But aggression is not a physical but a behavioural trait. Or at least so the ethological and sociobiological theories have it. And there are problems in treating behavioural traits as aspects of cultural evolution as distinct from the physical evolution of species. Although, since it is claimed that the synthetic theory applies in this area, the criticisms made above are relevant.

Aggression is said to be a behavioural phenomenon allegedly the product of genetic programming, itself the result of past adaptations and selection pressures. Man is aggressive when his innate conditioning is triggered off by an appropriate stimuli, such as population pressure, competition for resources and territory and competition for sex. But culture itself constitutes a selection pressure and is not merely a manifestation of the basic genetic composition of man. Here we have considerable difficulty in disentangling causes and effects in identifying the phenomenon and those conditions causal to it. If aggression is caused by a propensity to aggress, allegedly part of the human genetic composition, what is the connection between the inherited trait and cultural behaviour? More precisely, how can a propensity to aggress and aggression itself be distinguished? It is tautological to assert that the evidence for the former lies in observation of the latter.

What is necessary if we are to have a genuine theoretical explanation is a means of distinguishing the explanation and its terms of adequacy from the phenomenon that is the subject of explanation. In short, we need a statement, firstly of the causes of the alleged trait and not a rationalization of its alleged utility. It must be identifiable and susceptible to an explanation independent of its alleged manifestation. Secondly, we need a statement of the necessary and sufficient conditions that elicit the alleged phenomenon of aggression. And finally, since we are engaged in theoretical explanation, we need a law-like statement that offers a testable generalization about the incidence and occurrence of aggression. None of these conditions is forthcoming in sociobiological argument.

Instead we offered an *ex post facto* account that relies on an asserted functional relationship between aggression and specified social needs. If we refer back to Lorenz, for example, aggression is said to be *causally* necessary for the performance of certain functions in animal societies.[62] If it did not exist then neither would they. And, given this systemic relationship, it is easy to see the necessity for all behavioural manifestations. But the logic of this is not a causal one. It is simply the rather empty truism that if a given society did not behave in this way, that is, have these characteristics, then it would cease to be a society at all. A phenomenon is not explained by its alleged contribution to the existence of other phenomena. Such an argument is innately circular. The conditions for the 'survival' of a society are the same as those that that society manifests as its characteristic behaviour. If it ceases to manifest such conditions then it ceases to be that society.

Even if aggression is alleged to be a necessary condition for social cohesion, it is not explained in causal terms. Its utility in promoting the dispersal of population, a healthy breeding programme, the equitable distribution of resources, etc., are all rationalizations that confuse causes with effects. Aggression is defined rather than explained. Its actual explanation is side-stepped in the use of expressions such as nature, drive, instinct, motor mechanism, or unconscious motivation. These are synonyms for a propensity to act that can only be observed in terms of action itself. What *causes* aggression? Can it be understood in any way independent of the characterization of acts as aggressive and as functionally necessary to a species and its social organization? Can it be understood in genetic terms in the same way as the transmission of physical characteristics? The answer must be no. Neither the propensity to act in this way nor the conditions that elicit this behaviour are explained. A theoretical explanation of aggression would have to fulfil the logical and empirical conditions for a genuine theory discussed above in the context of the synthetic theory of evolution. If these are not provided, then we have a pseudo-explanation, which is really a conceptual scheme that gives us description and labelling as a substitute for knowledge.

Aggression is essentially a social act, however it is defined. It is described in terms of a language and an understanding peculiarly the product of a particular culture. And it has connotations of a normative and evaluative nature. As such, if we are concerned for an elucidation of its meaning as opposed to its explanation as a behavioural phenomenon, we look to our language and to the context in which it is used. In this sense it is not an 'objective' or scientific term, but part of the language in which we describe and evaluate our social practice. Its referents are cultural. Now when our understanding of aggression is taken from a language of description and social usage and applied to a context of explanation subject to quite different terms of reference and adequacy, a category mistake has been made. Science has its own language and rules and is not dependent upon terms and expressions found in everyday life to define and describe the phenomena it seeks to explain.

The depiction of animal behaviour in anthropomorphic terms is not a neutral or objective exercise. The claims that observation is untrammelled by preconceptions and that explanatory hypotheses are formulated subsequent to it are mistaken both in theory and in practice. A totally neutral observation is an impossibility, for what is deemed to have been observed is conditioned, firstly, by what we take to be our knowledge in that field and, secondly, by conjectural arguments to which we seek answers. The acceptance and rejection of empirical hypotheses are directly related to confirmation, or otherwise, of related observations. They serve both as subjects of explanation and as a test of explanatory hypotheses. In science, circularity is avoided by the method of testing adopted. Not all conjectures are potential bases for hypotheses; only those in principle susceptible to empirical testing are relevant to scientific investigation. Mere conjecture is avoided. Nor is a scientist committed to one conjecture in relating observations to theory. He can have several competing conjectures, some of which he hopes to eliminate. Without the system of testing through experiment and observation, he would indeed be caught in a circularity in which his observations necessarily followed his theories, for he would have no means of separating the explanation and its terms of adequacy from the phenomenon explained.

Now in ethology, studies of animal behaviour are formulated in language used to describe human activities. Aggression is an example of such usage. Of course this stems from the general assumption that there is no intrinsic difference in biological terms between human and animal behaviour. A common vocabulary can be adopted. As Fox puts it, 'One consequence of this view is that much of the quasi-intuitive behaviour of man can be studied in much the same way and by much the same methods as ethologists study the instinctive behaviour of other animals'.[63] But this exercise is circular. Assumptions made about human behaviour such as aggression, which are merely conjectural and dependent upon unproven and unexplained relations between drives, instincts, motor mechanisms and aggressive acts in stipulated social conditions (such as overpopulation, mating, competition for resources, etc.), are referred to the 'objective' study of species such as fish or rats. Their claims on territory, for example, are by analogy likened to inter-state competition for empire. Not surprisingly the conclusion is drawn that in terms of behaviour both men and other animal species are actuated by the same impulses. But neither the behaviour of animals, nor of men, is explained by this procedure. The attribution of rationalizing motives to the 'aggressive' behaviour of the robin in marking its 'territory' is no more explanatory than the attribution of territoriality as a reason for human aggression.

Indeed, the use of the term 'aggressive' begs the question, not merely of its causes, but of the very nature of the 'observed' behaviour of the animals in question. In the case of our own society we can evaluate the actions of others as aggressive or not, but this is the product of our experience, of the notion of rule-following and of an awareness of social mores. Our interpretations are based on a practical knowledge that in principle can be verified. In characterizing an act as aggressive we make a valuation and not a neutral scientific objective observation. The level of rationalization explicit in much of the sociobiological argument is dependent upon inferences based on a commonsense knowledge of human behaviour, and transferred to animal species. The 'findings' made from the study of animals are then transferred back to man. Such generalizations can only be validated if it can be shown in an empirically testable form that the alleged common behaviour is the product of a common set of stimuli acting on a common set of genetic attributes, innate to all the relevant species including man. The assertion that this is the case is not an acceptable substitute for an adequately tested theoretical explanation. Such an explanation would explain aggression by linking an identifiable phenomenon to a description and a set of causal conditions such that where these latter exist, then the phenomenon would occur. It may or may not be the case that one of the conditions is the molecular genetic process, but there is no evidence of this in the absence of a testable theory that makes it relevant. The same is true of the environmental conditions as alleged stimuli.

The kernel of such a theory lies in establishing a relationship between the genetic structure or genetic change and their causes, and in turn, their relation to the behaviour that allegedly springs from it. Putting it more concretely, if aspects of behaviour are asserted as produced by the stimulus of a given situation to an inherent inherited genetic programme, an appeal to behaviour itself does not establish this as true. This is particularly the case where 'behaviour' is mediated by a pre-existing social knowledge and is not scientifically neutral. We need to know in a testable form the postulated relationship between what are termed genetic forms and a level of action induced by environmental stimuli in which the former has a causal role. In any case, on the genetic side we need to know which conditions need to be satisfied so that a heritable form comes into existence. So far as mutations are concerned, these are not known at the moment. But even if this explanatory lacunae were filled, the link between genetic forms and social behaviour has still to be established.

If we turn to war as a behavioural phenomenon, we can see the difficulties in seeking a sociobiological explanation. The level of explanation is on interactions between individual members of a species explained in terms of an inbuilt genetic mechanism common to the species. It is hard to see how this process can operate in an age of total warfare where fighting largely ceases to be between individuals. Weapons of mass destruction, the deadly apparatus of war, the complex logistics and the intricate strategies involved in the deployment of nuclear weapons, on the face of it all appear to be impersonal factors. The major wars of this century have been fought by young men directed by their elders remote from the battlefield. Aggression may indeed be an element in hand-to-hand fighting, although this is an increasingly rare phenomenon in modern warfare, but it hardly seems to be a determinant of war itself.

Politicians act on a rationale that takes into account a multiplicity of factors including an appreciation of the relative balance of forces and of the intentions and capabilities of potential and actual opponents. Such a rationale in the event may be mistaken, and the outcome of the use of violence be far from what was intended. Yet it constitutes a rationale that is intelligible and that, providing there is sufficient evidence, allows us to approach an explanation of a particular war and of the actions of political leaders. There seems little evidence of atavistic impulses or unconscious drives in this cold reasoning. Of course, according to the sociobiological thesis, it is irrelevant. It is merely epiphenomenal. If this is the case, we need more than a mere assertion that wars are the result of a latent tendency to aggress.

Arguments that assert that war is a form of selection pressure designed to fulfil certain functional needs of a species by encouraging 'fitness' through selective breeding, are specious. Even if there was evidence of genetic change and adaptation in the human species during the brief time it has existed, and the even briefer time that war and social organization have appeared as human phenomena, it is impossible to attribute this to environmental factors in the absence of the kind of theory discussed earlier. War is not a combat between individuals, but a complex social activity. Can it be demonstrated that the survivors are genetically better endowed than the dead? Or that cowards contribute less to the gene-pool than heroes? If fitness is largely a function of selective breeding, it seems that war is counter-productive in that the chief casualties are the young and fit. In an age of nuclear weapons even this distinction seems to have disappeared. In fact no such proposition about biological fitness and human aggression can be sustained. And this is equally true of the converse argument that war is unbridled aggression and counter to the fitness of the species. Whatever is said of its functional or dysfunctional role in social relations, such arguments are not theoretical propositions but disguised ethical judgments.

Finally, the notion of action entailed by sociobiological explanations of social behaviour is suspect. Human action includes a wide variety of phenomena, including involuntary as well as voluntary acts. The rubric of action subsumes the physical functions of organisms as well as intended or purposive rational actions. In the case of animals, in the absence of access to animal 'reasoning', a wide variety of actions, including that of 'aggression', can be taken as involuntary. Anthropomorphic language derived from a context of usage that implies intention and purpose is used to describe animal behaviour. There is a misfit here between the use of such descriptive language and the assumption that animals are void of a capacity to learn, to reason and to express thought in linguistic form or, if not totally void, possess such capacities in a rudimentary and largely inaccessible form. The transfer back to the human species of findings derived from such anthropomorphically based studies treats man as akin to animals in that his actions too are unreasoned. The element of intention has somehow been dropped in this double shift. An appeal is made instead to instinct and non-reasoning faculties. But the majority of human actions, including that of aggression, are reasoned. An explanation of a war or an imperialist adventure is intimately bound up with an elucidation of reasoning, expectations, intentions and judgements of an evaluative character. Human actions have the connotation of intention and purpose as animal actions do not, unless translated into anthropomorphic language. Animal action or behaviour is not the same as human action for they do not have a common context of reference. A conceptual framework that subsumes both types of action is profoundly mistaken.

I began this study by saying that man is an animal. But an explanation of his actions is not fostered by the assumption that this is all he is. The simple reductionism of the sociobiologists' thesis of aggression and imperialism is inherently non-explanatory. It cannot explain the phenomenon of imperialism by reference to the biological nature of man, for this merely transfers the problem of explanation from one context to another. As we have seen, quite apart from the confusions and ambiguities of the sociobiological view, there is a theoretical hiatus in the argument. We have not explained the phenomenon of aggression, if phenomenon it be, by reducing the explanation to an assertion that man is aggressive because his nature decrees it. The dismissal of human reasoning as irrelevant to an explanation of human action is itself unreasonable. Schumpeter's comment that 'pretexts for war were always found. There is no situation in which pretexts are altogether lacking. What matters here is that pretexts are quite unsuitable to form links in the chain of explanation of historic events — unless history is to be resolved into an account of the whims of great lords',[64] ignores the fact that wars and imperialism are very often explicable in terms of the 'whims of great lords'. What Chaucer called the 'borrel folk' had, and have, very little say in such matters. Wars are not caused by soldiers, they are only fought by them. And this has serious consequences for the sociobiological argument and its conception of aggression.

NOTES AND REFERENCES

1 The most notable of these in Konrad Lorenz *On Aggression* (London, Methuen, 1966).
2 See, for example, R. A. Hinde *Animal Behaviour: A synthesis of ethology and comparative psychology* (New York, McGraw Hill, 1966) and V. C. Wynne-Edwards *Animal Dispersion in relation to Social Behaviour* 1962.
3 Lionel Tiger and Robin Fox *The Imperial Animal* (London, Secker and Warburg, 1972) p. 28.

4 For a more detailed analysis of genetic theory in terms of its status as an explanation see Michael Ruse *The Philosophy of Biology* (London, Hutchinson University Library, 1973) pp. 12-46.

5 See T. Dobzhansky, F. J. Ayala, G. L. Stebbins and J. W. Valentine *Evolution* (San Francisco, W. H. Freeman, 1977) p. 17.

6 I have relied on Ruse, *op. cit.*, pp. 99-101 for this account but the case of the peppered moth is commonly cited in the literature.

7 See, for example, Detlev Ploog 'Neurological aspects in social behavior' in Smithsonian Institute *Man and Beast* (Washington, Smithsonian Institute Press, 1969) p. 100.

8 See, for example, Robin Fox 'The cultural animal *ibid.*, pp. 277-95.

9 See Ploog, op. cit., p. 113 and Lorenz, *op. cit.*, pp. 213-14. See also J. M. Thoday 'Genetics and educability' in D. Brothwell (ed.) *Biosocial Man* (London, Institute of Biology, 1977) pp. 209-

10 See E. O. Wilson 'Comparative and aggressive behavior' in *Man and Beast, op. cit.*, pp. 184-210.

11 T. Dobzhansky in *Dobzhansky et al., op. cit.*, p. 29.

12 See, for example, Mary Midgley *Beast and Man* (Hassocks, Sussex, Harvester 1979) p. 95.

13 Fox, *op. cit.*, p. 291.

14 Tiger and Fox, *op. cit.*, p. 33.

15 *ibid.*, p. 37.

16 Glen MacBride 'The nature—nurture problem in social evolution' in *Man and Beast, op. cit.*, p. 49.

17 See, for example, J. Dollard *et al., Frustration and Aggression* (London, Routledge and Kegan Paul, 1944).

18 Konrad Lorenz 'Ritualized fighting' in J. D. Carthy and F. J. Ebling (eds) *The Natural History of Aggression* (London, Academic Press, 1964) p. 49.

19 See Ploog, *op. cit.*, p. 99.

20 *ibid.*, p. 101.

21 Wilson, *op. cit.*, p. 210.

22 See Frank B. Livingstone 'The effects of human war on the biology of the human species' in M. Fried, M. Harris and R. Murphy (eds) *War; the Anthropology of Armed Conflict and Aggression* (Garden City, New York, Natural History Press, 1967) p. 12.

23 *ibid.*, p. 13.

24 See Lorenz *On Aggression, op. cit.*, pp. 90-126.

25 Susanne K. Langer 'The great shift: instinct to intuition' in *Man and Beast, op. cit.*, p. 328.

26 See Fox, *op. cit.*, p. 288 and Hilary Callan *Ethology and Society* (Oxford, Clarendon Press, 1970).

27 Lorenz *On Aggression, op. cit.* and also E. O. Wilson *Sociobiology; the New Synthesis* Cambridge, Mass., Harvard University Press, 1975).

28 Lorenz *On Aggression, op. cit.*, p. 90 and pp. 176-84.

29 *ibid.*, p. 186.

30 Tiger and Fox, *op. cit.*, p. 209.

31 *ibid.*, p. 34.

32 Lorenz *On Aggression, op. cit.*, p. 211.

33 *ibid.*, p. 211.

34 *ibid.*, p. 203.

35 J. A. Schumpeter *Imperialism and Social Classes* (trans. Heinz Norden, Oxford, Basil Blackwell, 1951). First published in 1919.

36 *ibid.,* Chap. 5, 'Imperialism and capitalism' pp. 83 and 118.

37 *ibid.,* p. 6.

38 *ibid.,* p. 14.

39 *ibid.,* pp. 7 and 83.

40 *ibid.,* p. 29.

41 *ibid.,* p. 130.

42 Lorenz 'Ritualized fighting', *op. cit.,* p. 155.

43 Lorenz *On Aggression, op. cit.,* p. 214.

44 Livingstone, *op. cit.,* p. 13.

45 Lorenz *On Aggression, op. cit.,* p. 186.

46 I am indebted for this account of Japanese nationalist sentiment to Masao Maruyama *Thought and Behaviour in Modern Japanese Politics* (trans. Ivan Morris, London, Oxford University Press, 1963) and Richard Storry *The Double Patriots* (Chatto and Windus, London, 1957).

47 For example in 1937 the army blocked the appointment of Ugaki as Prime Minister and forced his resignation as Foreign Minister.

48 See Maruyama, *op. cit.,* p. 107.

49 See Marius B. Jansen 'Modernization and foreign policy in Meiji Japan' in R. E. Ward (ed.) *Political Development in Modern Japan* (New Jersey, Princeton University Press, 1968) p. 149.

50 See Joseph C. Grew *Ten Years in Japan* (London, Hammond and Hammond, 1944) p. 72. The British government abrogated the trade agreement between India and Japan on June 1933 seriously damaging Japan's cotton industry.

51 Maruyama, *op. cit.,* p. 114.

52 *ibid.,* p. 114.

53 See Jansen, *op. cit.,* pp. 181-3.

54 Cited in Maruyama, *op. cit.,* p. 146.

55 *Japan's Decision for War. Records of the 1941 Policy Conferences* (hereafter *Policy Conferences*) (ed. Nobutake Ike, California, Stanford University Press, 1967). 63rd Liaison Conference, 28 October 1941, Statement of Yamada Chief of the Navy Bureau of Supplies and Equipment, p. 192.

56 *ibid.,* 50th Liaison Conference, 3 September 1941, p. 131.

57 Ribbentrop had been urging Japanese leaders to attack Singapore for some time. See *Policy Conferences, op. cit.,* 20th Liaison Conference, 22 April 1941, p. 22.

58 *ibid.,* Imperial Conference, 6 September 1941, p. 139.

59 *ibid.,* p. 142.

60 This pact was signed on 13 April 1941.

61 *Policy Conferences, op. cit.,* Imperial Conference, 5 November 1941, p. 114.

62 Lorenz *On Aggression, op. cit.,* pp. 23 and 190.

63 Fox, *op. cit.,* p. 295.

64 Schumpeter, *op. cit.,* p. 43.

6

Explanation and Imperialism

In every one of the so-called test-cases examined in this book — the post-war arms race, the multinational corporations and national autonomy, Hitler's ideology and foreign policy, and Japanese imperialism in the 1930s — there has been an uneasy fit between the conceptual framework that in principle explains them and the actions and events that, nominally, constitute them. Only by a rigorous editing of the 'facts' could each such case be presented as an example or illustration of the associated 'theory'. Each theory presents a prismatic image of reality; they select and organize the 'facts'. And each theory makes a universal claim to knowledge. They purport to offer a general explanation of a class of phenomena termed imperialism.

Now these test-cases have been selected not simply because they present a challenge to the explanatory power of these models of imperialism. In this sense they are arbitrary. In principle, given the general nature of their claims, any nominal case of imperialism should be explicable within their terms. The common denominator in the selection of these test-cases is that in one way or another they fall within the commonsense rubric of imperialism. We have a prior understanding of them as phenomena. What is the relation between this level of understanding and the formulation of conceptual schemes and their evaluation as explanations? Do they transcend common sense?

Of course, successful theory does not turn on commonsense definitions. Such a theory presents through its own explanatory adequacy a description that makes sense only by means of the conceptual apparatus it deploys. We should obtain new knowledge from it. What we already 'know' in terms of the 'facts' or of a practical understanding provides us with one sort of 'explanation'. It need not be rigorous or even genuine, providing no great claim is made for it. But it is not the basis of a theoretical explanation even though it might form its point of departure by acting as a basis for conjecture.

And this is the central objection to these conceptual frameworks that assert an explanation of the phenomenon of imperialism. They do not advance our knowledge of human actions and experience. Instead of providing a genuine explanation that establishes new knowledge, they subsume what we already know and re-present it within the terms of their arguments and concepts. They give us a redescription of what we take to be reality in such a way as to make it impossible to separate the conceptual framework — the theory — from the phenomena it purports to explain. We are being asked to look at what we already know in a particular light. The 'explanation' and the phenomena to be explained are not logically or empirically independent of one another but are interdependent and inseparable. The facts cannot be stated in a manner shorn of the interpretation that selects and organizes them.

The test-cases are ambiguous and ambivalent; they are opportunities for explanation as well as constituting a form of 'explanation' based on our commonsense understanding. We begin with the possibility that they represent some form of imperialism without begging the question which form is relevant or productive of an explanation theoretical in nature. It is in this sense that they are neutral. In principle, all aspects of competition and conflict between peoples and states should be explicable by any one of the forms of imperialism I have considered in this study. The quest for power; the operation of economic forces; the ideas that possess men; and the innate nature of the human species; each and any one of them could explain these case-studies.

If we take the power-security hypothesis, for example, we can subsume all cases of competition between states within its conceptual framework. Such conflicts, of course, can be interpreted as economic, political, racial, religious, social, and so on, according to their ostensible concerns. But whatever the nominal content — the facts and the perceptions of the agents engaged in conflict — the underlying explanation lies in the security fears centring on the need to preserve the territorial integrity of the state or the identity of the group. All other aspects of inter-state competition can be reduced to this. Although its most obvious manifestations are arms races and war itself, ideological concerns and political beliefs are also related to chauvinism and to nationalist sentiment. The locus of social, economic and political action is the state, and the concept of the state assumes a central role in the relationship of theory to practice, in the realization of belief through action.

This is the case even for universalist ideological views such as that of Marxism—Leninism. Although the state is deemed to wither away in the end, the practical aspects of the ideology and its central focus are linked to the capitalist states. Capitalism has a state locus, and capitalism operates in a world dominated by capitalist states. Revolutionary action within them is designed to change their governance not their status *qua* state. Only with the achievement of communism and under unstated conditions will the state wither away. Socialist states are states too. And so problems of subversion, insurrection, terrorism and dissent become threats to security and security is linked to the fears of a regime for its political existence regardless of its ideological affiliations. The challenge to the state from its inimical and unstable environment is not simply a matter of relative military capacities; it has an ideological dimension too. And so the notion of security fears is extended from the preservation of national territory from aggression to the maintenance of its political system and its government. Such a concern has been part of the security problems of the state ever since nation-states came into being. Dynastic politics and religious affiliation were powerful sources of insecurity before the liberal and nationalist upheavals of the last century and the Marxism of this. A weak regime, civil war, the existence of radical dissent, and so on, have been exploited by statesmen as a means of extending national control over their dangerous environment. Intervention both friendly and hostile is a common occurrence in inter-state relations and can be seen as a means of control designed to make the interventionary power more secure. The point here is that such interventions and the phenomenon of ideological conflict and unrest all have a security dimension and can be interpreted in that light. It is their implication for security that is central. And in the nuclear age, with its inhibitions on the use of violence or its threat as a means of guaranteeing security, this aspect is particularly relevant.

Similarly, the concern of the state for its well-being, represented in its foreign economic policies, is directly related to security. The appearance of multinational companies has been seen both as a danger to the political independence of the state and as an extension of the power of the major capitalist states. They are manifestations of the attempt to control and stabilize the external environment by the major developed countries. Economic control is merely another facet of political control. In this sense they are part of the competition between states seen as the central phenomenon of the power-security hypothesis. The weaker nation-states find themselves dependent upon these companies, which are extensions of their home capitalist base. Caught in a mesh of dependent exchange relations, these countries are both economically exploited and made politically subservient to the interests of foreign powers. These last too need to create this type of relationship for the sake of their own political and economic stability. And they do this in competition. The penetration of American multinational companies into Europe was seen as a challenge to the autonomy of the European states. And, equally, their penetration of the Third World was seen as a threat to European interests. The response was the encouragement of European-based multinational companies and enhanced competition. In short, the economic independence of the nation-state was a prerequisite for a genuine security. Controlling those factors necessary to the needs of the national economy — return on foreign investment, external markets and sources of raw materials, etc. — was but another facet of national security.

Hitler, as we have seen, saw the solution to this problem in the creation of autarky for Germany. It involved him in seeking to create import substitutes regardless of the *economic* sense of such a policy. And when this appeared to be only partially successful he sought to create an economic hinterland under German control in Eastern Europe. Part of his reasoning was the vulnerability of the German economy to external pressure. It was not simply his characterization of the danger as emanating from international Jewry in control of the international money market, but the fact that after a military defeat that was only nominal Germany had been exploited through reparations and the manipulation of credit. Inflation and the massive unemployment of the thirties were the direct result of an economic dependence on external markets and sources of credit. German recovery after the war had been made possible by American loans and when the Great Crash occurred Germany was in a very difficult position. Not only economic but political instability was the result. If Germany was ever to be secure, let alone capable of a successful foreign policy designed to restore her position in the world, a condition of economic independence was essential. A view of Germany as a state surrounded by actual and potential enemies and suffering from the exploitation of its economic and political weaknesses by foreign powers permeated Hitler's reasoning. Security in his eyes consisted not only in 'possessing a strong army and a well-filled war chest' (to paraphrase Frederick the Great), but in a condition that insulated Germany from all forms of external pressure. In short, his imperialism and his concern for autarky can be subsumed within the power-security hypothesis. It was not peculiar to Hitler but was a view that prevailed in all states especially under the conditions of economic crisis prevailing at that time. Economic nationalism on this argument was simply a reflection of security fears.

This was also the case for Japanese imperialism and the concern of the Japanese government for the problem of ensuring both markets and supplies of raw materials. The collapse of the world market and the exclusion of Japanese goods had a bearing on Japanese imperialism as it had for Hitler's policies and the protectionist policies of the other imperialist powers. It was perhaps unfortunate that the attempt to restrain Japanese imperialism (and this was perhaps the case for sanctions against Italy also) took the form of the kind of pressure it was designed to overcome. The embargo on the supply of oil to Japan and the other economic measures taken by the United States and Britain both exacerbated the sense of economic weakness and made it imperative to secure independence in this respect. It was a challenge to the political autonomy of Japan and one that the Japanese government could not afford to meet tamely. To accept defeat meant a permanent subjugation to foreign political and economic dominance of the kind manifest in China and in the European empires. Security fears thus become central to an explanation of Japanese imperialism and place it within the rubric of the power-security hypothesis.

Equally the other models of imperialism can be used to 'explain' these case-studies in the same way. The point is that the same body of 'facts' can be interpreted quite differently depending upon the choice of conceptual framework. 'Facts' that are inconvenient to such interpretations are either revised and restated or dismissed as irrelevant as mere epiphenomena. The intelligibility of such an account of actions and decisions depends upon an understanding of the conceptual language of the model. It is this that confers meaning and significance upon the empirical level. The concepts employed appear to be specific to the account and not translatable into other models. While these four models of imperialism make universalist claims to explanatory authority and subsume all imperialist 'phenomena', on the theoretical level they appear to be incommensurable. On the face of it, we cannot synthesize or relate the power-security hypothesis and the economic imperialist thesis. In the former case, security fears are the mainspring of the resultant competition between states; in the latter, while this competition is unchallenged, it is the product of economic forces stemming from the nature of the capitalist mode of production. If fear is at all relevant, it is the fear of losing profits. But of course fear is irrelevant, for such forces are impersonal. Consciousness merely reflects them.

Similarly, commitment to ideological beliefs such as the socio-biological arguments in Hitler's national—socialism is not at all the same as the sociobiological thesis of imperialist drives. Whatever Hitler's reasoning, he was constrained to act as he did, as is the case for any human agent, by the dictates of his biological nature. That his beliefs took the form they did as a rationalizing argument, or a justification of the survival of the fittest as a principle of action, was only to be expected. It was merely a formal and unnecessary expression of the aggressive drives that motivated him. Believing in the principle of evolutionary survival through aggressive adaptation is not a necessary pre-condition of aggressive behaviour. Intra-specific aggression is explicable not through beliefs but by reference to an innate biological mechanism common to man and many other species. Wars, imperialism, economic competition, and indeed all forms of conflict, are subsumed within the sociobiological thesis of aggression and other arguments are irrelevant. If states seek power then it is because they, or rather their statesmen and subjects, rulers and ruled, are driven by the same biological forces. If they claim a lien on the world in the form of resources, markets and territory, then this is explained by their biological nature, whatever its nominal aspect.

We can see from this that all of these models of imperialism are reductionist in nature. They constitute not a way of looking at the world but worlds in themselves. Once we have grasped the conceptual apparatus and understood its language, we are equipped to interpret human actions and events accordingly. Intelligibility, making sense of the world and understanding are the products of such models. But there are problems in accepting them as explanations. The first set of problems concerns the internal consistency or coherence of the model and has to do with the logic of the postulated conceptual relations, while the second set is more fundamental and concerns its relation to the empirical level and its explanatory adequacy.

Let us look at the first type of problem. I said earlier that these models of imperialism are incommensurable. They are mutually exclusive, making universalist claims that deny any authority to rival schemes. On the theoretical level they are reductionist — asserting an exclusive objectivity for their central hypotheses. Yet, if we examine them as pieces of reasoning, their apparent conceptual autonomy and clarity dissolve. In the examination of each of these models we have seen many cases of ambiguity and circularity in the development of their conceptual relations and in the argument generally. The concept power, for example, was used in ways that were not necessarily compatible or consistent with one another. Power is at one and the same time a capacity and a performance; a condition for acting and action itself. Clearly there are difficulties in using this concept in an attempt to explain the phenomenon of imperialism if this ambiguity and inconsistency are left unresolved. If power is as power does, then apart from the innate tautology we can only have *ex post facto* assessment. If it is a necessary pre-condition for action distinguishable from action itself, then we need to identify it as a phenomenon independent of the phenomena we are seeking to explain and this in practice proves peculiarly elusive.

But while imperialism is identified with the quest for power, that is the attempt of the nation-state in competition with other states to control its unstable and inimical environment, the *raison d'être* of this activity is found in security fears. And these are not linked to individuals and their conceptions of security but are attributed to the nature of the nation-state itself. Such a conception of the state is taken as axiomatic by the power-security theorist. Yet this notion can be subsumed by the other models of imperialism. At the levels of the individual and of aggregate social groups, which include nation-states, the sociobiological thesis explains power-seeking in terms of human biology. Fear is a product of social and other environmental pressures acting on an instinctual or innate set of reflexes. Territorial expansion and its associated violence are its direct products. Similarly, the economic imperialist argument conceives of imperialism as a response to a fundamental contradiction in the capitalist mode of production, related to the need to create and realize surplus value. Capitalists are compelled to pursue what is conceived to be in their own interests to create surplus value from a finite pool of labour. They do not control this drive but are forced to follow its dictates. Hence the resultant competition and expansionist tendencies beyond the nation-state are explained in terms of an economic process that produces insecurity and fear among capitalists. And equally ideological imperialism, too, can be subsumed within the concepts of fear and insecurity.

Thus, although the underlying explanation in each case is different — ranging from the axioms of the power-security hypothesis to the more rigorous theoretical framework of economic imperialism and the sociobiological argument — the conceptual apparatus is curiously ambivalent. Each argument appears to overlap. What appear to be the same basic ideas occur in all these models. The basic explanation of fear differs, but the subsequent extensions of the argument, both conceptual and empirical, contain similar elements. They draw on the same ideas.

Perhaps the most perfect example of this kind of lateral synthesis is that of Hitler's ideas. Firstly, there is the biological element in the conception of race as the principal factor in determining human relations. In essence the ideology is based on biology in terms of the primacy of genetically endowed characteristics. Although Hitler believed in the force of environmental conditioning incorporated in his programme of germanization, the genetic basis for this was all important. No amount of conditioning would turn a Jew into an Aryan. Secondly, the power-security hypothesis enters into the view in the form of a conception of the world of states as inherently anarchic. The state consists of the basis for world politics and no higher interest or value exists beyond the national interest. Such a view is conflict-orientated and the struggle of all against all in the pursuit of national interests is considered to be the chief characteristic of world politics. The dangers to the state and its security are clearly recognized in this view, but while this constitutes a problem to the state it is conceived of as only one aspect of the wider problem of the preservation of the race. The state is impelled to expand not merely to achieve a condition of security but in order to establish a racial hegemony that is part of nature. The state is thus a racial state. Thirdly, some of the economic arguments in Hitler's expressions of his beliefs have similarities to the economic model of imperialism. The ideal condition for the state is autarky. Only thus is the state made secure from external pressures and constraints. Hitler's view of international capitalism is strikingly similar to the Marxist view. It was controlled by capitalists who sought to manipulate state economies through the operations of finance capital. While Hitler abhorred the socialist or Marxist solutions to an encroaching capitalism and rejected social revolution, he believed in a form of state capitalism that had remarkable similarities to the Soviet system. The interests of the state were paramount over sectional interests and this meant state intervention in industry, the creation of an economic structure that ran counter to the rationale of a free market economy, control over labour and its deployment, a high level of public investment in communications and in defence, and so on. The aim of course was not the sort of social justice that nominally at least was the goal of a socialist state, but a form of economy that was independent of any external constraint and free of any purely economic controls. Hitler once said that he would shoot all professors of political economy! He believed that economic activity was ancillary to the *raison d'être* of the state. Private enterprise had to be brought within state control for the good of the state. Its political consequences were too important to be left to the vagaries of industrialists and the market.

So in a sense Hitler and his thinking constitute a test of the adequacy of these models. His attempt to relate these ideas to a practical programme constitutes a kind of control for their adequacy. Where the conceptual framework appeared to be incoherent in terms of its internal structure it was modified. Race, for example, became a matter not simply of 'blood' but of spirit. The Jews became a 'race of the mind'. Where the facts appeared to be inconsistent with the theory, the latter was revised. The Soviet Union, initially conceived of as rotten and dominated by Jews and racially inferior, had to be revalued as their sucessful resistance to the German armies began to harden into victory. Scapegoats were found to account for the impending German defeat and these were not hard to find after the attempt on Hitler's life in July 1944. But the enemy within was not Jewish by then. Similarly, Hitler's pressing need for manpower as the war developed into its total form, together with his realization that his eugenic programme and natural population growth were unlikely to produce the 100 million Aryans he deemed necessary to sustain the New Order, led him to accept a programme of germanization. And so Poles, Czechs and even Russians were included in his racial categories as potential Aryans, provided a tenuous connection could be established with an Aryan ancestor.

The point is not merely that the demands of the situation produced a modification of the ideological principles, but that the principles themselves were sufficiently elastic as to permit such necessary modification. This flexibility is present in all of these conceptual schemes and gives us an indication of their character. It is this tension between the conceptual framework and the world of practice, in which one is interpreted and the other modified in the light of experience, which the case of Hitler strikingly illustrates, that reveals the nature of such theories. They are aids to understanding and sources of justification for action, as well as making claims to explain. They all have a prescriptive element to a greater or lesser degree. It is most obvious in the economic imperialist argument, but it is present also in the others. The power-security hypothesis gives an account of the world that warns against foolish idealism, or alternatively urges practical steps such as arms control as a means of avoiding war. The sociobiological view, in spite of its apparent determinism, stresses the importance of controlling aggression through substituting surrogates.

However, it is their nature as putative explanations that is my chief concern in this conclusion. The way in which we look at things presupposes a conceptual apparatus that, in a sense, precedes our understanding of them. We identify, classify, describe, and so on, as a matter of course. At this level there is no problem of imperialism. As I said earlier, we have a commonsense understanding. A wide variety of human phenomena can be subsumed under its rubric. Our problems arise when we wish to transcend our descriptions either by explaining or by justifying them. Descriptions themselves are neither true nor false, although they may be full or incomplete. They are simply recognizable in terms of our cultural and linguistic referents. They admit of comparison, analogy and metaphor. If any problems arise, they are those of identification, association and appropriateness. There are no clear criteria on which they may be resolved. We may validly agree to differ.

Now, while any enquiry that seeks to provide an *explanation* of empirical phenomena begins with tacit assumptions of their nature (a form of description as it were), it will proceed no further and constitute a genuine enquiry if it is bound by them. An explanation provides a re-description of phenomena, but it is rather more than that. For what is explained is a puzzle and if we assumed the answer in advance of our questioning then our enquiry would be circular. In short, there must be a problem associated with 'imperialism' that is not answered by our commonsense assumptions about it. And this problem takes the form of a question or questions, the answer to which is already known in terms of what would count as an answer. Whatever our conjectures and assumptions, they must in principle be referrable to some external test that qualifies one or more of them as adequate answers.

What counts as an appropriate description is largely a subjective matter. We can genuinely agree or disagree over its content for there are no criteria of appropriateness beyond our own individual recognition or the conventions of common sense. Poetry and art are relevant here. But what counts as an adequate explanation depends entirely on the existence of evaluatory criteria independent of a particular explanation or enquiry. If we do not know what these are in advance of our enquiries, then we cannot know what would count as a result. Our attempts at explanation would be directionless. To put it another way, any answer would count as an answer.

Hence these models of imperialism and their associated conceptual frameworks should in principle enable us to make empirical enquiries and arrive at testable conclusions if they are to possess any explanatory value or to qualify as explanations. We do not want mere descriptions of the world or a means of classifying phenomena; we want adequate explanations of human actions and experience. Now all of these models of imperialism offer an intelligible picture of the world. They are not lacking in meaning. Once we have understood them we have a recognizable state of affairs presented to us. As we have seen, while there are common assumptions and referents in these models, their theories and related descriptions are incommensurable. We cannot interpret the world as intelligible in terms of a power struggle arising out of security fears *and* as a fundamental conflict between competing capitalist systems; as the product of an atavistic biological drive *and* as corresponding to the precepts of national—socialism.

Faced with these incommensurable 'theories', we have no means of choosing or evaluating other than through an examination of their internal argument. Here ambiguities and circularities enable us to make some sort of criticism, but this kind of exegesis evades the central problem of their status as explanations. Essentially what is at stake is the postulated relationship between the conceptual framework and experience in terms of a characterization of imperialism that provides us with knowledge. The theory is in principle referrable to practice — the level of experience — and vice-versa. But what is the nature of this reference? Does it take the form of an empirical test that demonstrates according to prescribed rules and conventions a correspondence between hypothetical conclusions and empirical 'reality'? Are the associated 'facts' independent of the explanatory argument? As we have seen, the relationship between theory and 'reality' in these models constitutes a contrast between conceptual categories and analysis and empirical interpretation. The relationship is not explanatory in that the former explains the latter, as is the case of physical theories in the natural sciences and their process of empirical testing. The exercise turns out to be one of attempted coherence in that the two levels — that of conceptual analysis and that of the empirical 'facts' — are made compatible. But the selection and interpretation of the 'facts' are already conceptually formed. It constitutes an explanatory argument of sorts organized by the conceptual framework. And the conceptual framework is modified and propositions formulated that permit revision and qualification so that they do not either strangle the argument through excessive dogmatism or contradict the proffered interpretation. They are really mediated through a pre-existent commonsense understanding of the world. It is not a purely analytic or abstract argument but one that is constantly modified in the light of experience. The two levels are related in such a way as to preclude their separation in the form of a correspondence between theoretical statement and the facts that confirm or disconfirm it. 'Experience' — the level of interpreted facts or commonsense understanding — is conceptually formed and becomes a kind of rationalization referrable only to the concepts that fix their nature and significance. Such an exercise is essentially *ex post facto* and void of predictive capacity.

The central problem is whether actual empirical 'examples' *illustrate* or *demonstrate* the propositions derived from the conceptual analysis. If the former is the case, then clearly we are not presented with an empirical explanation of a theoretical kind on which we can base an understanding of the world. The conceptual world is clarified by reference to historical cases interpreted and formulated with conformity to the conceptual scheme in mind. They are selected and given a form of intelligibility prescribed by the theory. The method here has a vicious circularity. We are given an intelligible and coherent world (where the argument is sufficiently rigorous) that prescribes our way at looking at events. No reference to the conceptual framework can show this world to be true; it is merely intelligible.

If demonstration is required, then the conceptual framework must provide a source of generalizations and hypotheses deducible from the theory that are capable of empirical verification. Such generalizations are atemporal and applicable to classes of events in the same way as in scientific theory. The postulated relationship between theory and 'reality', in which the latter tests or falsifies the former, requires the formulation of not merely a general theory but derived *testable* hypotheses. The rationalizations of these models of imperialism do not in fact do this and hence cannot sustain a level of theoretical explanation. So, even if these models were coherent, it would not follow from this that they were also explanatory.

Although our knowledge is conceptually formed, this does not mean that a conceptual framework void of any means of external and independent criteria of adequacy constitutes an explanatory basis for knowledge. Without any grounds for establishing its explanatory adequacy, it provides a form of understanding that is essentially irrefutable. We either accept it or reject it as we will. There is no common ground on which to assess the rival claims of these models of imperialism in the absence of such criteria.

Throughout this book I have contrasted two modes of explanation: that associated with a generalizing theory, and that with the reasoning of individuals in time and place. Both are distinct and autonomous types of explanation subject to different criteria of reference and conditions of adequacy. They seek to answer different questions. The former is concerned with establishing causal relations and the explanation of classes of events; the latter is concerned with establishing what was the case for a specific type of action. Theory is atemporal and seeks to formulate general laws. Reason-giving explanation is innately temporal and confined to the specific. The point is not that one mode is superior to the other, or that they are complementary in some way, but that they seek to do quite different things in the conduct of an enquiry. There are, as I have suggested in the course of this book, elements of both in the models of imperialism I have considered. As general theories, they fall short of the requirements and conditions of theoretical explanation. Their generalizations are pseudo-generalizations and their empirical references illustrative and circular.

Let me conclude by turning to the other mode of explanation and seeing how this relates to the problem of imperialism. Theoretical explanation is concerned with events and not actions. To put it another way if they are concerned with human action this is conceived of as independent of reasoning. In a sense, it counts as an event. Reason-giving explanation, however, is essentially concerned with the type of action that is intended, purposive, motivated or reasoned. And it is the connection between that reasoning and the action or decision itself that is the subject of its enquiry.

The relation between intention and action is one that explains what the action really was, as opposed to what we may conjecture about it. It does not suppose that the consequences of action correspond to a state of affairs that the agent actually intended. Clearly he believed, or his reasons might assume, that there was a connection between his actions and the achievement of what is desired. In one sense, his formulation of ends presupposes that he was in possession of the means if he contemplates an action. Otherwise such ends are merely vaguely expressed desires, or aims, without any clearly expressed or understood conditions for their realization. The point here is that where action is linked to the attainment of a state of affairs the agent is making some sort of connection between ends and means.

Now, while the *agent* may do this without prejudice as it were, the observer in making his enquiry is not constrained to assert the same kind of reasoning. He is not concerned with establishing a proper relation (whatever that might be) between ends and means. If he is so concerned, then implicitly or explicitly his enquiry entails establishing the necessary and sufficient conditions for the attainment of a given state of affairs conceived of as a class and within the rubric of a covering law explanation. The agent is postulating action as a means of achieving a desired state of affairs similarly is applying some general notion of causality in that he thinks that he can satisfy most if not all of the conditions necessary for success. In practice, such reasoning is not theoretically rigorous. To the agent his reasons *are* good without the need for such reference. But if the observer wishes to interpolate *his* judgement as to their adequacy, then he is under the obligation of making his theoretical presuppositions explicit and subjecting them to the appropriate test. For he is seeking to assess the reasoning of the agent in the light of an adequate theory of action that falls within the covering law type of explanation. And an assessment of the results of action — of consequences — implies this sort of explanation.

Reasons for the agent are what he deems to be relevant and reasonable; and citing them is sufficient to explain what the related action actually was. We need go no further. Any claim that they are adequate or reasonable on grounds other than his holding them need not be investigated. Of course, such assessments are made in the world of practice and the justification of action is an important part of the reasoning of agents. Such justification is not usually made in terms of an appeal to a validated theoretical argument that can authoritatively prescribe practice, although sometimes this claim is made, but by reference to normative or ethical grounds. Such a justification remains what it is — justification. Whether the ends sought or the means adopted are ethical depends upon an acceptance of common values. Alternatively, the relation of means to ends may be referred to a commonly held principle of rationality, as in the case of the maximization of profits in economic theory. But, whatever the reference, it does not involve explanation. It is sufficient to cite the reasons held in order to explain the action, without any assessment of them as good or bad, reasonable or unreasonable.

It will be objected that this argument reduces explanation of human actions to only one class of data — namely reasons — and that this necessarily excludes all other phenomena or forms of reference. The point is not that I wish to reduce all explanation of human action and experience to the phenomenon of human reasoning but that such reduction, if reduction it be, stems from the prior insistence on criteria logically independent of the phenomenon that is the subject of explanation. In short, no answer to a question is adequate if it is not referrable to some kind of test. This necessarily means that questions have to be formulated with a test in mind. So an account of human action needs must refer to grounds on which it can be evaluated if it is to count as an explanation. What are these grounds? They constitute evidence of reasoning for this is the only external reference possible for reasoned action. This is not to deny that other references are possible for other human phenomena, although they have to be made explicit. As we have seen, the contrasted mode of explanation — that of theory — has quite distinctive evaluatory criteria. But when we talk of action we are talking of intentions, motives, reasons, purposes, and so on. Such talk is not external to the agent but is derived from his own reasoning whatever form it takes. Where there is evidence of this, then we have in principle a testable explanation. Where there is not, we cannot talk of explanation. Where the surviving evidence is confused, contradictory, partial or incomplete, the question of adequacy depends upon additional conventions being applied to an assessment of the evidence.

The crucial question for an explanation of this kind is whether there can be a reference to evidence of reasoning. This is a constitutive rule for this mode. It stipulates what is to count as evidence — the facts we deem relevant and that we select. But the regulative rules are those that apply to its assessment and here there is room, as there is in scientific enquiry, for debate. Such debate, however, is within a genuine discourse and takes place on common ground. Its conclusions are provisional and tentative. Knowledge is created but not a certain knowledge.

So I am not saying that the only proper subject of enquiry into human behaviour is human actions and experience treated in this manner. Rather I am saying that if we make such an enquiry then its results must be assessible in terms of external reference to evaluatory criteria. There may be a number of different modes of explanation each with its own distinctive set of such criteria. Human action can be examined in different ways and reason-giving explanation is only one of them. It is claimed here, however, that such a mode of explanation satisfies both the general criteria for explanation and provides us with specific criteria for the assessment of good and bad explanations of human actions.

Turning back to the phenomenon of imperialism, we can see that this form of explanation is directly related to the perceptions and decisions of individual agents. It will be recalled that in the account of an imperialist ideology the crucial connection was between Hitler's reasoning and his decisions and actions. In so far as a reconstruction of his reasoning was possible based on surviving evidence, then we are able to explain what he actually did. And this is equally true for the other models of imperialism − or rather for their applications. Security fears and economic motivation can be understood in terms of the reasoning of the agents. An explanation of imperialism is thus available to us not as a general phenomenon explicable in terms of theory and hypothesis, but as an aspect of human action in terms of the reasoning of individual agents. It is this world, or rather their conceptions of it, that furnishes the clue to an explanation of the phenomenon of imperialism. All of the so-called test-cases are in principle explicable in these terms.

Certainly such an explanation is not general or based on any theory of human behaviour or its rationality. Such a theory in any case would have to satisfy quite different criteria. The knowledge derived from an adequate theoretical explanation of human conduct would be as far removed from our present knowledge as scientific knowledge is removed from our commonsense understanding of the physical world. There is a sense in which we can say that the sun rises and claim to have knowledge of that phenomenon quite independent of any claims that science may make. But while this does not prevent the dual existence of a theoretical and a historical knowledge of human experience the former must be more than a re-description of the latter.

While such theories have yet to be found and evaluated, we can be satisfied with a form of knowledge of human action that, however limited in scope and tied to specific individuals and situations, nevertheless provides us with a communicable understanding. We can enter into the consciousness of human agents through the surviving evidence of their reasoning and conduct an enquiry into the rationale of action fully as rigorous and 'scientific' as enquiry in the natural sciences. The knowledge obtained is as grounded and tenable as that created through scientific enquiry.

An account of human action is as good or bad as the nature of the evidence of reasoning to which it is subjected as a test. And so accounts of the imperialism of the past provide us with an elucidation of the rationale of the imperialists. Such a rationale is not imposed on them either through a theoretical overview of the kind I have discussed in this book, or through the rationalizations of the putative 'observer'. It is derived from what survives into our present as evidence of their reasoning. It is *their* imperialism that constitutes both the problem and the subject of our enquiries.

Bibliography

GENERAL

Angell, N. *The Great Illusion* London, Heinemann, 1910
Aron, R. *The Century of Total War* London, Verschoyle, 1954
Aron, R. *The Imperial Republic* London, Weidenfeld and Nicolson, 1975
Bennett, G. *The Concept of Empire: Burke to Attlee 1774-1947* London, Black, 1962
Brailard, P. and de Senarclens, P. *L'Imperialisme* Paris, Presses Universitaires de France, 1980
Kedourie, E. (ed.) *Nationalism in Asia and Africa* London, Weidenfeld and Nicolson, 1971
Koebner, R. *Empire* Cambridge, Cambridge University Press, 1961
Koebner, R. and Schmidt, H. *Imperialism: The Study and Significance of a Political Word 1840-1960* Cambridge, Cambridge University Press, 1964
Lichtheim, G. *Imperialism* Harmondsworth, Penguin, 1974
Mommsen, W. J. *Theories of Imperialism* London, Weidenfeld and Nicolson, 1980
Moon, Parker T. *Imperialism and World Politics* New York, Garland, 1947
Nadel, G. H. and Curtis, P. (eds) *Imperialism and Colonialism* London, Macmillan, 1964
Thornton, A. P. *Imperialism in the Twentieth Century* London, Macmillan, 1978
Winslow, E. M. *The Pattern of Imperialism: A Study in the Theories of Power* New York, Columbia University Press, 1948

IMPERIALISM AS POWER

Ayers, M. R. *The Refutation of Determinism* London, Methuen, 1968
Barringer, R. E. *War-Patterns of Conflict* Cambridge, Mass., MIT Press, 1972
Barry, B. (ed.) *Power and Political Theory* London, Wiley, 1976

Beaufre, A. *Deterrence and Strategy* New York, Praeger, 1966

Bell, E., Edwards, D. U. and Wagner, R. H. (eds) *Political Power* Glencoe, Free Press, 1969

Biddle, W. F. *Weapons Technology and Arms Control* New York, Praeger, 1973

Blainey, G. *The Causes of War* London, Macmillan, 1977

Brodie, B. *War and Politics* London, Cassell, 1975

Buchan, A. P. *War in Modern Society* London, Fontana, 1966

Buchan, A. P. *End of the Post-War Era: A new balance of world power* London, Weidenfeld and Nicolson, 1974

Carlton, D. and Schaef, C. *Dynamics of the Arms Race* London, Croom Helm, 1975

Carr, E. H. *The Twenty Years Crisis 1919-1939* London, Macmillan, 1940

Easton, D. (ed.) *Varieties of Political Theory* Englewood Cliffs, NJ, Prentice-Hall, 1966

Eisenstadt, S. N. *The Political Systems of Empires* New York, Free Press, 1969

Foucault, M. *Power/Knowledge* Brighton, Harvester, 1980

Gallois, P. M. *The Balance of Terror* Boston, Houghton Mifflin, 1961

Gallois, P. M. *Paradoxes de la Paix* Paris, Presses du Temps Present, 1967

Garnett, J. C. (ed.) *Theories of Peace and Security* London, Macmillan, 1970

George, A. L. *Deterrence in American Foreign Policy: Theory and Practice* London, Columbia University Press, 1975

Gray, C. S. *The Soviet—American Arms Race* London, Saxon House, 1976

Greenwood, Ted *et al. Nuclear Proliferation; motivations, capabilities and strategies for control* New York, McGraw-Hill, 1977

Halle, L. J. *The Cold War as History* London, Chatto and Windus, 1970

Halperin, M. H. *Contemporary Military Strategy* London, Faber, 1973

Holst, J. J. *Security, Order and the Bomb* Stockholm, Universitetsforlaget, 1972

Horowitz, I.L. *War and Peace in Contemporary Social and Philosophical Theory* London, Souvenir Press, 1973

Jones, R. E. *Nuclear Deterrence* London, Routledge and Kegan Paul, 1968

Kaufmann, W. W. (ed.) *Military Policy and National Security* London, Kennikat Press, 1972

Kissinger, H. A. (ed.) *Problems of National Security; A book of readings* New York, Praeger, 1971

Lasswell, H. D. and Kaplan, A. *Power and Security; a framework for political inquiry* New Haven, Conn., Yale University Press, 1950

Legault, A. and Lindsey, G. *The Dynamics of Military Balance* Cornell University Press, 1976

Lukes, S. *Power; A Radical View* London, Macmillan, 1974

Martin, L. W. P. *Arms and Strategy; an international survey of modern defence* London, Weidenfeld and Nicolson, 1973

Midlarsky, M. N. *On War; Political Violence in the International System* London, Collier Macmillan, 1975

Morgan, P. M. *Deterrence; A Conceptual Analysis* London, Sage, 1977

Morgenthau, H. J. *Dilemmas of Politics* Chicago, University of Chicago Press, 1958

Morgenthau, H. J. *Politics Among Nations* New York, Alfred Knopf, 1951

Nagel, J. *The Descriptive Analysis of Power* New Haven, Conn., Yale University Press, 1975

Northedge, F. S. *The Use of Force in International Relations* London, Faber, 1974

Nye, J. J. and Keohane, R. *Power and Interdependence* Boston, Little, Brown, 1976

Parsons, T. and Shils, E. A. (eds) *Towards a General Theory of Action* New York, Harper and Row, 1965

Pierre, A. *Nuclear Politics; The British Experience with an Independent Strategic Force 1939-70* London, Oxford University Press, 1972

Polsby, N. W. *Community Power and Political Theory* New Haven, Conn., Yale University Press, 1963

Rakove, M. L. *Arms and Foreign Policy in the Nuclear Age* London, Oxford University Press, 1972

Roberts, A. *Nations in Arms* London, Chatto and Windus 1978

Rosecrance, R. N. *Strategic Deterrence Reconsidered* London, International Institute for Strategic Studies, 1975

Russell, B. *Power: A New Social Analysis* London, Allen and Unwin, 1938

Sanders, R. *Politics of Defence Analysis* New York, Dunellen, 1973

Schelling, T. C. *Arms and Influence* New Haven, Conn., Yale University Press, 1966

Walsh, M. N. (ed.) *War and the Human Race* Barking, Elsevier, 1971

ECONOMIC IMPERIALISM

Amin, S. *Imperialism and Unequal Development* Brighton, Harvester, 1978

Avineri, S. (ed.) *Karl Marx on Colonialism and Modernization* New York, Doubleday, 1968

Baran, P. A. and Sweezy, P. M. *Monopoly Capital* New York, Monthly Review Press, 1966

Barnet, R. J. Muller, E. *Global Reach: The Power of the Multinational Corporation* New York, Simon and Schuster, 1974

Barratt Brown, M. *After Imperialism* London, Heinemann, 1963

Barratt Brown, M. *Essays on Imperialism* Nottingham, Spokesman Books, 1972

Bergsten, C. F. Hurst, T. and Moran, T. H. *American Multinationals and American Interests* Washington, DC, Brookings, 1978

Blake, D. and Walters, R. S. *The Politics of Global Economic Relations* London, Prentice-Hall, 1976

Bosch, J. *Pentagonism: A Substitute for Imperialism* New York, Grove Press, 1968

Boulding, K. E. and Mukerjee, T. (eds) *Economic Imperialism* Ann Arbor, University of Chicago Press, 1972

Bukharin, N. I. *Imperialism and World Economy* London, Merlin Press, 1972, first published 1917

Cohen, B. J. *The Political Economy of Imperialism* London, Macmillan, 1974

Emmanuel, A. *Unequal Exchange — A study of the imperialism of trade* London, New Left Books, 1972

Fieldhouse, D. K. *The Theory of Capitalist Development* London, Longmans, 1967

Franko, L. G. *The European Multinationals* London, Harper and Row, 1976

Ghadar, F. *The Evolution of OPEC strategy* New York, Lexington, 1977

Gilpin, R. *US Power and the Multinational Corporation* New York, Basic Books/Macmillan, 1975

Grierson, E. *The Imperial Dream* London, Collins, 1972

Gunder-Frank, A. *Capitalism and Underdevelopment in Latin America* New York, Monthly Review Press, 1969

Hahlo, M. R., Smith, J. G. and Wright, R. W. *Nationalism and the Multinational Enterprise* Leiden, Sijthoff, 1973

Hilferding, R. *Das Finanzkapital* Vienna, 1910

Hobson, J. A. *Imperialism; A study* (revised edn) London, Allen and Unwin, 1968, first published in 1902

Hodgart, A. *The Economics of European Imperialism* London, Arnold, 1977

Hodges, M. *Multinational Corporations and National Governments* London, Saxon House, 1974

Horowitz, D. *Imperialism and Revolution* London, Allen Lane, 1969

Hudson, M. *Super-Imperialism* New York, Rinehart and Winston, 1968

Jalee, P. *The Pillage of the Third World* New York, Monthly Review Press, 1967

Kemp, T. *Theories of Imperialism* London, Dobson Books, 1967

Kindleberger, C. P. *Power and Money* London, Macmillan, 1976

Knorr, K. *Power and Wealth* London, Macmillan, 1973

Kolko, G. *The Roots of American Foreign Policy* Boston, Beacon Press, 1969

Lall, S. and Streeten, P. *Foreign Investment: Transnationals and Developing Countries* London, Macmillan, 1977

Lenin, V. I. *Notebooks on Imperialism Collected Works* Vol. 39, Moscow, Progress Publishers

Lenin, V. I. *Imperialism: The Highest Stage of Capitalism* Moscow, Progress Publishers, 1966, first published 1917

Liska, G. *Imperial America* Baltimore, Johns Hopkins University Press, 1967

Luxemburg, R. *The Accumulation of Capital* (trans. A. F. Schwarzchild) London, Routledge and Kegan Paul, 1951, first published 1913

Mack, A., Plant, D. and Doyle, U. (eds) *Imperialism, Intervention and Development* London, Croom Helm, 1979

Madelin, H. *Oil and Politics* London, Saxon House, 1975

Magdoff, H. *The Age of Imperialism* New York, Monthly Review Press, 1969

Mazrui, A. *Africa's International Relations; the diplomacy of dependency and change* London, Heinemann, 1977

Melotti, U. *Marx and the Third World* London, Macmillan, 1977
Nkrumah, K. *Neo-Colonialism: The Last Stage of Imperialism* London, Mason, 1965
Odell, P. *Oil and World Power* Harmondsworth, Penguin, 1970
Owen, R. and Sutcliffe, B. (eds) *Studies in the Theory of Iperialism* London, Longman, 1972
Radice, H. (ed.) *International Firms and Modern Imperialism* Harmondsworth, Penguin, 1975
Rhodes, R. I. (ed.) *Imperialism and Under-Development* New York, Monthly Review Press, 1970
Robbins, L. C. *The Economic Causes of War* London, Jonathan Cape, 1939
Rosen, S. and Kurth, J. R. *Testing Theories of Economic Imperialism* Lexington, Heath, 1974
Rothstein, R. L. *The Weak in the World of the Strong* New York, Columbia University Press, 1977
Sweezy, P. M. *The Theory of Capitalist Development* London, Dobson, 1946
Vernon, R. *Sovereignty at Bay* New York, Basic Books, 1971
Winslow, E. M. *The Pattern of Imperialism* New York, Columbia University Press, 1948
Wolfe, M. *The Economic Causes of Imperialism* London, Wiley, 1972

IMPERIALISM AND IDEOLOGY

Broszat, M. *German National Socialism 1919-1945* S. Barbara, Clio Press, 1966
Butler, R. *The Roots of National Socialism 1783-1933* London, Faber, 1941
Carr, W. *Arms, Autarchy and Aggression 1933-1939* London, Arnold, 19
Cecil, R. *The Myth of the Master Race. Alfred Rosenberg and Nazi Ideology* New York, Dodd Mead, 1972
Gasman, D. *The Scientific Origins of National Socialism* London, MacDonald, 1971
Goebbels, J. *The Goebbels Diaries 1942-1943* (trans. Louis P. Lochner) London, Hamish Hamilton, 1948
Hiden, J. W. *Germany and Europe 1919-1939* London, Longmans, 1977
Hildebrand, K. *The Foreign Policy of the Third Reich* London, Batsford, 1973
Hitler, A. *The Speeches of Adolf Hitler 1922-1939* Vol. II (trans. Norman H. Baynes) London, Royal Institute of International Affairs, Oxford University Press, 1942
Hitler, A. *The Testament of Adolf Hitler. Hitler—Bormann Documents Feb-April 1945* (ed. F. Genoud, trans. R. H. Stevens, intro. H. Trevor-Roper, London, Cassells, 1960
Hitler, A. *Mein Kampf* (trans. R. Mannheim) London, Radius/Hutchinson, 1969
Irving, D. *Hitler's War* London, Hodder and Stoughton, 1977
Jones, T. *A Diary with Letters* London, Oxford University Press, 1954

Liddell Hart, B. H. *The Other Side of the Hill* London, Cassell, 1948
Nazi Conspiracy and Aggression Washington DC, US Govt Printing Office, 1946-48
Neumann, F. *Behemoth; The Structure and Practice of National Socialism* London, Gollancz, 1942
Nolte, E. *Three Faces of Fascism* New York, Holt Rinehart, 1965
Pois, R. (ed.) *Alfred Rosenberg Selected Writings* London, 1970
Rauschning, H. *Germany's Revolution of Destruction* London, Heinemann, 1939
Rauschning, H. *Hitler Speaks* London, Butterworth, 1939
Reitlinger, G. *The House Built on Sand* New York, Greenwood Press, 1975
Rich, N. *Hitler's War Aims* Vol. I *Ideology, the Nazi State and the Course of Expansion,* Vol. II *The Establishment of the New Order* London, Deutsch, 1973/4
Schmokel, W. W. *Dream of Empire, German Colonialism 1919-1945* New Haven, Yale University Press, 1964
Schmidt, P. *Hitler's Interpreter* (ed. R. H. C. Steed) London, Heinemann, 1951
Snyder, L.L. *Roots of German Nationalism* Bloomington, Indiana University Press, 1978
Speer, A. *Inside the Third Reich* London, Macmillan, 1970
Sontag, R. J. and Beddie, J. S. (eds) *Nazi—Soviet Relations 1939-1941* Washington, DC., US Dept of State, 1948
Stachura, P. D. *The Shaping of the Nazi State* London, Croom Helm, 1977
Trevor-Roper, H. *Hitler's Table Talk 1941-44* London, Weidenfeld & Nicolson, 1953
Warlimont, W. *Inside Hitler's H.Q. 1939-45* (trans R. H. Barry) London, Weidenfeld and Nicolson, 1964
Weinberg, G. L. *The Foreign Policy of Hitler's Germany* Chicago, Chicago University Press, 1970

SOCIOBIOLOGY AND IMPERIALISM

Alland, A. *Evolution and Human Behavior* New York, Natural History Press, 1967
Ardrey, R. *The Social Contract* London, Fontana/Collins, 1970
Ashley, M. M. F. (ed.) *Man and Aggression* London, Oxford University Press, 1968
Berkowitz, L. (ed.) *Roots of Aggression* New York, Atherton Press, 1969
Butow, R. J. C. *Tojo and the Coming of the War* Princeton, Princeton University Press, 1961
Callan, H. *Ethology and Society* Oxford, Clarendon Press, 1970
Carthy, J. D. and Ebling, F. J. (eds) *The Natural History of Aggression* London, Academic Press, 1964
Chapple, E. D. *Culture and Biological Man* New York, Holt, Rinehart and Winston, 1970
Crowley, J. B. *Japan's Quest for Autonomy, National Security and Foreign Policy 1930-1938* Princeton, Princeton University Press, 1966

Dunn, L. C. *Heredity and Evolution in Human Populations* Cambridge, Mass., Harvard University Press, 1962

Feis, H. *The Road to Pearl Harbor* Princeton, Princeton University Press, 1950

Fried, M., Harris, M. and Murphy, R. (eds) *War; The Anthropology of Armed Conflict and Aggression* New York, Natural History Press, 1967

Friedrich, H. *Man and Animal* London, Paladin, 1971

Grew, J. C. *Ten Years in Japan* London, Hammond and Hammond, 1944

Iriye, A. *After Imperialism. The Search for a New Order in the Far East 1921-33* Cambridge, Mass.

Japan's Decision For War. Records of the 1941 Policy Conferences (trans. and ed. Nobutake Ike) Stanford, Stanford University Press, Calif. 1967

Jones, F. C. *Japan's New Order in East Asia — its rise and fall 1937-45* London, Oxford University Press, Royal Institute of International Affairs, 1954

Lebra, J. C. *Japan's Greater East Asia Co-Prosperity Sphere in World War II. Selected Readings and Documents* Kuala Lumpur, 1975

Lerner, M. *Heredity, Evolution and Society* Princeton, Princeton University Press, 1968

Lockwood, W. W. *The Economic Development of Japan; Growth and Structural Change* Princeton, Princeton University Press, 1954

Lorenz, K. *Behind the Mirror* London, Methuen, 1977

Lorenz, K. *On Aggression* London, Methuen, 1966

Mackenzie, W. J. M. *Biological Ideas in Politics* Harmondsworth, Penguin, 1978

Maruyama, Masao *Thought and Behaviour in Modern Japanese Politics* (trans. Ivan Morris) London, Oxford University Press, 1963

Maxon, Y. C. *Control of Japanese Foreign Policy — a study of Court—Military Rivalry 1930-1945* Berkeley, University of California Press, 1957

Midgley, M. *Beast and Man. The roots of human nature* Hassocks, Sussex, Harvester, 1979

Morley, J. W. (ed.) *Dilemmas of Growth in pre-war Japan* Princeton, Princeton University Press, 1972

Morley, J. W. (ed.) *Japan's Foreign Policy 1868-1941 A Research Guide* New York, 1974

Nish, I. H. *Japanese Foreign Policy 1869-1942* London, Routledge and Kegan Paul, 1977

Oakamoto, Shumpei *The Japanese Oligarchy and the Russo-Japanese War* New York 1970

Otterbein, K. (ed.) *The Evolution of War* Cambridge Mass., HFAF Press, 1970

Royama, Masamuchi *Foreign Policy of Japan 1914-1939* Westport, Conn., Greenwood Press, 1973

Russell, W. M. J. *Violence, Monkeys and Man* London, Macmillan, 1968

Scott, J. P. *Aggression* Ann Arbor, Chicago University Press, 1958

Schumpeter, J. A. *Imperialism and Social Classes* Oxford, Basil Blackwell, 1951, first published 1919

Shillony, Ben-Ami *Revolt in Japan; the Young Officers and the February 26th 1936 Incident* Princeton, Princeton University Press, 1973

Smithsonian Institute *Man and Beast* Washington, DC, Smithsonian Institute Press, 1969/71

Storry, R. *The Double Patriots: A Study of Japanese Nationalism* London, Chatto and Windus, 1957

Storry, R. *Japan and the Decline of the West in Asia 1894-1943* London, Macmillan, 1979

Thorne, C. *The Limits of Foreign Policy* London, Hamish Hamilton, 1972

Tiger, L. and Fox, R. *The Imperial Animal* London, Secker and Warburg, 1972

Totten, G. O. *The Social Democratic Movement in Pre-War Japan* New Haven, Conn., Yale University Press, 1966

Ward, E. R. (ed.) *Political Development in Modern Japan* Princeton, Princeton University Press, 1968

Wilson, E. O. *Socio-biology; The New Synthesis* Cambridge, Mass., Harvard University Press, 1975

EXPLANATION AND IMPERIALISM

Anscombe, G. E. M. *Intention* Oxford, Blackwell, 1957

Ayala, F. J. and Dobzhansky, T. (eds) *Studies in the Philosophy of Biology; Reduction and Related Problems* London, Macmillan, 1974

Brown, D. G. *Action* Toronto, University of Toronto Press, 1968

Brown, R. *Explanation in Social Science* London, Routledge and Kegan Paul, 1963

Care, N. J. and Landesman, C. (eds) *Readings in the Theory of Action* Bloomington, University of Indiana Press, 1968

Danto, A. *Analytical Philosophy of History* Cambridge, Cambridge University Press, 1965

Dray, W. *Laws and Explanation in History* London, Oxford University Press, 1957

Feigl, H. and Maxwell, Grover (eds) *Minnesota Studies in the Philosophy of Science* Vol. III, Minneapolis, University of Minnesota Press, 1962

Gardiner, P. *The Nature of Historical Explanation* London, Oxford University Press, 1952

Geach, P. T. *Mental Acts* New York, Humanities Press, 1957

Hampshire, S. *Thought and Action* London, Chatto and Windus, 1959

Hempel, C. G. *Aspects of Scientific Explanation and other Essays* Glencoe, Free Press, 1965

Hook, S. (ed.) *Determinism and Freedom in the Age of Modern Science* New York, New York University Press, 1958

Korner, S. (ed.) *Explanation* Oxford, Blackwell, 1975

Korner, S. (ed.) *Practical Reason* Oxford, Blackwell, 1974

Louch, A. R. *Explanation and Human Action* Berkeley, University of California Press, 1966

Nagel, E. *The Structure of Science* New York, Harcourt Brace, 1961

Popper, K. *Conjectures and Refutations* New York, Basic Books, 1963

Pringle, J. W. S. *Biology and the Human Sciences* London, Oxford University Press, 1972

Quine, W. V. O. *Word and Object* Cambridge, Mass., MIT Press, 1960

Rescher, N. (ed.) *The Logic of Decision and Action* University of Pittsburgh Press, 1967

Ruse, Michael *The Philosophy of Biology* London, Hutchinson University Library, 1973

Ruse, Michael *Socio-Biology; Sense or Nonsense* Dordrecht, P. Reidel, 1979

Ryan, A. (ed.) *The Philosophy of Social Explanation* London, Oxford University Press, 1973

Ryle, G. *The Concept of Mind* London, Hutchinson University Library, 1949

Studdert, Kennedy G. *Evidence and Explanation in Social Science* London, Routledge and Kegan Paul, 1975

Taylor, C. *The Explanation of Behaviour* London, Routledge and Kegan Paul, 1964

Taylor, D. M. *Explanation and Meaning* Cambridge, Cambridge University Press, 1970

Taylor, R. *Action and Purpose* Brighton, Harvester, 1980

Winch, P. *The Idea of a Social Science* London, Routledge and Kegan Paul, 1963

Von Wright, G. H. *Explanation and Understanding* London, Routledge and Kegan Paul, 1971

Index

DATE DUE

DEMCO 38-297